studies in jazz

Institute of Jazz Studies
Rutgers—The State University of New Jersey
General Editors: Dan Morgenstern and Edward Berger

1. BENNY CARTER: A Life in American Music, *by Morroe Berger, Edward Berger, and James Patrick, 2 vols., 1982*
2. ART TATUM: A Guide to His Recorded Music, *by Arnold Laubich and Ray Spencer, 1982*
3. ERROLL GARNER: The Most Happy Piano, *by James M. Doran, 1995*
4. JAMES P. JOHNSON: A Case of Mistaken Identity, *by Scott E. Brown,* Discography 1917–1950, *by Robert Hilbert, 1986*
5. PEE WEE ERWIN: This Horn for Hire, *as told to Warren W. Vaché Sr., 1987*
6. BENNY GOODMAN: Listen to His Legacy, *by D. Russell Connor, 1988*
7. ELLINGTONIA: The Recorded Music of Duke Ellington and His Sidemen, *by W. E. Timner, 1988; 4th ed., 1996*
8. THE GLENN MILLER ARMY AIR FORCE BAND: Sustineo Alas/I Sustain the Wings, *by Edward F. Polic,* Foreword *by George T. Simon, 1989*
9. SWING LEGACY, *by Chip Deffaa, 1989*
10. REMINISCING IN TEMPO: The Life and Times of a Jazz Hustler, *by Teddy Reig, with Edward Berger, 1990*
11. IN THE MAINSTREAM: 18 Portraits in Jazz, *by Chip Deffaa, 1992*
12. BUDDY DeFRANCO: A Biographical Portrait and Discography, *by John Kuehn and Arne Astrup, 1993*
13. PEE WEE SPEAKS: A Discography of Pee Wee Russell, *by Robert Hilbert, with David Niven, 1992*
14. SYLVESTER AHOLA: The Gloucester Gabriel, *by Dick Hill, 1993*
15. THE POLICE CARD DISCORD, *by Maxwell T. Cohen, 1993*
16. TRADITIONALISTS AND REVIVALISTS IN JAZZ, *by Chip Deffaa, 1993*
17. BASSICALLY SPEAKING: An Oral History of George Duvivier, *by Edward Berger,* Musical Analysis *by David Chevan, 1993*
18. TRAM: The Frank Trumbauer Story, *by Philip R. Evans and Larry F. Kiner, with William Trumbauer, 1994*

19. TOMMY DORSEY: On the Side, *by Robert L. Stockdale, 1995*
20. JOHN COLTRANE: A Discography and Musical Biography, *by Yasuhiro Fujioka, with Lewis Porter and Yoh-ichi Hamada, 1995*
21. RED HEAD: A Chronological Survey of "Red" Nichols and His Five Pennies, *by Stephen M. Stroff, 1996*
22. THE RED NICHOLS STORY: After Intermission 1942–1965, *by Philip R. Evans, Stanley Hester, Stephen Hester, and Linda Evans, 1997*
23. BENNY GOODMAN: Wrappin' It Up, *by D. Russell Connor, 1996*
24. CHARLIE PARKER AND THEMATIC IMPROVISATION, *by Henry Martin, 1996*
25. BACK BEATS AND RIM SHOTS: The Johnny Blowers Story, *by Warren W. Vaché Sr., 1997*
26. DUKE ELLINGTON: A Listener's Guide, *by Eddie Lambert, 1998*
27. SERGE CHALOFF: A Musical Biography and Discography, *by Vladimir Simosko, 1998*
28. HOT JAZZ: From Harlem to Storyville, *by David Griffiths, 1998*
29. ARTIE SHAW: A Musical Biography and Discography, *by Vladimir Simosko, 2000*
30. JIMMY DORSEY: A Study in Contrasts, *by Robert L. Stockdale, 1998*
31. STRIDE! Fats, Jimmy, Lion, Lamb and All the Other Ticklers, *by John L. Fell and Terkild Vinding, 1999*
32. GIANT STRIDES: The Legacy of Dick Wellstood, *by Edward N. Meyer, 1999*
33. JAZZ GENTRY: Aristocrats of the Music World, *by Warren W. Vaché Sr., 1999*
34. THE UNSUNG SONGWRITERS: America's Masters of Melody, *by Warren W. Vaché Sr., 2000*
35. THE MUSICAL WORLD OF J. J. JOHNSON, *by Joshua Berrett and Louis G. Bourgois III, 1999*
36. THE LADIES WHO SING WITH THE BAND, *by Betty Bennett, 2000*
37. AN UNSUNG CAT: The Life and Music of Warne Marsh, *by Safford Chamberlain, 2000*
38. JAZZ IN NEW ORLEANS: The Postwar Years through 1970, *by Charles Suhor, 2001*
39. THE YOUNG LOUIS ARMSTRONG ON RECORDS: A Critical Survey of the Early Recordings, 1923–1928, *by Edward Brooks, 2002*

40. BENNY CARTER: A Life in American Music, Second Edition, *by Morroe Berger, Edward Berger, and James Patrick, 2 vols., 2002*
41. CHORD CHANGES ON THE CHALKBOARD: How Public School Teachers Shaped Jazz and the Music of New Orleans, *by Al Kennedy,* Foreword *by Ellis Marsalis Jr., 2002*
42. CONTEMPORARY CAT: Terence Blanchard with Special Guests, *by Anthony Magro, 2002*

"Terence Blanchard is a very gifted musician and a good role-model for musicians coming up today. I'm one of his biggest fans. Whenever I see him play or when I hear one of his movie scores, it just makes me feel very proud." —**Sonny Rollins**

"For those of us who have been on the scene for a long time, we're always very proud to see a young talented gentleman like Terence come on the scene." —**Clark Terry**

"Terence was a big influence on all of us. He and Wynton Marsalis were probably the two biggest idols of all the high school jazz musicians in the mid- and late 1980s." —**Christian McBride**

"Terence is the man! He's one of my favorites. The thing I love about Terence is that he has his own style, his own voice. It's a very personal sound with great dexterity." —**Roy Hargrove**

"Terence has this wonderful warmth to his sound, which reflects his character too. And I have a great admiration for his writing abilities, not only with his group, but with the scores that he's written for film."
—**Dave Holland**

"Terence brings another sensibility to the field [of film scoring], and I think he does a great job." —**Wynton Marsalis**

"Terence is out there writing those movie scores for Spike Lee and others and I think it's great—and he's great at it!"
—**J.J. Johnson**

"I'm very honored that I've been able to work with Terence and have a true collaboration. He's very important to my filmmaking. Terence's music fills in the holes and lifts it up to another level." —**Spike Lee**

"Terence is a killer trumpet player, a great musician, composer and arranger. He does everything and he does it well!" —**Ray Brown**

Contemporary Cat

Terence Blanchard
with Special Guests

Anthony Magro

Studies in Jazz, No. 42

The Scarecrow Press, Inc.
Lanham, Maryland, and Oxford
and
Institute of Jazz Studies
Rutgers—The State University of New Jersey
2002

SCARECROW PRESS, INC.

Published in the United States of America
by Scarecrow Press, Inc.
A Member of the Rowman & Littlefield Publishing Group
4720 Boston Way
Lanham, Maryland 20706
www.scarecrowpress.com

PO Box 317
Oxford
OX2 9RU, UK

British Library Cataloguing in Publication Information Available

Library of Congress Cataloging-in-Publication Data

Magro, Anthony, 1976–
Contemporary cat : Terence Blanchard with special guests / Anthony Magro.
p. cm. – (Studies in jazz ; no. 42)
Includes bibliographical references, discography (p.), filmography (p.), and index.
ISBN 0-8108-4323-4 (alk. paper)
1. Blanchard, Terence. 2. Jazz musicians—United States—Interviews. I. Rutgers University. Institute of Jazz Studies. II. Title. III. Series.

ML419.B575 M34 2002
781.65'092—dc21

2002006433

∞™ The paper used in this publication meets the minimum requirements of American National Standard for Information Sciences—Permanence of Paper for Printed Library Materials, ANSI/NISO Z39.48-1992.
Manufactured in the United States of America.

CONTENTS

ACKNOWLEDGMENTS

This book would not exist in its current form if not for the extraordinary cooperation I received. I am indebted to all those whom I interviewed for giving their time and sharing their memories. They are Edward Simon, Troy Davis, Wynton Marsalis, Donald Harrison, Billy Pierce, Mulgrew Miller, Cyrus Chestnut, Carl Allen, Reginald Veal, Rodney Whitaker, Joe Henderson, Clark Terry, Benny Golson, Curtis Fuller, Dave Holland, Ray Brown, Dave Grusin, Alex Steyermark, Kasi Lemmons, Michael Cristofer, Bill Fielder, Paul Jeffrey, Christian McBride, Nicholas Payton, Jeanie Bryson, David Pulphus, Eric Wright, Benny Green, Geoff Keezer, Wilson Turbinton, and Kenny Barron.

Special appreciation goes to Branford Marsalis for the sort of candid interviews that writers covet; to Spike Lee for directing my own personal adventure; to Sonny Rollins for sharing his incomparable musicality and personality on the same night; and to Wilhelmina Blanchard, Alice Douglas, Roger Dickerson, Martha Francis, Willie Metcalf, Ellis Marsalis Jr., and Robin Burgess for their New Orleans hospitality. I also wish to express gratitude to Robin for entrusting me with her approving green light.

A special thank you to the photographers who generously contributed their art to this book: David Lee, David Bartolomi, Hans Neleman, Jack Vartoogian, and David Leung. More special thanks to Gino Larice for his cover design and to David Wagman for his editorial wisdom.

The assistance I received from Jason Lampkin, Roderick Harper, Melinda Summers, Erika Duffee, Colleen Slattery, and Roberto Yangosian is well regarded.

I would like to extend love to my mother for her enduring support and to my father for his trusted counsel. Love also to Tammie Maraldo for the comfort she gives in being there; to Nathan Downer for a blissfully enlightening introduction; to Jennifer Arseneau for conveying the virtue of patience; to Neil J. Price for his help in launching this project; to Lee Cash for always being in my corner; and to Jason Stephens for his open ear and helpful suggestions.

Finally, and especially, I am beholden to Terence. His giving personality and astonishing artistry intersected with my inspiration. I thank him for an experience I will forever treasure.

PREFACE

Still high on the music, a few people drift to the bar for last call, but mostly everyone has gone home by now. The band is on the road in Toronto near the end of their Canadian sweep. They are performing songs from their best-selling new album, a tribute to Billie Holiday. Their leader, enjoying its commercial success, is grinning on the cover of the latest *Down Beat* magazine.

He is somewhere in the spacious three-story club, replete with another bar above and a restaurant beneath. When he emerges from the basement bathroom, leisurely climbing the stairs, a little preoccupied, reeling perhaps from his performance, there is a quiet gracefulness to his movement but nothing to suggest the warmth of his humility. He is an imposing presence; his thick frame, stylish attire, and aloof demeanor render me timid in his company. But I was so wowed by his musicianship that I felt compelled to tell him so.

That evening I exchanged flattery for acknowledgments with Terence Blanchard on an empty stairwell at the Top O' the Senator, but our first close encounter occurred a year later, in 1995, when I interviewed him at that same club.

Out of that meeting came an opportunity to write this book, which was a challenge that inspired me. In addition to the usual demands of writing a biography—researching, interviewing, transcribing, and editing—I would be required to keep pace with a consistently prolific subject.

The fact that Blanchard is an active, modern musician was very attractive to me. It is important to document and learn about jazz artists, but retrospectives of careers long ago far outnumber books about the new and exciting ones. Jazz is thriving in the twenty-first century, as popular as it's been in forty years. So to explore one of today's leading musicians, one that we can actually embrace and enjoy, promised to be relevant and refreshing.

Now entering the second half of his life, Blanchard is in his prime, braced for infinite possibilities and success. But because he has already amassed such an impressive and diverse body of work, some assessment of his life and career is in order.

I began spending hours upon hours interviewing him in his Garden District home in New Orleans, at various venues and hotel rooms in New York, Detroit, Montreal, and my hometown of Toronto, or, as a last resort, on the phone when he was too far to reach in person.

Over the years, Terence was an accommodating subject. He gave his time whenever I requested it, and he never ordered content restrictions on our conversations. Predictably, he relates tales about his formative years in New Orleans, his cherished time with Art Blakey, and his numerous collaborations with Spike Lee. He also speaks openly about his family, including his father's fatal illness and the sudden death of his close friend, Miles Goodman. However, Terence's divorce from his first wife, Jackie DeMagnus, was an area of reticence. My instinct was not to push him, knowing his thoughts and feelings had been openly articulated in his music, *Romantic Defiance*, which is far more interesting anyway.

And that is precisely the appeal of Terence Blanchard—his music. Jazz is intellectual and intricate with unlimited possibilities, and its complexities can be rewarding to audiences. Still, when explored by some of its musicians, there have been charges of indulgent, esoteric playing—alienating listeners with thorny improvisations, loose harmonies, and abstract melodies.

Blanchard and the musicians in his band perform for an audience. There is an expressive and lucid sophistication to their playing that resists the temptation of technical esotericism. Then there is something to be said for his stage presence: a jovial entertainer in the tradition of prebop performers, Terence engages spectators with his dry, improvisational humor and storytelling abilities. The quiet and introverted boy from New Orleans now elicits laughter and levity from stages around the world, which is just as important, he feels, as presenting good music.

As a trumpeter, Terence has created his own sound through the instrument, a warm and dexterous crooning quality that both musicians and singers like to bounce off of. It was fully developed after his successful but laborious embouchure change, the most dramatic period of his career.

A composer of considerable range, Terence has forged solid footing in the precarious film industry, complementing his jazz recordings with several scores. In fact, with over thirty to his credit, no jazz musician has composed for more films than Blanchard.

En route to such distinction, he formed relationships with the jazz elite and top Hollywood directors and composers, many of whom, in addition to granting interviews, are discussed thoroughly in this book. *Contemporary Cat: Terence Blanchard with Special Guests* is made up of numerous voices as dozens of artists speak about Terence and their work together in previously unpublished words. This book seeks to illuminate those collaborations, what motivated them, what challenged them, and the colorful anecdotes that came out of them.

Tracing Terence's career through interviews with those who know him best lends authenticity and intimacy to this book. Its style also allows for more color and free-form discussion. More than chronicling Terence's jazz and film projects, conversation explores compelling social issues like the segregated South and why African Americans are rarely seen in jazz audiences today. Its far-reaching scope delves into the civil rights movement and how its leaders Martin Luther King and Malcolm X have influenced the artists of this book.

One of the perks of such comprehensive interviewing was a rare opportunity to meet and converse with so many great artists whom I have long admired. Appealingly, they all came forth without prodding. They were all happy to do it—an indication of the respect Terence garners among his peers.

After fifty years, Sonny Rollins remains inspired and active on the jazz performance circuit. So many generations have been so fortunate to experience his music live. During his career, he has accumulated an enormous songbook with such popular fare as "St. Thomas." Invariably, the calypso rhythm induces dancing in the aisles, but you know you are watching a special performer when he announces that the previous tune was written by his friend Thelonious Monk. The expression may be cliché, but Sonny Rollins is truly a walking history of jazz. He is the last of the great Giants.

Now in his seventies, his energy remains remarkably boundless in performance. He still plays with the vigor and endurance that he has long been reputed for, exploring the entire stage, shuffling his shoulders and bopping his head like a pigeon. It is truly a sight to behold. But when the music stops and he emerges from his trailer, he shows his age, moving languidly to his van. Still, he stops to sign autographs and pose for snapshots. He is remarkably open for a musician of his stature.

Later that evening, to my delight, Mr. Rollins accepted an impromptu interview. He was thrilled to speak about Terence, whom he considers to be an exemplary musician and person. When Terence learned of his mentor's flattering remarks, he was so overcome with honor as if he had been ceremoniously confirmed into the pantheon of jazz musicians.

PREFACE

I had the privilege of engaging Joe Henderson in an hour-long telephone conversation from his home in San Francisco. For decades he was considered one of jazz's best-kept secrets until he achieved tremendous exposure in the nineties, winning three Grammy Awards.

In 1998, he gladly received an invitation to perform on Terence's Sony Classical debut recording, an amalgamation of jazz and film music. A lifelong fan of movie soundtracks, *Jazz in Film* is among Henderson's most inspired playing, and his lyrical exchange with Terence on André Previn's "The Subterraneans" is magical.

Shortly thereafter, toward the end of a long bout with emphysema, the tenor titan spoke passionately about his ambitions and how Terence, a musician twenty-five years his junior, has inspired him. Sadly, Mr. Henderson passed away on June 30, 2001, of heart failure, and *Jazz in Film* was his last recording.

Jazz in Film would also be one of the very last recorded performances of the very talented Kenny Kirkland. When Branford Marsalis propositioned him to join his brother Wynton's first band, Kirkland was already one of the most respected young pianists on the New York scene. His star would rise with Wynton and later with Branford's quartet, but there was a feeling that he had yet to realize his full potential.

Kirkland's death in November 1998 came out of the blue. It had shocked and anguished his closest friends. He was only forty-two, but a weak heart that was exasperated by drug use had claimed his life.

Terence was on the road in Birmingham, England, when he was informed of the sad news. He always had a great deal of fondness for Kenny's musicianship, but he mourned the passing as a loss of a friend whose company he enjoyed.

Over the course of working on this book, several of Terence's collaborators passed away, including the legendary J. J. Johnson, whose influence on trombone was so enormous that he set a standard to which all successors strove.

In the last years leading up to Johnson's curious retirement, he remained prolific with live performances and studio recordings, including *Let's Hang Out*, featuring Terence on three tracks. He thought highly of Terence as a trumpet player, but as a onetime film composer, he was particularly impressed with Blanchard's scores. Johnson's retirement in 1998 saddened the jazz community, but his violent suicide left it reeling.

For twenty-five years, film producer Marvin Worth had persisted to see the making of *Malcolm X*. And he was prepared to make another enduring commitment to bring Miles Davis's story to screen.

Worth had been so impressed by Terence and his music for *Malcolm X* that he had already committed him to write the score. Actor Wesley Snipes was said to be interested in portraying Miles, but there were too many conflicting ideas about the subject, and the script underwent endless rewrites. Worth was experienced in fighting these types of battles, but he would lose a bigger one to cancer, dying in April 1998. Consequently, the Miles Davis film project is stuck in limbo.

When Terence flew to California in the summer of 1996 to cowrite a score with Miles Goodman, there was no way to know that he would ultimately finish it by himself. While working together out of Goodman's Brentwood home studio, Terence's friend and mentor died suddenly and unexpectedly. Terence was there to witness his collapse, and he vividly recalls the details of the harrowing incident.

I had hoped to speak with both of Terence's parents, but his father was too ill to converse. When I arrived at the doorstep of their New Orleans home on a cool January afternoon in 1996, Mrs. Blanchard opened the door with a quizzical half-smile and welcomed me in. Although Terence had told her to expect me, she seemed uneasy about the function of my visit. She sat me down at her kitchen table and politely excused herself for a moment to attend to Mr. Blanchard, who was bedridden in a nearby room. When she returned, she rigidly lowered herself into a chair across from me and smiled nervously. I wanted to make her more comfortable, so I improvised a question about her grandchildren that brought a warm smile to her face. She responded enthusiastically about Terence Jr. and Olivia (granddaughters Sidney and Jordan were not yet born).

Wilhelmina Blanchard is an authentic New Orleanian. Her accent is not thick, but there is a soft, southern cadence in her voice. From then on, her words flowed voluntarily. For two hours, she recited her fond memories of raising her only child, a smart and obedient boy who enjoyed going to the movies, watching wrestling, and playing football.

Mother and son look alike and remain close today. She takes pride in his life and career, laughing at the days when Terence's trumpet playing was so unbearable to everyone's senses that they had him practice in the backyard.

Occasionally, she excused herself to attend to her husband, one time bringing back a framed photograph of him. His resemblance to Terence is also unmistakable.

Regrettably, our conversation is dated by the death of Joseph Oliver Blanchard, her husband of thirty-seven years. He was a good father, says Mrs. Blanchard, who reared his son on his own strict moral code despite his desire to pamper him. His passion for music was so strong that it helped galvanize Terence to become a professional musician, a goal Mr. Blanchard had once set for himself.

Although I was unable to speak with Terence's father, Terence's maternal aunt, Alice Douglas, who was an active participant in his upbringing, provided a wonderful complement to those years. Like her sister, there is a soft-spoken kindness in Mrs. Douglas's voice. And while she too was unfamiliar with taking a stranger down memory lane, she seemed happy to make that trip.

The winter months of 1996 were brutal. Much of the United States and Canada were bombarded with snowfall. During this time, I began my initial research in New Orleans. It was unseasonably cool there too, often dipping into the thirties, but it was still a pleasant escape from Old Man Winter.

Until I was settled, I stayed with Terence and his soon-to-be wife, Robin, in their exquisite home on Prytania Street. The Garden District, in Uptown New Orleans, is an elite nineteenth-century residential neighborhood. Their grand, pink-colored house was said to have once belonged to slave plantation owners.

Terence's pianist, Edward Simon, who was still new to the band, was also staying there. He was stuck in town after their gig at the House of Blues because all flights to his home in Pennsylvania were postponed. Edward is a gentle, introverted man who chooses his words carefully. Other than music, he has a passion for language and culture. We enjoyed watching *Gandhi* together on videotape.

Robin is a fabulous cook, but Terence's favorite spot to eat is a late-night hangout fifteen minutes east of the city on Chef Mentour Hiway called We Never Close. His passion for po' boys (New Orleans–style sandwiches on long French bread) rallied us into his fully loaded Volvo sedan for regular visits to the drive-thru. Terence's choice po' boy is fried oysters and shrimps topped with Tabasco-infused mayonnaise. He was "tickled pink" to be home, just recently moving back after fifteen years in New York.

One night, he strolled briskly and confidently through the musical streets of the French Quarter, where he was greeted with a few head bobs of recognition. He led us all to Preservation Hall on St. Peter Street, the most famous jazz joint in the city. Although it attracts capacity crowds on a nightly basis, its décor is simple if not rundown. A small number of battered wooden benches were already occupied when we arrived, so we sat on the floor with our backs pressed against the peeling, dingy walls. This wasn't the Cotton Club. But Terence ensured us of a good time. After all, his friend and homeboy Leroy Jones was playing that night, a dazzling trumpeter/singer who was also happy to be home after a long tour with Harry Connick Jr.'s big band.

I awoke the next day to Terence's stereo. He is an early riser and enjoys listening to music first thing in the morning. He would play jazz but also Stravinsky and John Williams's *Schindler's List.*

One evening, at my request, he played selections from his own album *Romantic Defiance.* We each had our favorites: Edward, who has a predilection for ballads, made an obvious choice with "Unconditional." I favored the dark, haunting urgency of "Divine Order." Interestingly, Terence selected a bouncy number called "Focus."

The recording of his newest album, *The Heart Speaks*, had just been completed. It was still a couple of months away from release, but Terence played it for me, directing my attention to the end of "Congada Blues." He was excited about the finished product and looked forward to touring the music.

Earlier that day, he and Edward took the St. Charles streetcar to the Quarter to add to his already massive music collection. They returned with the complete sessions from Miles Davis's seminal 1965 date at the Plugged Nickel. The newly released material was a point of giddiness for Terence, who wasted no time loading the discs in his state-of-the-art stereo.

When the music stopped, we discussed the two great quintets Miles led. I preferred the edition with John Coltrane, while the musicians cited a stronger affinity for the freer framework of the mid-1960s group. To my surprise, the next morning I awoke to the music of *Kind of Blue.*

Although Terence was on hiatus from the road, he was very busy. When not composing in his home studio for HBO's *Soul of the Game*, he was in California interviewing for the romantic comedy *'Til There Was You* or in New York recording on pianist Billy Childs's album *The Child Within.* Still, he was constantly listening to music. Mid-1960s Miles Davis in his car; Thomas Newman's *The Shawshank Redemption* in his living room; live recordings of Louis Armstrong in his studio. Terence broke into a chaffing laughter when he described Pops's minstrel presentation, but then he quickly straightened up and exclaimed, "He could play!"

Bassist David Pulphus, a young bachelor in his early twenties, drove around in style in his brand new Pathfinder—for his instrument, he said. He lived nearby in a New Orleans shotgun (a house whose architecture is characterized by several rooms joined in a straight line from the front to the back). He dropped by frequently and unannounced, usually to play action-packed video games "to vent all of that hostility," we joked.

When Terence returned from California, his longtime drummer Troy Davis, who lived eighty miles northwest, in Baton Rouge, drove down with his wife. The quartet was together, and although they spoke of renting some space to rehearse, they went to the gym instead to work out.

On the weekend, we were treated to a visit by Terence's children. His daughter, Olivia, was a shy and precious three-year-old, and his son, Terence Jr., on the brink of turning eight, was talkative and curious. They live with their mother in the city and visit frequently. A room that I was sleeping in would be furnished for them.

I settled into a charming bed-and-breakfast on nearby General Pershing Street in the Uptown neighborhood where Terence's mom was raised. Finding my way around town was made easy by the hospitality of my interviewees. After my conversation with Terence's aunt, Alice Douglas, she kindly drove me to the campus of the University of New Orleans (UNO) where I was to meet her old friend Ellis Marsalis. They had attended Dillard University together with another pianist/educator and integral figure in Terence's formative years, Roger Dickerson. A professor in occupation and demeanor, Mr. Dickerson, like the Blanchards, still lives in the same house that Terence spent countless hours inside practicing.

Ellis Marsalis, who presided over jazz education at UNO, had been a prominent figure for the city for decades. Since his days at Xavier University and then more famously at the New Orleans Center for Creative Arts (NOCCA), he has been lionized for instructing more than a dozen of the world's top jazz musicians. He retired from UNO in 2001 and was succeeded by one of his former students, Terence Blanchard.

With fifty years of musical experience, Mr. Marsalis still performs regularly in his own band and occasionally with his four musician sons. Ironically, his career as a pianist and bandleader got a marketing boost when his eldest sons, Branford and Wynton, burst onto the jazz scene with striking fanfare in the early 1980s.

I first met Branford Marsalis at the 1996 Montreal Jazz Festival. He was there that summer with his father touring their excellent album, *Loved Ones*. I had crept backstage to proposition him for an interview, and he quite generously invited me to his home in New Rochelle, a short commute from Manhattan.

It had been more than a year since Branford quit *The Tonight Show* in California, but he did not appear to be settled in this house; cardboard boxes were everywhere. In one room, presumably the dining room, is where I waited for him. He was held up from a round of golf—a new hobby he was passionate about. There was a well-rounded selection of books in a nearby case—he is a voracious reader nicknamed "Book"—but the most eye-catching to me was the autobiography of Miles Davis. I wondered whether all jazz musicians considered it requisite reading.

When Branford arrived, he apologized for his tardiness. He was hungry, though, and before we began he quickly fixed himself a bowl of cereal. It would be the first of two conversations—his friendship with Terence is genuine, and he thinks of him fondly.

Our first meeting transpired just days after the TWA Flight 800 tragedy that had claimed the wife of his friend and mentor, Wayne Shorter. We sat on the porch of his suburban house located in a serene community with an adjacent pond. Friendly passersby engaged him in conversation about his golf game, his last tour stop, and his favorite baseball team, the New York Mets. He was popular in the neighborhood but not in a manner specific to a famous entertainer.

The scene was innocuous enough, but an hour later I had been jolted by his strong, caustic views on music, greed, vanity, and racism. His brutal honesty, irreverent humor, and the complexities of his character give this book charismatic spice.

For a man so regularly burdened with so many people making requests for his time, Wynton Marsalis was remarkably affable and accommodating. Interestingly, he and Terence, two of the greatest trumpeters in the world, were by their own admission two of the worst. They were eleven when they met, playing together as third-stringers in a big-band summer camp in New Orleans.

Less than ten years later, they were both in New York making a name for themselves by igniting the 1980s jazz resurgence. Their rivalry has been played up in the media, but they have a friendly and sincere respect for each other.

For all of his success as a jazz musician, this book is as intrigued by Blanchard's cinematic endeavors in Hollywood. What started as a novel assignment performing on the soundtracks for Spike Lee's early "joints" quickly blossomed into a celebrated career as a film composer.

My background in short filmmaking as a writer and director had equipped me with a high regard for the relationship of music to movies. The best film music fleshes out a director's vision. It can communicate the vital nuances that language or pictures cannot, giving audiences greater insight and heightened emotional attachment to the characters and story.

Directors are infamous for lamenting over their film's score because music is an art too complex for the average filmmaker to create or even mold. They are often subject to vulnerability and compelled to place a great deal of trust in their composer. Thus, a director–composer relationship is a delicate and often difficult collaboration.

After partnering with more than a dozen directors, Terence has a career filled with revealing insights into the collaborative process and why it is often the most troublesome of all filmmaking alliances.

It was the winter of 1997, and I had just seen my idol, Spike Lee, in person for the first time. He was sitting in his familiar perch at Madison Square Garden watching his beloved Knicks battle their nemesis Reggie Miller and the Indiana Pacers.

He had been a hero to me since my formative years. The resilience and fortitude he demonstrated in launching his feature filmmaking career was a constant source of inspiration. Additionally, the mighty resistance he withstood from Hollywood's studios for artistic control of his films had shaped my own aesthetics.

I was to meet with Spike that winter to discuss Terence and their work together, but he had been bogged down with his own projects and had postponed our interview. But it was with great curiosity that I watched him that afternoon, particularly after stoppages in play. He was in the midst of production of a documentary called *4 Little Girls*, and in an effort to fully utilize his time, he was scribbling notes, reviewing materials—working in a room of twenty thousand basketball fans. It was an image so strikingly unconventional that I developed a new appreciation for the demands of his schedule, which would deter our talk until 2001. In March of that year, he was between films (but still working on a TV project about Black Panther Huey P. Newton) and could accommodate an hour-long interview.

A meeting was scheduled at his advertising office, Spike DDB, on Madison Avenue, but he was detained that afternoon at Studio One, a postproduction facility on nearby Broadway. He rescheduled the interview there after his session and invited me to sit in with him until it was finished.

He was on the eighth floor of the Brill Building at the end of the hall, in Studio C. I entered the dark and hushed room where a panel of filmmakers reviewed footage of actor Roger Smith as Huey Newton. It has been said of Spike that he sees you before you see him. He is very attentive to his surroundings, not unlike his hero, Malcolm X.

Colorfully dressed in an orange sweater, green cords, and a black and orange Knicks toque, Lee gestured me over to him and pointed to an empty chair at his side. We shook hands, and I sat down and reveled in the fortuity of observing him at work.

They were sound-editing the picture, which can be a long and tedious procedure, so in between directing his staff, Spike engaged me in small talk.

He is a sober person; he speaks slowly in a low monotone. There are occasional bursts of enthusiasm that may be accompanied by his trademark cackle. When he smiles, it's usually in only one corner of his mouth. He is polite and avoids using profanity.

Amid the perfect pandemonium of Times Square, Spike Lee and I stood on a Broadway sidewalk fifty feet south of 49th Street waiting for his driver to arrive. His celebrity was demonstrated by curious gazes and giddy laughter from passing pedestrians. A pair of young women stood at the intersection staring and grinning, then waving at him. Spike waved back and then glanced down at his watch. In just an hour (the amount of time he had committed to me), he had to be at the Garden; the Celtics were in town.

His plan was to go home first, a thirty-minute drive through the stifling traffic, then another half hour back to the arena. We hopped in the back seat of his Mercedes SUV—his personal driver, Earl, was at the wheel—and we began our interview.

Spike's relationship with Terence dates back to the late eighties. They had known each other through the Marsalis brothers and became closer on the set of his 1990 jazz movie, *Mo' Better Blues*. Terence has written the original music to every one of his films since—a point of pride for the director. Lee is a loyal man who cherishes longtime partnerships.

When we arrived at his home on the Upper East Side off Lexington in the Sixties, Earl parked behind a black Lincoln Town Car, and Spike excused himself to speak with its driver. He returned to fetch a canvas book bag he carried, asked me to wait for him in the other car, and then vanished into his century-old townhouse.

As I waited, our new driver, a chatty white man in his fifties, queried me about Spike. Having never driven him before, he was only familiar with Lee's bad rap in the media as an antiwhite, cantankerous time bomb. But after meeting him, he, too, started to doubt its validity.

When Spike reemerged a few minutes later, he was, of course, still sporting the Knicks toque but had changed into his Latrell Sprewell jersey. For a man so serious, there was something unusually charming about him walking toward us (with the humorous saunter of his *Do the Right Thing* character, no less) dressed in the gay abandon of this blue, white, and orange apparel.

Terence has often accompanied Spike to the Garden, and despite being an equally ardent sports fan, he remembers how amusing it is to watch Spike demonstrate his passion for Knicks basketball. But his move to New Orleans in late 1995 squashed the regularity of those outings. Actually, when Terence told him he was moving, Spike, the consummate New

Yorker, was disappointed and could not fathom why he would want to leave the city.

So whenever club dates bring Terence back to New York, Spike makes every effort to visit him at the venue. More than collaborators, they are friends, and while he thinks of Terence as one of the premier film composers, he marvels at his trumpet playing and considers him a jazz musician first.

Yet to think of Blanchard as only one or the other, to judge him on his jazz music only or his film scores only, would be inappropriate. Each part makes up the whole.

My book thus presents Terence as a uniquely diverse talent with a myriad of remarkable achievements and musical associations. I hope that my rendering of the story of Terence Blanchard and his special guests evokes for its readers some of the same joy and profundity associated with their music and movies.

INTRODUCTION

The Dangling Carrot

Hit 'em hard and wish 'em well.

—*Bill Fielder*

June 28, 1995: The Toronto sun has set by now, but the insufferable humidity lingers into the evening. As millions of people across Canada's metropolis seek refuge from the sweltering summer heat, 120 jazz fans squeeze into their favorite haunt, the amply air-conditioned Top O' the Senator. On tonight's marquee: the Terence Blanchard Quartet.

The lights are low, the stage is vacant, and the Dangling Carrot is well out of reach, as the capacity crowd settles in their seats and orders cold drinks. Rather than taking solace in the respite they are now enjoying, the music lovers wear flabbergasted expressions and chatter endlessly about the outside humidity permeating the club.

When the band appears on the small but intimate stage, they are accompanied by distracted applause, as idle conversation lingers on. But as Blanchard and company burst into "The Premise," filling the room with its distinctively crisp and warm sound, an enchanting look welcomes them in. These four musicians, with their acoustic instruments, snuff out the audience's preoccupation with the weather and capture their undivided attention. Unfortunately, such a riveting performance is threatened when someone begins tampering with the room's impeccable temperature. Yet when a gust of hot air strikes the crowd, no one complains; not a single person seeks relief. In fact, they all seem to welcome it; Terence Blanchard is on fire.

Considering he is the culprit, Blanchard embraces the new climate and nourishes it all night long. Flushed and sweaty, it is a small price to pay, for the Dangling Carrot has now moved within his grasp.

After blazing past the midnight hour, the trumpet virtuoso finally stops blowing. He reintroduces his band, says goodnight, and steps off the stage to a spectacular embrace of firelike crackling applause.

Before vanishing up the stairs to their private lounge, Blanchard and his rhythm section turn to acknowledge the audience's adoration with a variety of grateful gestures. But gratitude is not what this exhilarated crowd wants. Their expression of affection surges into a relentless pursuit for more music. It does not matter that the musicians have now departed; these enthusiasts will not be denied.

Down the stairs they come; the straight-faced bassist, David Pulphus, appears first. He is followed by the ever-bopping and always-smiling drummer, Troy Davis. There is a momentary gap before the pleasantly serene pianist, Edward Simon, emerges with their leader. Suddenly, Blanchard's fingers snap out the tempo to "Dear Old Stockholm," and the full house, rewarded to approval, quietly return to their seats to indulge in the moment. They may hope the evening will last forever, but at its inevitable end, there isn't a disappointed face in the crowd. All are indeed grateful to Blanchard for producing a brand of heat unique to a midsummer night in Toronto, Canada.

CHAPTER ONE
THE BIRTH OF A JAZZMAN

> I was lucky in the sense that I always knew what I wanted to be, even from a very young age.
>
> —*Terence Blanchard*

Once upon a time, in a land not too far away, a musical creation evolved into America's most distinguished art form. Settled on the last southern stretch of the Mississippi River, New Orleans, Louisiana, is recognized as the birthplace of jazz.

According to music historians, jazz was first heard on the streets of New Orleans during the last decade of the nineteenth century. While the art form was developed in the United States, its origins are found in the African roots of those who created it. There have always been a large number of African American musicians, but at the turn of the twentieth century, music in some southern areas was all but considered a black profession. For blacks, music, and especially jazz, functioned as an emotional release from the legalized racism they had to endure.

During its early stages, jazz was essentially dance music with a strong foundation of the blues. It was a music free from traditional structure, as musicians improvised variations of rhythm and harmony according to the way their spirit moved them. Indicative of the time, whites generally dismissed this new creation as a crude and chaotic fad, going as far to denounce it as "the devil's music." Such public rebuke initially confined jazz to a notorious, sixteen-block district of New Orleans called Storyville.

Infamous for its wild dance halls, extravagant whorehouses, and all-night cabarets, the whole district was alive with music. Storyville attracted the city's finest musicians, all of whom emerged as pioneers in the evolution of jazz: Buddy Bolden, Freddie Keppard, Bunk Johnson, Red Allen,

Johnny Dodds, and Sidney Bechet. The three most dominant influences were pianist Ferdinand Joseph "Jelly Roll" Morton, cornetist Joseph "King" Oliver, and the Crescent City's greatest son, trumpeter/vocalist Louis Armstrong. To his peers, Armstrong was known simply as "Pops," a genial term used to describe his superior talent. Many music historians credit Armstrong as the artist responsible for eventually implementing rhythmic and melodic order to the so-called crude and chaotic beginnings of jazz.

As jazz flourished (not only in New Orleans but across the country and around the world), the Crescent City was counted on for its supply of polished jazz musicians. In 1917, however, the secretary of the navy deemed Storyville's red-light district a self-contained kingdom of vice. New Orleanians witnessed the shutdown of the district and the demise of their city as the jazz capital of the world. The music then sailed north along the Mississippi River, arriving in Memphis, St. Louis, Kansas City, and Chicago. It also spread to Dallas and its new capital, New York City, where it thrived for the better part of the next fifty years.

Jazz could still be heard in the French Quarter, but New Orleans did not produce a major jazz artist after Louis Armstrong followed the music to Chicago in 1922. Coleman Hawkins, Lionel Hampton, Charlie Parker, J. J. Johnson, and Miles Davis originated from the Midwest; Duke Ellington, Count Basie, Art Blakey, Sonny Rollins, and Clifford Brown from the Northeast. The Carolinas combined to produce Dizzy Gillespie, Thelonious Monk, and John Coltrane. Dexter Gordon and Charles Mingus made up a duo from California; Lester Young hailed from Mississippi, Cannonball Adderley from Florida, and Ornette Coleman from Texas.

This deficiency was attributed to the city's growing preference for new musical forms such as rhythm and blues, and fusion. However, fusion music—an integration of rock 'n' roll and jazz—did not merely thrive in the French Quarter. It became a popular genre for musical domains everywhere.

During its first seventy years, jazz survived ill repute and premature deaths of its pioneers to become America's greatest contribution to world culture. Yet, in 1969, when the frenzied popularity of rock infiltrated jazz, it immediately plummeted into a vast abyss. It was an era that would last ten-plus years, but at the time, many musicians, critics and fans alike, believed that jazz would be permanently cannibalized.

Then in the early 1980s, jazz and its favorite city came full circle. After a drought of sixty years, a powerful stream of New Orleans jazz musicians started surfacing in the most reputable conservatories in the country. Performances before capacity crowds in clubs and concert halls followed. Once again, the world was watching the city by the river. New Orleans began unleashing one talented jazz artist after another, spawning a timely revival in the music. This incredible movement in American music history is known as the 1980s jazz resurgence. Emerging at the forefront of this action was a young man who grew up in the Crescent City's Ninth Ward on Odin Street, Terence Blanchard.

Born March 13, 1962, Terence Oliver Blanchard soon knew that he wanted to become a professional musician. Growing up in a musical city certainly helped him realize such a goal, but it was the discipline and the determination instilled by his father that truly shaped Terence.

Joseph Oliver Blanchard studied opera and revered classical music. As a young man in the mid-1930s, he sang opera in and around New Orleans with a group called The Harlem Harmony Kings. As his aspirations of a permanent career in opera began to mount, segregation and bigotry thwarted them: discrimination against blacks who desired careers in opera and classical music was common. When the great Charles Mingus grew up in a Los Angeles ghetto studying cello, saxophonist Buddy Collette convinced him to switch to bass: "You're Black!" exclaimed Collette. "You'll never make it in classical music no matter how good you are. If you want to play, you've got to play a 'Negro' instrument."[1]

Forced to give up his dream, Blanchard then sold insurance for most of his life, an occupation that provided a stable income for his family. Still, he managed to remain active in the local music scene directing church choirs. At one Sunday morning performance, Blanchard met a lovely space filler in the choir named Wilhelmina Ray, whom he courted to be his bride.

Wilhelmina Ray, an authentic New Orleanian, was born in the Uptown section of the city in 1930. Although more than thirty-five years have passed since she resided there, Mrs. Blanchard yearns to return.

The Blanchards still live on Odin Street, in the same house where Terence first blew random riffs out of his trumpet. Nowadays, the doors don't swing open as often. Once filled with relatives, the house now shelters only Mr. and Mrs. Blanchard. But Mrs. Blanchard's memories of those days are fresh, and she shares them gladly. In a way, visiting Terence's mother is like listening to his music: it soothes, excites, and engages.

MRS. WILHELMINA RAY-BLANCHARD: I was born right here in New Orleans, Louisiana—Uptown, on General Taylor Street. And the house is still there, 2918 General Taylor. And after living in that house for a number of years, we lived on the 2800 block of General Taylor Street for twenty-two years. And that's where we grew up. And I love Uptown: "There's nothing like Uptown!"

CHAPTER ONE

I was the second oldest of four children. I had an older brother and a younger one, but they have both passed. And of course, there's my younger sister, Alice.

Mrs. Alice Ray-Douglas: My sister and I have been close since we were little girls; she's my best friend. We depend on each other. It's just the two of us living now, so we have to.

Mrs. Blanchard: Our mother was a disciplinarian, but our father was just the opposite. He was very quiet and didn't have much to say. My mother was a strong Baptist and whatever she said was law and gospel. Therefore, we had to dance by her music. No matter what we did Saturday night, we all had to go to church the next day and Sunday School, too; that was a ritual in my mother's house. But I wouldn't have wanted it any other way. The values that she taught me have shaped my whole life, and I loved her for that.

My father worked long hours as a plantsman for Standard Oil, but he was there for his children at all times. And he was a child at heart, playing more games with us than we did with each other.

Mrs. Douglas: Our father was very quiet, but he must have spent all of his spare time with us. And that was really important to us. He played the guitar and sang a beautiful bass. He never had any formal training; it was just a very natural talent. We actually have a lot of musicians in the family, especially on my father's side.

I began taking piano lessons when I was very young, then I went on to major in music at Dillard University. I went on to teach at three different high schools for a total of thirty-three years. My background is mostly classical piano, but we had several cousins who were singers.

Mrs. Blanchard: My parents wanted me to go to college—and I did, too—but I only finished high school. And that was my mistake. I only wanted to go to the college where all my friends were going, which was a boarding school. My parents couldn't afford it, but as youngsters you don't understand "can't afford." So I decided not to go at all because I thought I was hurting my parents, but I ended up hurting myself.

After I finished high school, I worked at the cleaners as a checker. I liked that job because I was constantly meeting people. I like people and I like to talk. When customers would come in, my face would say, "Talk to me." I could strike up a conversation in a minute.

But everything wasn't always so pleasant, you know, with segregation. There was this one rich lady that came to the cleaners regularly, and she would always compliment my coat that was hanging up on the wall. But she didn't know it was mine because every time she came in, she'd ask the white employees if it was their coat. They all said no, but they didn't know whose it was. I never said anything. Finally, after she couldn't figure out whose coat it was, she said to me, "Do *you* know whose coat that is?" And

I said, "Well yes, it's my coat." But she didn't believe me, "How can *you* afford a coat like that?" And I said, "I learned how to sign my name."

◆

Joseph Oliver Blanchard, the second of three children, all boys, was born in St. Martinville, Louisiana, in 1914 to Gabriel and Cauliest Blanchard. His father was known as "Red" because of his Indian coal-black hair, fiery red mustache, and his sandy-colored beard. Red enjoyed wrestling and boasted that he had never been "throwed" by any of his opponents. Relentlessly, Cauliest wrestled with whatever challenge came his way and always succeeded in conquering that which he set out to do. Tragically however, he was killed in a rice mill accident mere months after his youngest child was born. In an attempt to provide a better future for her three boys, Gabriel packed up her family and headed east for New Orleans.

MRS. BLANCHARD: Although his name is Joseph, we've been calling him Oliver all his life. It wasn't until we saw his birth certificate that we discovered his name was Joseph Oliver.

He left St. Martinville for New Orleans when he was twelve. Oliver was only two when his father was killed, so he never really knew his daddy. He got caught in one of those machines. I never met his mother, but I understand she was a midwife back in those days.

I never wanted to get married, and I was late getting married. I never really wanted a husband. I know it's odd and I don't mean to sound selfish, but I always used to think that I didn't *need* one. I think this was all because someone very dear to me had a terrible experience with her husband. It put a damper on men for me. And now I sit down and wonder all the time how Oliver ever caught up with me. I guess it was love.

We met in November of '59 when he came to our church to direct our choir. I couldn't sing, but I was in the choir; I was a space filler. I know the Lord didn't give me a voice because he knew I would drive everyone crazy. Oliver sang opera with a church group and traveled locally.

TERENCE BLANCHARD: He studied a great deal; he's a guy with a serious passion for music. People that knew him in his prime said he had a wonderful voice. He wanted to be an opera singer but didn't pursue it because of the racial stigma during those times. But he never became embittered; he sang in New Orleans every chance he got. The music was the only thing that he focused on. That's what I saw growing up.

Although he didn't really talk about it much, I knew he was frustrated by it. I think it also had a lot to do with the fact that he didn't know what to do or where to go; you see that a lot in the South. There's a lot of talented kids who can do some great things, but they're just sitting at home. They never had someone to tell them to go to New York or to see a certain teacher or musician.

MRS. BLANCHARD: Oliver is seventeen years older than me and had already been married. His wife passed because of a brain aneurysm. They had a child but it was still-born, so Terence was really his only child.

He was a young man when he married his first wife; he was only seventeen. Oliver was the type of person who needed to be married. I told him that I didn't want to get married, but he insisted. I don't know what kind of magic he used on me, but in a year's time we were married. Actually, it was in June of '61.

TERENCE BLANCHARD: It's kind of hard to describe, but to me, their marriage has been amazing. Like any other marriage, they had their problems and differences, but unlike many, they were able to overcome them. Growing up, it never seemed to me like they could ever break up. I guess everybody wants their parents to be that way. I just happen to be one of the lucky ones.

MRS. BLANCHARD: Originally, we were going to name Terence after Oliver's father. But I thought Cauliest was a rather odd name, so I started looking at one of those name books. When I saw the name Terence, it stuck with me—I liked it. So when Oliver came to the hospital, I told him I was going to name the baby Terence Oliver.

Terence was a very good baby. I never had any problems with him at all. With Oliver, he was more of a toy than anything. Of course, Terence was our only child, so Oliver spoiled him rotten.

MRS. DOUGLAS: Oh, he was very excited over his *one* son, his *only* child. He did everything for that little boy, and my sister, too—everything. I mean, they would even go as far to carry his school books. That's when I stepped in and reminded them that we wanted Terence to be a *boy*. They were going to make a sissy out of him! Since no one wanted that, they finally stopped.

MRS. BLANCHARD: Wherever Terence wanted to go, his daddy took him. I remember when the movie *Chitty Chitty Bang Bang* came out, Terence was about six, and they went to see that movie more times than I can count on all my fingers. They went to a lot of movies; Terence really loved them. Whatever movie he wanted to see, his daddy took him at least two or three times.

TERENCE BLANCHARD: He took me to see *Fiddler on the Roof* because he thought it was something I should see—and it was. [singing] "If I were a rich man . . ." He loved the music. Then he took me to see *Jungle Book* and *Chitty Chitty Bang Bang*—all that kind of stuff. But I really wanted him to take me to the wrestling matches, which he wouldn't do. Everything had to be a cultural experience. He was the type of guy who wouldn't let me play with toy guns. I remember he saw me chastise a cat in the street one day, and he jumped in my shirt about it. I knew he was a humanitarian, but I was like, "It's only a cat."

Sadly, over the last five years, Oliver Blanchard has become ill with transient ischemic attacks (TIAs). These attacks cause a brief interruption of the blood supply to part of the brain, resulting in a temporary impairment of vision, speech, sensation, or movement. Typically, the episode occurs suddenly, lasting for several minutes or, at the most, for a few hours. Treatment is aimed at preventing a major stroke, which occurs in approximately 30 percent of TIA patients within the first five years.

Mrs. Blanchard: He's completely bed-ridden now. He doesn't talk; he doesn't walk; he doesn't respond to hardly anything anymore. At one time he would respond to something on the television, but not anymore. For a while it wasn't so bad because he'd be up and around. I have to do everything now. But I want to take care of him myself. I don't like to leave him, and everybody fusses at me because I stay home.

When Oliver took ill, I would play Terence's music for him, and believe it or not, he knew the difference if I changed the music and put someone else on. At the time, it wasn't too bad because he walked around. But now, being in the bed all the time, well . . .

Terence Blanchard: My dad was a real passionate man in terms of loving his son. We did a lot of things together, especially when I was young. But while I was playing with Art Blakey, I remember I came home one time and I kind of became his friend. He heard me on the phone talking to somebody about going to a club for a jam session and he said, "Hey, let me take that ride with you." I wasn't sure if he should come but he was like, "Come on, let me come with you." He just wanted to be one of the fellas. So he came, sat at the bar, and fell asleep. He had a couple of drinks and that was it!

Mrs. Douglas: Terence was an ideal child to have. His mother could always sit down and talk with him, not at him. He wasn't the kind that would just fly off. It didn't really take much to make him happy. He was respectful and quiet at all times. I don't mean to say that you could just run over him. You could get Terence to do what you wanted him to do, but he'd always let you know what he thought he should do. The thing about Terence was that he was always very focused on what he wanted, which was to be a musician.

Terence Blanchard: A lot of people say that about me, but I did have an interest in sports. When I was in elementary school, I thought I was going to be a football star. I was playing Little League football and became quite serious about it. I was even picked to be on one of the All City teams. I played on the line, both offensive guard and tackle. Actually, we didn't have enough people for both offensive and defensive squads, so I played linebacker, too. I had a lot of fun playing the game until my father took me out. A lot of kids were getting hurt, some even paralyzed, which really scared my father. That's when music became a dominant thing in my life.

Mrs. Douglas: Terence's father was a musician and naturally, he wanted Terence to become one, too. But he wanted Terence to play classical music, not jazz.

Terence Blanchard: I loved the fact that there was always music played in my house. My dad was very instrumental in developing my appreciation for music. He'd always be playing his records. But I hated the fact that it was mostly opera and not the popular music of my time that I heard in the streets. And we would always argue about music. I would always talk about how great Miles Davis and Clifford Brown were, and he would always say, "Yeah, yeah, yeah, but I can't hear no melody." While we never really settled this issue, I learned as an adult to love the fact that my dad never disrespected my opinions. He would always encourage me to stick by what I believed in and make my case.

Mrs. Blanchard: Since my sister was a music major, Terence would go to her for anything he didn't understand. She would coach him along at times. My husband had a great deal to do with Terence's musical development, too. There were a lot of influences on Terence, and his daddy pushed him more than anybody.

Terence Blanchard: My family helped out a lot. They supported me in every way, which was great. They never really forced anything on me, but my father did push me to practice a lot when I was a kid. And I hated the fact that my lessons were based on boring exercises and classical études designed to build strength in my hands. My dad would come home tired after work and make me practice while he sat on the sofa listening to every note. When one of the many notes I played—in any piece of music I was learning—seemed out of context with the rest, he would stop me and say, "Stop and go back; that didn't sound smooth." But I loved the fact that these lessons got me to the point where I could play a piece of music on my own in public, even if my dad felt the need to start me on my practicing regimen two months prior to any scheduled performances.

I hated practicing, but he instilled a discipline in me. If it weren't for my father, I don't know where I'd be. His diligence helped me to build the confidence I needed to perform in public.

Mrs. Douglas: I wasn't fortunate enough to have children, so I really feel like Terence is part my child, especially since we all spent so much time together when he was young. My sister worked, so in the summer I would go over to the house to look after Terence and my other nephew, Eric. And with me, you had to drink milk and eat vegetables. And they hated it. They always wanted soft drinks and hamburgers. Soft drinks for lunch, soft drinks for dinner. Terence recently admitted to me that they used to call me "The Vegetable Queen" behind my back.

Terence was very young when he started playing piano, and I had read that it's not always the best thing for the family to start a youngster in music. So I said to my sister, "Let's get somebody else." We contacted Martha Francis.

MARTHA FRANCIS: Terence's aunt also taught music, and she said to me, "Martha, I think Terence has *something*, but I don't think I should teach him because I'm too close. Would you teach him?" Of course, I said yes.

I always knew that Terence had *it* from the beginning. I've been teaching since 1954, and during that time you sometimes get a feeling that, "Hey, this kid's going to . . . ." Well, I always felt that about Terence.

He caught on very fast, definitely faster than the average child. The thing I noticed most with Terence was that he was very conscientious for such a young boy. I used to play the pieces for him, and he'd come right behind me and play them perfectly. That's when I realized he had a good ear, and I explained to him that it was a gift, but I told him that in order to become a musician, you must be able to read. From then on, I never played the pieces for him again. I just put them in front of him so he could learn to read.

TERENCE BLANCHARD: Mrs. Francis had a great effect on me. She was a great teacher, but what I remember most was her patience and the way she could motivate me.

MRS. BLANCHARD: Terence started out on piano with Martha before he even started school. He was always over at Martha's house because she had four boys. We were next-door neighbors, and sometimes he wouldn't even come home for supper.

TERENCE BLANCHARD: Going over there was like going to my second mother's house. She used to discipline me just like my mother would. I remember she had a lot of friends who played piano as well. We lived right next door, in one of those double houses, and my bedroom wall was right up against their living room wall. So late at night I could hear them playing piano; it was like a piano house!

MARTHA FRANCIS: Terence was like a fifth son to me. He used to come over and play with my boys all the time. I can still picture this one incident when they were about eight or nine. Having four boys, I had two bunk beds on each side of the room. And I remember them coming downstairs to ask me for some towels. I didn't give it much thought because I was busy doing something, so I said, "Yes, you can take the towels."

The next thing I heard was this big bang and then a loud scream. So naturally I ran upstairs to see what was going on. As it turned out, they were playing "Superman," jumping from the top of one bunk to the other. They had tied the towels around their necks using them as capes. My two oldest boys went first, and they had made it. Then it was Terence's turn. But instead of jumping to the next bed, he fell right smack in the middle of the floor!

TERENCE BLANCHARD: Man, that's funny. I forgot about that. We had a lot of fun. Her son Mark and I were the same age, and he was always getting me to do crazy stuff like that. I remember he was so strong for a little kid. But that was my last jump!

MRS. BLANCHARD: Terence never talked much as a boy and still doesn't. With Terence, you have to be able to push that little button, then he'll decide to talk. Sometimes he'll take over an entire conversation, but if you don't know how to push that little button, then you won't get anything out of him. As much as Terence has traveled, he doesn't talk about it. Of all the people he's met, he doesn't talk about them. But that's his nature. Terence was always more or less a loner than anything. I mean, he had friends but was never what you'd call close to anybody. I think that he's a little more outgoing now because of the field that he's in. But his daddy was like that, too. Oliver had friends, but he liked to stay to himself. Terence is very much like him.

TERENCE BLANCHARD: It's true. I think it's probably because I was an only child, so I got used to being alone. The older I get, the more I value friendship. But sometimes that workaholic in me keeps me from getting close with people because whenever I have a free moment and think I should be calling somebody or getting in touch with a friend, my mind is going, "Well, you could be doing this or working on that." It's a work ethic I get from my dad. He was a workaholic, too, but I look at that as being one thing that hurt his health. But you know, also, when I was a kid in elementary school, I got good grades and wore glasses when they weren't fashionable. I was always ridiculed about that stuff, and I guess I never really felt like a kid who fit in with the popular kids. So after a while it just became part of the routine, and I didn't really mind it. But it all changed when I got to junior high and high school.

MRS. BLANCHARD: Terence was always a good student, but when he got to junior high school he began to—as old folks used to say—smell his oats. Teachers started calling me because of his behavior. It wasn't that he was a bad kid; it was just that he'd finish his work before all the other children and then tantalize them. I had two or three teachers tell me, "He's not a bad little boy, but he's got to learn to stay quiet." Then the teachers started giving him extra work, but Terence still finished before the others.

◆

Racial injustice and the American South have long been synonymous. Until President Lyndon Johnson passed the Civil Rights Bill in 1964, blacks were confined to the poorest sectors of the economy by way of legalized segregation.

For a forty-year period, beginning at the end of World War I, several thousand black southerners uprooted to the North in hopes of escaping social disharmony and realizing greater economic opportunity. In most cases, the migration manifested itself in two steps: a move from a rural farm area to a southern city and then to a northern city, primarily New York, Chicago, and Detroit.

Many of those who participated in this massive migration prospered economically from the move, even though the reduction of racial seclusion was minimal. It may have been illegal, but societal pressures restricted blacks from residential choice. Segregated schools and discrimination in the workplace also lingered on in the new black community.

Mrs. Blanchard: At one time, my husband wanted to leave the South for some town in Michigan. He worked for Sears & Roebuck for years selling insurance, and they were willing to transfer him there, but I told him, "No way." I didn't want to go up in the cold! Besides, I have some cousins that live in Chicago and St. Louis, and the ones from St. Louis had come down to visit us because they had heard terrible things about the South and how we were treated. But they were shocked when they got here because they realized it wasn't nearly as bad as they had thought. Then one year I visited Chicago, and, to me, the living situation *there* was horrible. I found it to be more segregated there than I did in New Orleans.

Indirectly, by never venturing to the so-called Promised Land, the Blanchards probably preserved their son's musical destiny. By staying in New Orleans to raise their only child, they gave Terence the opportunity to mature in one of the most musical cities in the world.

Terence Blanchard: I think New Orleans is one of the greatest places to learn from, especially during the time I was growing up. I got an opportunity to hear musicians play live in a traditional style *every* day. On the way home from school, I used to love walking down Bourbon Street. Some of the clubs used to have twenty-four-hour music—it was amazing! I would hear Teddy Riley play, guys like Emery Thompson and Danny

Barker. Obviously, I couldn't go in and have a drink, so I'd stand right outside the door and listen. Then when I got home I could listen to Clifford Brown and Miles Davis records. This way I could see right before my eyes how the music had evolved over time.

Also, there were a lot of teachers around at the time; it was a healthy period. I knew I wanted to be a musician from very early on, but I really didn't have any teachers. I mean, I had piano teachers, but no one to really teach me how to play on chord changes or how to compose—you know, the creative aspects of the music. So when I ran into those guys I was in heaven. I felt like I was learning a lot every day. And the thing that I always try to reiterate is that we didn't get instruction from one particular person; it was a well-rounded and well-orchestrated thing.

There was Alvin Batiste who taught [saxophonists] Donald Harrison and Branford Marsalis. Roger Dickerson was my composition and piano instructor. George Jansen taught me and Wynton [Marsalis] trumpet, Bert Braud theory and analysis, and of course Ellis Marsalis was teaching everybody jazz. These guys knew what they were doing. They had gone abroad and studied very hard and wanted to give something back to the community. And I commend all of them for that because so many of us will just abandon our communities nowadays.

Terence received the kind of instruction and exposure to jazz unique to New Orleans, a city where accomplished jazz musicians conduct assemblies in elementary schools. While in third grade, Terence sat in the gymnasium of his school, Mary D. Coghill Elementary, awestruck by Alvin Alcorn, the trumpeter who gained international fame in Kid Ory's Creole Jazz Band. Alcorn had an attractive tone and subtle style not unlike Miles Davis's, but he was also known for occasional bursts of exhibitionism. That afternoon he showcased the instrument's exciting repertoire of slurs, smears, and growls, inspiring an eight-year-old to make a lifelong commitment.

Terence Blanchard: Seeing Alvin Alcorn turned my life around. I'll never forget it! From that day on, I wanted to be a trumpet player. The thing that amazed me was that I could see this guy's mouth at one end of the instrument and hear all this *stuff* coming out the other end. I remember him bending notes and the way he phrased. I couldn't do *that* on the piano.

Studying piano with Mrs. Francis was cool—and I'll never forget her—but you know, as a kid, it kind of got boring and a little frustrating. But the funny thing was, I couldn't readily get out of it because she lived next door! So I had to constantly go to my lessons. But when Alvin Alcorn came to my school, he really woke me up; he caught my attention. I mean,

I had heard trumpet players before, but seeing Alvin Alcorn was really the first time I had heard the trumpet by someone who could *play* it. And I think that's what caught my ear.

That day I remember running home after school to tell my parents that I had to have a trumpet. But they were a little upset because they had just rented a piano.

MRS. BLANCHARD: When Terence first got his trumpet, my mother and father were living with us at the time, and my mother said to me, "He's not going to play that in the house, is he?" And I said, "No way! He can go in the backyard and practice." But it wasn't too long before my mother began to actually enjoy it. She used to sit down on the couch and listen to Terence practice all day long.

MRS. DOUGLAS: Playing music was just a part of the family. But what fell on Terence, well . . . .

Note

1. Grover Sales, *Jazz: America's Classical Music* (New York: Da Capo, 1992), 184.

CHAPTER TWO
LITTLE CATS

Terence was a thorough little cat!

—*Willie Metcalf*

It had been two years since Terence heard Alvin Alcorn play, and he was still buzzing from the epiphany. Armed with his first trumpet, and eager to improve, the youngster had another chance meeting with his newfound hero.

Terence and his father were in their car slowing to an intersection, where, stopped at a red light, was Alcorn. "Hey, Alvin," Mr. Blanchard yelled out. They had known each other for years, both being of the same age and active in the musical community. "This is my son here; he plays trumpet now. Do you think you could give him some lessons?"

The established musician, then in his sixties, rolled down his window and dryly replied, "No, I can't do that. He has to learn it himself."

Alcorn's advice lingered in the impressionable boy's mind, shocking and confusing him. But Alcorn was not trying to dishearten the child; he was simply speaking from experience.

A self-taught "street musician" from New Orleans, Alcorn never reaped polished instruction from one of the many conservatories for jazz now throughout the country. During his formative years in the 1920s, aspiring jazz musicians learned their craft without the aid of written music and formal instruction. Education was primarily obtained through the study of phonographic recordings and live performances. Terence Blanchard came from a completely different generation, one that emphasized music education in schools, one that would prove Alcorn's statement to be inaccurate.

Music education in 1970s New Orleans was flourishing. As schools were beginning to implement programs in music, camps for youngsters were growing in popularity. At the age of eleven, Terence took part in a summer music camp held at Loyola University.

> **Mrs. Douglas:** Since I was a music teacher, I used to hear about a lot of music programs for youngsters. That's how I heard about Loyola's summer music camp. Loyola is one of the better universities in New Orleans, so I assumed it would be a good thing for Terence. So right away I enrolled him in that. And he loved it.

> **Terence Blanchard:** My aunt was very helpful as I was growing up. She was always getting me involved in local musical activities like music camps and stuff like that. One summer, before the sixth grade, she enrolled me in a summer camp at Loyola University. That's where I met Branford and Wynton [Marsalis].

◆

Gumbo and New Orleans, carnivals and Mardi Gras, Marsalis and jazz—they all go hand in hand. Born in the Crescent City on November 14, 1934, Ellis Marsalis Jr. majored in music at Dillard University. The first instrument he played was clarinet before switching to saxophone. While at Dillard, he settled on piano, an instrument that has inspired him for the last fifty years.

His father, Ellis Sr., was not a musician but an influential local businessman who owned, among other things, a family motel in the Jefferson-Parish district. In the 1950s, much to his discontent, his son ran an unsuccessful jazz club out of the motel called Music Haven. After six months, Ellis Jr. realized that "business was not his thing" and joined the marines for two years. In 1958, he married his wife, Dolores Ferdinand, and on August 26, 1960, the first of their six sons, Branford, was born.

Like his father, Branford began on clarinet and by the age of fifteen had switched to the alto saxophone. However, unlike his father, Branford settled on the illustrious woodwind. While attending Southern University, he studied under Alvin Batiste for one year before transferring to the Berklee College of Music in Boston.

Branford's younger brother Wynton (named after piano legend Wynton Kelly) was born on October 18, 1961. Predictably, he began playing music as a youngster, and despite evolving into a jazz traditionalist and purveyor of such musical values, Wynton found his early development enlightened by performing in an assorted range of ensembles. As a teenager, the trumpeter led a funk/R&B band called the Creators, listened to fusion music, and played with the New Orleans Civic Orchestra. Upon graduation from the New Orleans Center for Creative Arts (NOCCA) in 1979, Wynton furthered his studies at the Juilliard School in Manhattan and then as a member of Art Blakey's Jazz Messengers.

By the summer of 1981, after Branford's abbreviated gigs with Lionel Hampton and Clark Terry, the brothers Marsalis were musically reunited in the Jazz Messengers' front line. Their stint together in the famous hard-bop band is well represented on the Grammy-nominated album *Keystone 3*.

> **Branford Marsalis:** When we were with Art Blakey's band, I was always having arguments with Wynton. Wynton said that I should play tenor instead of alto because all that I did was play in the middle to lower register of the alto, that I never used the upper register, that I wasn't playing it like an alto, so why bother playing it? I said, "You are wrong. I am working on a concept, so shut the fuck up." Then he said that he was starting a band, and if I didn't have a tenor, I wouldn't be in the band. I got a tenor. Three minutes after I blew it, I knew that he was right all along.[1]

Over the next four years, Branford and Wynton lived together in New York City, growing closer as brothers and collaborators by maturing and performing side by side (mainly under the highly successful heading of the Wynton Marsalis Quintet).

In early 1985, Branford was introduced to Sting, then lead singer of the wildly popular rock band the Police. Shortly thereafter, the British rocker ventured his popularity to assemble a new band that would better communicate his artistic sensibilities. He hired top-fleet jazz musicians—Marsalis and pianist Kenny Kirkland among them—and promptly recorded his solo debut, *Dream of the Blue Turtles*.

Wynton's quintet eluded disbandment for a few more months until Branford and Kirkland quit the band to tour with Sting. Their departure caused a rift between the siblings that took years to subside. Wynton was disappointed to lose his brother, his kindred spirit, but devastated to see him join a pop band.

> **Branford Marsalis:** Wynton's not too fond of pop music, and [he was upset because] he had written all this music for a band that no longer existed. He had set aside a period in his life that he had dedicated to that band, and none of it ever materialized. I mean, he had the next record all written out, and then we left and that music was gone; it was never played, and it never will be played. And it was very hard on him to find a new band because it's hard to find jazz musicians. It's not hard to find pop musicians; you can find them crawling through every crack in the world, you

> know, literally thousands of them ready to take gigs. Albeit not great musicians, but you don't have to exactly be a technical wizard to play three chords a song. But with jazz musicians, there's just not many of them, and it's not like there was a pile of people in the talent pool who were ready to step up and play that kind of music in that kind of style. As a matter of fact, Wynton's next record [*J Mood*] is like a complete 180 from *Black Codes from the Underground* because he couldn't find musicians who could play that style of music. I mean, Marcus Roberts is not gonna play like Kenny Kirkland, and Todd Williams ain't gonna play like me; they can't play that style of music. So he ended up writing a whole new thing. So I can understand why he'd be upset; shit, I'd be upset, too.

Since their disagreeable split, both Branford and Wynton have strived to achieve their own interpretation of success. Reputed for his technical mastery, Wynton nonetheless has an astounding ability to articulate feeling through his trumpet. An integral part of the 1980s jazz resurgence, Marsalis is a multiple Grammy Award winner and the only jazz artist ever to be awarded a Pulitzer Prize (for *Blood on the Fields*). Consequently, he has been surrounded by media hype and celebration—attention he has unequivocally earned.

While Branford has taken a considerably different route than his younger brother, he, too, played a pivotal role in the rebirth of jazz in the 1980s. Along the way, he explored many diverse musical styles. Such eclectic taste, of course, notes Branford's early jazz recordings with Blakey, as well as Herbie Hancock and Wynton, but his departure from the latter's quintet confirmed his desire to take chances outside jazz.

The global appeal of Sting kept Branford actively performing throughout their three-year collaboration, but Marsalis concurrently pursued his own projects. During a break in filming *Bring On the Night*, a documentary made in France on the evolution of Sting's group, Branford skipped to London to finish recording his first classical album, *Romances for Saxophone* with the English Chamber Orchestra. In the fall of 1986, Columbia Records released Branford's *Royal Garden Blues*, a jazz piece that won a Grammy nomination. The title track was made into a music video by an up-and-coming young filmmaker named Spike Lee, marking the first collaboration in a series of many between the two artists.

Branford has also been musically linked to Miles Davis, the Grateful Dead, Buckshot LeFonque, Bruce Hornsby, and the rapper Guru, but his most widespread exposure began on May 25, 1992, when he was beamed through millions of television sets across the world as musical director of *The Tonight Show with Jay Leno*.

Branford Marsalis is indeed a mammoth contemporary talent but also an engaging personality. While part of his appeal can be attributed to his poignant wit and infectious storytelling skills, his penchant for saying what he thinks in the bluntest of terms is downright riveting.

The Marsalis musicians do not stop there. The fourth son, Delfeayo, is a brilliant trombonist/producer, while the baby of the family, Jason, is an emerging young talent on drums. With so many musicians raised under the same roof, one might assume that the roof must have been that of Carnegie Hall. As Branford explains, that was not quite the situation.

BRANFORD MARSALIS: We didn't really have a music household; it was just a regular household with a bunch of kids screaming, hollering, you know, needing to be disciplined. And when we needed to be disciplined, we were. Music was something everybody in New Orleans does, and we just did it. The idea of becoming professional musicians had nothing to do with it. To me, it was just a hobby until I was nineteen.

WYNTON MARSALIS: I remember when I first met Terence. We were in a music camp at Loyola, and me and him were like third-stringers in this big band. We sat way on the end—it was sad. I mean, we were terrible. At the time, I wasn't too interested in learning jazz. I wanted to play basketball.

TERENCE BLANCHARD: Me and Wynton were the *worst* players in the section. And I'll never forget it because Wynton was a little intimidating back then. He had a fresh mouth when he was a kid, and that made me a little nervous. He was also a year ahead of me—he was going into the seventh grade, while I was going into the sixth. We played in the concert band together, but we sat all the way at the end holding conversations.

BRANFORD MARSALIS: That shit always sounds good: "The *worst* player in the section." But Wynton *was* one of the worst players. He was terrible. Terence was real quiet, shy. I remember, man [*laughing*], he had a big head and we used to tease him all the time. But everybody teases everybody in New Orleans. That's the way it was; that's the way it is.

WYNTON MARSALIS: We always bugged him about his head, but he never got mad; he was cool. Terence was a real nice guy, and I wish I had some crazy story to tell about him when he was young, but I don't. He never really messed around or anything like that. I mean, he wasn't one of them geeks; he was just cool and intelligent. He always made intelligent decisions. He would always be practicing—he was real serious about practicing. When we were growing up in New Orleans, me and Terence were the only ones truly serious about the music. Terence was the only cat I knew that I could talk intelligently with about the music. All the other guys were just talking bullshit. That is until I met Marcus Roberts.

Terence Blanchard: I've known those guys for a long time. When we were kids, Wynton was this little skinny kid with a big afro, and Branford had short hair because it wouldn't grow. Branford's an easy-going guy, very laid back—too laid back for some people. They'll say, "Branford, come on, we got to do this!" And he'll be like, "*OK*, just chill, I'll get it done."

Branford Marsalis: We were musicians, so we had a lot in common. We were in bands together. Terence joined this funk band that I was in, [called The Creators], but it wasn't like we sat around and practiced music all day. It wasn't even like I practiced at all. We were just partners. I used to go to his house and hang out. I don't remember what we did, but since we're from New Orleans, we probably didn't do shit. People in New Orleans didn't do anything. You just go to somebody's house and you watch TV. We'd go outside and throw a football around, or we used to walk to the campus of Southern University in New Orleans and look at all the college chicks.

One thing that I like about Terence is that in a lot of ways, he was the opposite of the way we were. I mean, we were very boisterous and Terence is real quiet. And if you got to know anything about Terence, you were privileged to know that. He's just a very quiet person; he keeps his shit close to the vest—not very much different than what he is now.

Terence Blanchard: When we were in school together, people used to think me and Branford were brothers. We had an interesting relationship because our personalities were very different. Actually, I was compared more with Wynton. But me and Branford were always hanging out at the student center, playing pinball and all kinds of stuff like that. Then when we were living in Brooklyn, we hung out all the time, going to baseball games together.

Branford Marsalis: Terence and I lived around the corner from each other. We used to see each other every day. I mean, he had a wife and a kid and I had a wife and a kid. I would take my kid, put him in a stroller, and walk over to Terence's house. The two kids would play and we'd talk about baseball, the Saints, and not a whole lot about music. We were definitely close. Then he moved to New Orleans—well, I left Brooklyn, divorced my wife, and moved to California, so that killed that. Shit happens.

Terence Blanchard: It was the kind of thing where you just sort of grow apart, I guess. You just start getting busy; you start doing other things. He went out west; you know, I was traveling and never really went out there. Then I moved to New Orleans, so you know, we don't get a chance to see much of each other anymore.

Branford Marsalis: Me and Terence have a very similar sense of humor, and unfortunately, we're both New Orleans Saints fans. He gets a little more emotionally wrapped up in it than I do. I mean, he would throw his television set out the window. I don't get to that level, but we're very passionate about it.

It may be difficult to envision Terence giving way to such a demonstrative display—at least when not performing somewhere on a stage—but beneath the reticent surface is a passionate man. More than sports and music, Terence delights in world culture; he is inquisitive and deeply spiritual. At times, he is a stirring conversationalist or an amusing humorist complete with impressions. His passion is probably innate, honed early by his father until it flourished when he discovered the trumpet. For it is through the horn that Terence expresses his most powerful emotions.

MRS. BLANCHARD: Before high school, Terence got to the point where he became so involved with music that he was always practicing or performing somewhere. I remember he always wanted to go to St. Augustine, which is a private Catholic high school, because he wanted to be in their marching band. And whenever the band played, Terence's daddy was there. Oliver was very proud. He showed up wherever Terence played.

TERENCE BLANCHARD: I was fourteen when I first played in a night club. I wasn't playing jazz, but it was a very exciting experience because here I am, fourteen years old, playing in an after-hours club and everybody's worried about the police coming in and grabbing me. Somebody handed me a beer and said, "Don't drink it, just hold it—it'll make you look older." So we played the set, and then my dad turned up and the MC called out, "Terence Blanchard, your father is at the door!" I just tried to sneak out as best as I could.[2]

MRS. BLANCHARD: Terence even played his trumpet in church. On Saturday night, he would play with the marching band, then on Sunday morning he played in church. The thing that was so amazing was that I never had to wake him up that morning. He had himself up and ready to leave on time every week. He loved playing that trumpet.

MRS. DOUGLAS: When Terence was playing his trumpet in church, the organist wanted him to learn how to transpose. So he said to Terence, "Come over to my house and I'll show you." And before long, Terence was taking the head note and going from page to page just transposing.

One day, his mother and I were listening to him in the other room. "I don't want it in that key!" he said to himself. "I'll put it in that key!" I thought, "Oh, my goodness, I can't even do that!" That's when I called Roger Dickerson.

Roger Dickerson and Ellis Marsalis were my classmates at Dillard University. They're *very* good musicians—excellent. Ellis has the soft, beautiful touch playing jazz. And Roger, too. One of the things that impressed me about Roger was that he was so self-disciplined. When the gang of us would go out on the weekends, Roger wouldn't leave his house until he played his scales so many times.

I thought Roger would be able to help Terence with his writing. So I said, "Roger, I know you don't teach youngsters, but you have got to listen to my nephew." He said, "OK, Alice, you know I don't teach them, but I will listen." And then after listening to Terence, he said, "I'll teach him myself." That's when I really knew Terence must have been *something*.

Roger Dickerson: When I took Terence on as a private student, we started right away on piano and composition. Terence came to me when he was just beginning high school, but he was already very serious about what he wanted to do. He had a kind of self-motivated inner drive where he was doing things to develop himself that had nothing to do with a deadline or a certain agenda. He did it because he wanted to realize his talents. And that is something that is very rare. And I think it's almost a forgone conclusion when you see such dedication in a person that success will soon attach itself to that particular musician. There are not too many people like Terence who are willing to give that kind of time and serious dedication; they want things overnight.

We began working on composition because he was writing a "big" score for the St. Augustine band. It was *Rocky* or something very popular like that. Terence worked really hard, and it paid off rather well. But after he began coming here, Terence wanted to get into NOCCA.

Terence Blanchard: The summer before the ninth grade—I was like fourteen—we were all playing with Willie Metcalf at his camp, and I couldn't believe how much better Wynton was.

Wynton Marsalis: I started getting serious. I was taking lessons and practicing like four to five hours a day. When Terence heard me play, he was like, "Whoa, shit!" You know, all shocked.

Terence Blanchard: I was like, "Damn, what happened to you?" That's when I began to feel like I was playing catch-up to them. They had developed so quickly, and I felt like I was way behind. I was like, "Where did that period go? What was I doing while they were getting their shit together?" I felt like I had no time for bullshit, that I had a lot of work to do. So I wanted to know what the deal was. Wynton said, "NOCCA, bro. NOCCA." And I was like, "What the hell is NOCCA? What does *that* mean?" But when I found out, I went home, and just like with Alcorn and the trumpet thing, I said to my parents, "OK, now I got to go to NOCCA."

◆

NOCCA, the New Orleans Center for Creative Arts, describes itself as one of the finest preprofessional arts high schools in the country. And that is not a boast. Since its founding in 1973, NOCCA has unleashed dozens of the world's leading jazz musicians. Aside from Terence and the brothers Marsalis (Branford, Wynton, Delfeayo, and Jason), the institution's prestigious alumni include Donald Harrison, Kent Jordan, Victor Goines, Jesse Davis, Reginald Veal, Harry Connick Jr., Marlon Jordan, Nicholas Payton, and Aaron Fletcher.

In spite of reveling in its impressive list of graduating jazz greats, NOCCA also nourishes careers in the fields of visual arts, dance, theater, and creative writing. Thus, it is the home of the Crescent City's most artistically talented youth. Admission to the school requires a comprehensive audition and more than adequate grades. Once enrolled, students take academic courses in the morning at their regular high school and then head to NOCCA for a long afternoon of intensive study in arts training.

Terence Blanchard: I had to switch high schools because St. Aug wasn't allowing their students to go to NOCCA. I ended up having to switch to [a public school called] Kennedy. I didn't get to NOCCA until my junior year of high school, and Wynton and Branford had already been there a couple of years.

Branford Marsalis: I used to tease Terence for going to St. Aug even though I started out wanting to go there. [In those days], if you were a black child growing up in New Orleans and went to St. Augustine, you were ruling the roost, you were on top of the food chain.

People had known about us coming up and the St. Aug band director just naturally assumed that we would all go there because they had the best talent that the city had to offer. They have a great marching band but had a terrible music program. I went to De La Salle High School, which was predominately white.

When I went to take a placement test [at St. Augustine], I had all these questions [to ask the band director] like, "What are the requirements that you would have of me as a student in your band?" And the guy was like, "Requirements? You can march, can't you?" And I said, "Yeah."

"Well, that's all you need."

All the kids from St. Aug used to tease me: "Man, why you go to school with all them white boys?"

"Y'all out there marching; I'm learning to play music. Who's going to be laughing in the end?"

Terence probably remembers that. He wasn't lost on that. It didn't take him long to figure out that if he was going to play music, he had to get the hell away from those fools.

Terence Blanchard: I had to argue with my parents for a whole year before I got to go to NOCCA. But when I got there, that's when I started my walk, my quest.

Before NOCCA, such a robust commitment to the arts was a rare entity in New Orleans. Fortunately for the welfare of jazz, this undertaking has proved prosperous. In fact, thanks to a major fund drive, the institution relocated into a new, $18-million facility in 1998. For all its plaudits and prestige, when Terence's long-awaited arrival to NOCCA finally materialized, it was actually considered a senseless move.

Terence Blanchard: They had a lot of problems when the school first opened because everybody thought that by being an arts school, you'd go over there and do nothing but goof off all day. So a lot of teachers didn't push students to go to the school when I was going to it.[3]

Branford Marsalis: The fact that they made the program from 1 P.M. to 6 P.M. was really good because it separated the guys who really wanted to be there from the guys who thought it would be easy. You had to give up some of your private time in order to attend the school.

Donald Harrison: They taught us from the beginning of music to the end of music. We learned the guts, the insides of the music. They don't stand for any lollygagging. If you're not woodshedding and practicing and trying to develop to become proficient at all the techniques of music, then you have to leave the school. You have to learn the whole scope of music.[4]

Terence Blanchard: NOCCA was probably the first place I went to as a kid that really sparked some fire into me. My piano teachers had done it earlier, but this was an intensive classroom environment, so it was very different. Never, on a daily basis, had I been so excited about something. We were moving at a very rapid pace, learning a lot every day. It was an amazing thing to be a part of.

During my first year at NOCCA, I remember having a serious temperature, so my mom wanted me to stay home, but I wanted to go to school. Prior to NOCCA, if I had the slightest temperature, I was staying home!

I think what really made NOCCA great for me was meeting other kids who shared the same thoughts and rituals as me. Before I went to NOCCA, people used to look at me kind of strangely. They'd say, "Look at that cat—he's quiet; he doesn't say nothing; he just carries that horn around." But when I started going to NOCCA, I saw people there like me who were interested in the same things. I got the chance to be inspired by other kids my age. Donald Harrison, Wynton, Branford, and all the other people that were there, we supported each other. It wasn't an ego thing where it would be like, "Who the hell are you talking to?" It wasn't like that. We all respected each other. It was one of the healthiest, most artistic environments I've ever been in. It was really great.

Branford Marsalis: NOCCA *was* great because NOCCA wasn't a jazz school. Jazz was one of the subjects that you took. We took classical music, harmony, and theory with Dr. [Bert] Braud, and all that stuff. Basically the school fostered an atmosphere of creativity, adventure. We weren't subjected to the limitations that you are in a conventional school.

Wynton Marsalis: I hung out at NOCCA all the time, especially since my father was teaching there. Back then, he couldn't get regular gigs, so he had to teach. New Orleans doesn't support its musicians; it's a sad thing.

Ellis Marsalis: I could get gigs, but not for the kind of music that I wanted to play—they were hard to come by. There were a lot of guys making good money playing R&B, but I wanted to play jazz. But everybody was leaving New Orleans, and [jazz] players were getting fewer and fewer. Edward Blackwell, who I was playing with, left for New York in 1960. Then I started playing with Jimmy Black, but he left around '63. So consequently, the opportunity for me to make a living playing jazz was slim to none. So with that situation and because I was certified through university to do so, I got into teaching. Another plus to teaching was that it afforded a consistent paycheck. But looking back, I probably could have made the same money hustling gigs. It was just that having a family, it would have been too sporadic to do.

In 1964, I took a teaching job that was not in New Orleans. So we all had to move to a very small town in Louisiana called Breaux Bridge. I was making $4,200 a year, which was big money at the time. Not to mention that as a schoolteacher, you also get all the benefits like hospitalization, retirement. And all of it was a learning experience for me, too, especially in ways that I didn't anticipate. I was there for two years until I ended up on the wrong side of the politics. So we moved back to New Orleans. But when we moved back, things had changed. While we were in Breaux Bridge, the Lyndon Johnson administration passed the civil rights bill, so all the legal aspects of segregation went out the window; musicians who couldn't work with each other were all of a sudden allowed to do so. I started working at the Claiborne Club, which was the same club I had worked at before but lost the job because of segregation.

In 1967, I joined Al Hirt's band; he was pretty hot at that time. I also started working at Xavier University where I developed this course in Afro-American music. Three years later, I left Al Hirt's band and began teaching full-time at Xavier. Then sometime around August of '73, a friend of mine, Alvin Batiste, called me up telling me about some new school that was opening up. He said I should go interview for it. And my wife said it was a good idea too, so I went.

There were a bunch of people there for the job, but they hired me. And that turned out to be NOCCA. I had no idea that kids in the 1970s were interested in jazz. But it was great because it was like a lab for me. I was able to experiment with a lot of different things. We had a faculty that had the complete trust of the principal. We were able to change things around to suit what was best for the students. And there was a common understanding with the NOCCA kids that when you graduated and went to whatever conservatory, at the end of the first semester you had to come back and report. We'd put all of the students in a room and say, "OK, tell us what we didn't do." We'd get reports from someone in Cleveland, Manhattan, everywhere. They'd tell us what we needed or what was missing, and then we'd go about improving the curriculum on that basis. So by the time the NOCCA kids graduated, they were prepared to get into the best conservatories in the country.

I worked at NOCCA for twelve years, and while I was there, a parade of people came through. Terence was one of them. He came to NOCCA looking for a career in music. And the thing I remember most about Terence was that it was obvious that he was an extremely talented person. I was glad that I had a chance to be involved in his development.

TERENCE BLANCHARD: Ellis had a great effect on me. I mean, he really introduced me to the music. Before I started going to NOCCA, I was listening to electronic music, like Return to Forever and Weather Report. Ellis turned my head around. The first thing he gave me was a tape of Miles Davis's called *Someday My Prince Will Come.* He told me to listen to the piano player, Wynton Kelly. He and Roger Dickerson wanted to make a piano player out of me. But I took it home and listened to Miles. That's when I really started getting into Miles.

ROGER DICKERSON: Terence is very talented on piano, and he could have been a pianist if he wanted to. Ellis thought so, too, and so we tried to make a piano player out of him, but trumpet was his choice.

TERENCE BLANCHARD: The next thing Ellis gave me was this Clifford Brown record called *Sweet Clifford.* It was like culture shock. I had never heard anybody play trumpet like that. I took it home and kept it for so long that when I gave it back, the cover was all worn. Jazz was still a serious mystery to me. I'd listen to the records over and over, just the drums or just the piano, to figure it out. John Coltrane scared me to death! But my two main musical influences have been Clifford Brown and Miles Davis. When I was a kid, I walked, ate, slept, everything Miles Davis. He was it for me! Miles was the kind of person who spoke his mind—and that's how he played. He didn't meander—simple and to the point. The thing about Miles was that economy was his thing, but it was done in such a complex fashion. That's the thing that caught my ear; it's what made his music interesting to me. A lot of people can get up there and play a few notes, but the notes that Miles chose to play, and where he placed them, was the thing that made it interesting. You can really hear that on *Porgy and Bess* throughout the album. There's great arrangements in there, and then all of a sudden Miles will come in with the perfect note that just seems to fit. And that's the magic that he always seemed to have. I got a lot of enjoyment out of Miles's albums, even the stuff he did near the end, like *Tutu* and *Amandla*. I've listened to them all, and I still think they're great albums. But people made the mistake of classifying them as jazz albums. And Miles Davis himself would tell you he wasn't playing jazz. He knew that he was playing R&B. I think he changed his style because he had an interest in other styles of music. And the reason why I say that is because when I met Miles the first thing out of his mouth was, "Keep doing what you're doing!" So that let me know that he was aware that he was just doing a different type of music and that jazz wasn't dead. You know, he had done jazz in his past and wanted to do something else.

◆

Many have fervently debated the issue: Was Miles Davis an important apostle for change or a false prophet? A decade after his death, he is remembered as an artist of admirable exploits, one who experimented with a myriad of musical styles. Yet, many allege that, in leading the fusion movement, Miles provoked the most destructive dearth in jazz history. Wynton Marsalis, one of his most ardent admirers, bemoaned, "He was like a great general who went over to the other side."

Ellis Marsalis: The 1970s was producing fusion, and nobody was talking about jazz. There was nothing out there. Nobody was talking about Miles, either. Miles wasn't even playing! The last thing Miles did was *Bitches Brew*, and after that he basically retired and didn't come back until the 1980s. Coltrane died in '67, and everybody else was like chasing behind them little clone Tranes. I mean, there was nothing out there! It was just fusion. Wynton and Branford weren't interested in jazz. Nobody really was.

Branford Marsalis: I always wanted to be a rock star first. When I was a kid, I wanted to play in funk bands; I didn't want to play jazz. When I went to play with Sting, people asked my father what he thought, and he said, "I'm surprised he even played jazz at all." I came back to jazz because I love it. I love them both. But if I look at the things that I'm going to wind up doing for the rest of my life, it's going to be playing jazz, not those other things. Those other things are cool, but they have more limitations. Jazz is limitless.

Terence Blanchard: When I started out, I played in a lot of funk bands—that's what I was into. Before NOCCA, I wasn't really into jazz. Even when I started getting into it, I was still playing funk because there weren't that many gigs for me to play jazz. At that time, in the 1970s, everything was Top 40. We didn't see any young musicians playing jazz, so we had to find support in each other.

I remember people tried to discourage us. They'd say, "Why do you want to play jazz? You're not going to be able to survive." But my feeling was "Well, I'm not trying to make money; I just want to play. I want to be happy playing the music." I became a musician because I love to play the music and that, culturally, what I do will have an impact on other people. Now, the amazing thing is, lately I've been having these unbelievable encounters with people at my shows. This one guy told me that he met his wife at one and that they love the music and play it all the time. Then they had a son and named him Terence. Hearing those kinds of stories from people is *extremely* flattering. It gives you an entirely new perspective on your responsibility to your art.

Part of being an artist is disregarding the conventional wisdom of practical people, dealing with the rhetorical "Why don't you get a real job?" But New Orleans's intimate size and historical roots yield a certain sense of cultural awareness, providing more opportunity for youngsters to pursue careers in the arts.

Roger Dickerson: There's a camaraderie in New Orleans. And so, when Branford (who is my godchild) was young, I gave private lessons. We are all close in the sense of a community. But the great thing about living in New Orleans is that everyone gets the chance to play and develop and to work with some really great people. Ellis and I used to talk about the process that's been operating here all the time—something that I like to call an organic process. Because of certain elements here—the culture, community, and energy—New Orleans has turned out musicians for centuries. This city is kind of a channel for that. And when you're working with students, you sense you're contributing to the development of such a rich musical legacy.

Ellis Marsalis: There's definitely a camaraderie here. I knew Terence before he even started coming to NOCCA. I knew a lot of them: Victor Goines, Donald Harrison, Jesse Davis, Reginald Veal. And I had a great relationship with all the kids, sort of like a big brother. They were in all kinds of bands in the summer, and I watched them all from a distance. Willie Metcalf had a jazz summer camp that was like an apprenticeship situation. Willie would help the kids play Charlie Parker and other stuff like that. And that's what the kids need now; they need more people like Metcalf.

Willie Metcalf: I'm what you call a "street musician" because I've never been formally trained. I've been playing music [all my life]. Actually, I'm the oldest bebop piano player in New Orleans. But coming from Detroit, I hung out with cats like Tommy Flanagan, Barry Harris, Paul Chambers, Curtis Fuller, Betty Carter, and we'd share what we had. We learned through trial and error. And for me, that's the way it's supposed to be—share your craft!

When I was living in Detroit, I checked myself into a rehabilitation program because I had a drug problem. During stages of my life, I was a functioning addict, but I finally recognized that I couldn't continue being one. The rehab program thought New Orleans would be good therapy for my recovery because that's where the music began, the birthplace of jazz.

When I first came down to New Orleans, I was doing some things with [saxophonist and educator] Kidd Jordan, who opened a lot of doors for me. I started doing some workshops and later founded the Academy for Black Artists. That's where I met Terence, Wynton and Branford, Donald Harrison, all those young cats. I've always liked being around the younger cats because they have such great enthusiasm and they like to get excited. Although Terence was quiet and didn't say much, I could always sense his enthusiasm through his dedication. And that's cool. Branford and Wynton, on the other hand, they were cocky like me.

I thrive on results and try to bring out the best in every musician that I teach. But with Terence, I didn't have to do anything. All I had to do was *show* him because he was so hungry to learn. When I saw that he was determined like that, well, I was satisfied. His parents used to ask me all the time, "How's he doing? Is Terence doing all right?" I told them Terence was on the right path—that's all I could say. But I mean [*laughing*], I didn't really think that path would lead him to where he is today.

Martha Francis: Once Terence started attending NOCCA—he doesn't know this—but I began to keep up with his accomplishments. Whenever there would be articles or pictures of Terence in the newspaper or magazines, I would clip them and show them to my students. Once a student of mine said, "Well, *I* had a teacher who taught Harry Connick Jr.!" And I said, "Well, OK, that's *fine*." The truth is, Terence has done my dear old heart good.

◆

Clearly, New Orleans embodies a strong sense of community, but for decades, the city had not provided its homegrown products an opportunity to stay and flourish. During this unfortunate dry spell, dozens of exceptionally talented New Orleans musicians fled their birthplace for prestigious conservatories in Boston, New York, and, in Terence's case, New Jersey.

Terence Blanchard: New Orleans is a strange animal where it has a lot of talent but it doesn't have the following to support it. There are not enough jazz lovers in the city to support the national acts. And it's frustrating since it is the birthplace of jazz.

One of the biggest things that frustrates me about New Orleans is when I walk down the French Quarter and hear pop music. Some of those guys are my friends, but it's a drag. But the tradition has been lost for a long time. There are a lot of musicians in New Orleans who can play, but they just stay in New Orleans and don't really apply themselves. No one really ventured forth like Wynton. Wynton and the rest of us were the first in a long time who really wanted to do something different musically. And in order to do that, we unfortunately had to leave New Orleans.

My father wanted me to go to school in New Orleans at Loyola. It was my mom who talked to him and made him understand that I needed to go away to school. My mother is a tough person. She was tough on me and tough on my father. She didn't understand the music I was into, but she *did* understand that I was serious about it, which I really appreciated. The interesting thing about my relationship with my parents was that my father was the one who got me interested in music, who had all the knowledge about it, but it was my mother who understood that I had to study abroad. She knew I had to be my own person and have my own experiences away from home. My father didn't really understand that; he wanted me where he could touch me.

Mrs. Blanchard: It was hard for me to see Terence go away to college, but it was even harder for his daddy. We always knew that once Terence left, he would never come back. See, Terence had a scholarship to Loyola, and Oliver was determined to see Terence go there. But I was just the opposite because I knew what had happened to me as a child, and I didn't want to see the same thing happen to Terence. So my sister and I went shopping to buy a trunk and everything. When Oliver came home, we were packing and he said, "What's going on?" But I think in the back of his mind he knew Terence was going to leave.

Terence Blanchard: It was all I talked about. It was a big step leaving New Orleans, but I didn't realize it at the time because the only thing I thought about was starting my career. But I kept wondering why everybody was so sad. I was like, "I'm just going away to school." Everybody was packing up stuff, acting like there was a death in the family.

◆

At seventeen, Wynton Marsalis didn't cook much, but his Manhattan apartment on West 99th Street and Broadway was a welcoming lodge for friends staying in New York. Brother Branford and Donald Harrison frequently came down from Berklee College in Boston to hang out there. In the spring of 1980, when still in high school, Terence stayed at the apartment, too. He was in New York to audition as a finalist for the Presidential Scholars in the Arts Program.

Terence Blanchard: That was my first time in New York, and I didn't really know what to expect. First of all, Wynton's apartment was so damn small. I couldn't believe it! But it was just a crazy experience being in that city. I mean, there were literally millions of people everywhere. I had never seen anything like it. I stayed with Wynton for a few days, and he was cool 'cause he was glad to have some company. He took me with him to his brass rehearsals and to a couple of clubs. I got to hear a lot of music, which was great for me. I didn't win that scholarship, but I ended up getting one to Rutgers University.

MRS. BLANCHARD: Terence was very fortunate because Roger and Ellis were very instrumental in helping him get into Rutgers University.

ROGER DICKERSON: After Terence graduated from high school, I was talking to him about where he was going for college. And he didn't really have anything worked out in terms of a scholarship. But we ended up getting something for him. Ellis and I had a friend on the faculty of Rutgers.

ELLIS MARSALIS: I knew Bill Fielder, and I knew that he was a hell of a trumpet player and instructor. Whenever he'd come to town, Wynton used to hold him at our house for four- to five-hour lessons.

BILL FIELDER: When I was driving down to New Orleans, I was still working at Southern University [in Baton Rouge]. Wynton, I would say, was very erudite and very aggressive. Actually, Wynton had said to me, "One of my friends, man, I would like for him to attend Rutgers University." So I heard Terence play and I was very much impressed. Also, I thought Terence was an astute, cordial young man. He was always sitting down and reading as many books as possible, mostly philosophical books. And similarly to Wynton, Terence is very goal oriented. And to see a couple of kids at that stage who knew exactly what they wanted in life was quite remarkable.

ELLIS MARSALIS: Terence was a good student; I didn't have any doubts that he could make it into Rutgers. With some of my other students, I wasn't too sure. They had the talent musically but lacked the discipline. But Terence had it all. He always manifested all the elements required to become a professional musician: the right attitude, tremendous talent, intellect, and a tremendous amount of self-discipline. And it made sense for him to go there because he would be able to study with a great trumpet teacher and be close enough to New York to launch his career. To me, that was logic. The only matter of concern was some luck and the right contacts. Well, in a matter of two years, he was practically running Art Blakey's band.

◆

In August 1980, a month before classes began, Terence sat in an airplane grounded on the runway of New Orleans International Airport. As he awaited takeoff, the young eighteen-year-old envisioned a more monumental launch; he was about to embark on a journey destined to fulfill a lifelong desire. Just hours later, however, he had already faced his first setback.

"The school didn't have any housing for me," remembers Terence, who was met at the Newark Airport in New Jersey by Paul Jeffrey. Jeffrey, a saxophonist/arranger and director of the Rutgers jazz program at the time, invited the shelterless Terence into his home until something could be arranged. This little glitch in housing administration proved to be a blessing in disguise, as Terence was provided with a spectacular opportunity.

> **TERENCE BLANCHARD:** Paul was playing with Lionel Hampton off and on, and Lionel called to say that they had a gig to do in Philadelphia. And Paul said to me, "Why don't you come along—and bring your horn." So we drove to New York and caught the band bus right outside Lionel's apartment building. There was Rickey Ford, Curtis Fuller, Frankie Dunlop, all those guys. When we got to Philadelphia, one of the trumpet players, Jeff Davis, was playing around on stage before the gig, so I went up there and pulled out my trumpet. Then Hamp walked up behind me and heard me playing with Jeff and asked the piano player, Zeke Mullins, to play a blues with me. And after I'd played, Hamp said he was going to call me with some work, but I didn't expect anything. But right before school started, he called me to start doing some gigs.[5]

> **CURTIS FULLER:** When Terence started playing with Hamp's orchestra, I could hear that he was going to be a great player. He had a little Dixie influence in him, but you could also hear Freddie Hubbard and Woody Shaw. There were a lot of trumpet players who could play in the band, but they were older and their playing was set in their own way. Whereas Terence, his playing was more investigative, sort of like a young Clifford Brown or Lee Morgan. He was searching. And I was very impressed by that because that's also me all over again. Duke Ellington told me, "I'd rather hear you make a mistake than hear somebody else play perfectly." That's what Trane saw in me and Lee Morgan. The two of us, Lee and I, we could be risky and have a great time. So that's what impressed me with Terence, and it is no surprise to me that he has become the great trumpet player and writer he is today.

> **PAUL JEFFREY:** Lionel Hampton saw tremendous potential in Terence and thought he was already a great musician. Actually, he said to me, if Terence had a tuxedo that night, he would have hired him right on the spot.

◆

Known simply as Hamp, the living legend Lionel Hampton is a walking history of jazz. Born in 1909 in Louisville, Kentucky, he first came to prominence as a drum prodigy in the 1920s. By 1930, Hamp was playing with Louis Armstrong and began tinkering with the vibraphone. Pops took a liking to the sound, got him to play a solo on "Memories of You," and, as a result, spun the wheels in motion of Hamp's true career.

Over the next seven decades, Hamp became the first musician to establish the vibraphone as a jazz instrument, played with a Who's Who of jazz giants, and, through his band, propagated many notable youngsters.

In 1980, eighteen-year-old Terence Blanchard became his newest young discovery. Over the next year and a half, Terence spent most of his time shuttling between gigs with the Lionel Hampton Orchestra and school at Rutgers. Playing in the legendary orchestra prompted Terence to proclaim Hamp as "the master of swing!"

Undoubtedly a swing machine, whether it was leading his orchestra through world tours or playing in smaller bands with Benny Goodman, Art Tatum, and Oscar Peterson, Hamp will always be regarded as an influential leader of the music. In 1998, still inspired and active on the performance circuit, Lionel Hampton received a National Medal of Arts from U.S. president Bill Clinton.

> **Curtis Fuller:** I first met Terence before he joined Hamp when he was still in high school in New Orleans. I was there to inaugurate the Louis Armstrong Park with Count Basie when Ellis Marsalis told me about these two great kids he had—you know, up-and-coming stars who had their own band. So when I went to the house to meet them, it was Branford and Terence. Ellis then had to go back to work, so he told the kids to hang with me. So they took me to some game machine place, and they played pinball. I immediately took a liking to Terence; he had the personality that I like. He was a wonderful little kid—he's still like the little kid with big cheeks—and to watch him grow so fast has just been incredible.

In playing with Hamp, Terence's career was off to an auspicious start. The dream gig supplied him with the confidence and exposure every young musician needs. But the teenager, just a couple of weeks removed from his parental nest and Crescent City stomping grounds, had difficulty adjusting socially to the northern American lifestyle.

> **Bill Fielder:** Yes, Terence did have some problems at first. People in the Northeast are not as cordial as those from the South. I would say they're more of a plastic type. But in time, because Terence has this gregarious type of personality, he made the proper adjustments.

> **Terence Blanchard:** When I moved up there, the things I had grown accustomed to were gone. People were more to themselves, which I wasn't used to. New Orleans is the kind of place where it's very friendly, the people are very open, and you get a family kind of feeling just being there. That's one of the reasons I moved back [in 1995]. I didn't know how

much of an effect New Orleans had on me personally until I left. When I went to Rutgers, I was looking for that same kind of feeling, but I didn't know too many people up there at first. I got lonely. And the people that I did meet were from a completely different environment. It was like learning a whole new culture.

BRANFORD MARSALIS: Northern cities are constantly looking for the next new thing; they're like suckers for hype. But the thing about southern cities is that they don't change, and they're not very tolerant with different things. I mean, New Orleans is a very provincial town. Their views on sex, their views on politics, their views on race—they're just very antiquated people. And after growing up in that kind of environment, I never even imagined myself as a younger person staying there with that kind of backward mentality. But now that I'm older and understand it, I love going home much more than I ever did. I can accept it for what it is rather than being mad because it's not what I want it to be. But it wasn't until I moved up here [New York] that I realized how thin people's skin is. You grew up down there, you had pretty thick skin. But I mean, you want to play jazz, you come to New York. You know, kids from Chicago got to leave home; kids from Toronto got to leave home; kids from Montreal got to leave home—it ain't no big deal.

◆

In the midst of his sophomore year at Rutgers, Terence was presented with an extraordinary offer and, at the same time, a great dilemma. Art Blakey, prolific drummer and bandleader, wanted Terence to assume his coveted trumpet chair in the Jazz Messengers. But to accept the position, Terence would have to leave Rutgers prematurely.

MRS. BLANCHARD: Before Terence went away to school, I stressed to him that he should *finish* college. This way if he didn't make it in the music world, he would always have something to fall back on. But that didn't go very far with him. During that second year, he wanted out.

TERENCE BLANCHARD: My mom kept after me, telling me that I needed something to fall back on. And I hated that. I was going after it with such a vengeance that I didn't even think about anything else. It was like, by you telling me that it seems that you think I *am* going to fail.

BILL FIELDER: When I was younger, one of my objectives was to always be one of the major trumpet players in jazz. But I was circumvented from that by my parents. My mother cried and cried and my father said, "Oh, no, you don't want to live that type of lifestyle." See, my mother was a teacher and my father was a pharmacist, so they wanted me to be a music teacher. But I didn't really want to be nothing but a jazzman. I was actually approached by Art Blakey twice back in the 1960s to join his band, but I turned him down both times. I listened to my parents and became a teacher. And to this day, I think that's the one thing I regret.

I knew Terence was very dedicated to his father and his mother, and that was, of course, something I could appreciate, but I told him, "Look here, man, you can always come back to school and finish, but this may be your big chance."

Mrs. Blanchard: At first, I didn't want to go along with it, but after I realized how determined he was, I gave Terence my blessing. I guess you could say it worked out pretty good. I'm very proud of my baby. (He hates it when I say "my baby.")

Terence Blanchard: When I decided to leave Rutgers, I remember my father being on the phone screaming at me. My mother talked to him again; actually, some of the musicians did as well. They made him understand that leaving school wasn't the end of the world for me.

Me and my father had the kind of relationship where he apologized for it all later on. He said, "I'm really proud of you because you've always been your own person. If you had listened to me, you probably still would have been in New Orleans."

Roger Dickerson: Terence's parents were very happy for him because there was always something there for them to see. I mean, Terence was always in good company. He was here [with me] then with Ellis at NOCCA, and then he went up to New Jersey to study at Rutgers. He then got into good company with Lionel Hampton and then Art Blakey. I mean, Terence took over Art Blakey's group. He was running the band! I remember a friend telling me he saw Terence in New York, and he said, "Man, I couldn't believe it; there's Terence calling the tunes in Blakey's Messengers!" Although in matters of this kind, you never really know where it's all going to lead. There is always the mystery of what is going to happen to your child. All those years you love and educate them and you tend to wonder and worry.

After Terence left, I would sometimes see his father at the supermarket, and he was always happy to see me. I asked him if he had heard from Terence lately, and he said, "Yeah, you know, he thinks he's as big as those guys up there in Manhattan." And I said, "Well, he is. He's just as good as they are." I remember he looked back at me like I was crazy. He said, "Really? My son?" And I said, "Yes."

Terence Blanchard: I knew leaving school was a very big jump, but I also knew that I was making the right move. I don't believe in the "have something to fall back on" mentality. I mean, no school can re-create the atmosphere of a working musician.

CHAPTER TWO

Notes

1. Dave Helland, "The Marsalis Tapes," *Down Beat* (November 1989): 18.
2. David Yeats, "New Orleans Rhythm Kings," *Blues & Soul* (1984): 45.
3. Lee Jeske, "Profile: Terence Blanchard," *Down Beat* (August 1983): 44.
4. Gene Kalbacher, "Youth Marches On with New York Second Line," *Hot House* (October 1984): 13.
5. Yeats, "New Orleans Rhythm Kings," 45.

CHAPTER THREE
SENDING A MESSAGE
The Art Blakey Years

> Young musicians need a lot of experience, and Art was the only bandleader that I ever knew who let the sidemen call and write the tunes. He was a propagator of the music!
>
> —*Terence Blanchard*

In early 1982, shortly before Terence Blanchard turned twenty, his career took its most significant turn to date. Also around this time, exciting opportunities developed for Terence's crony, Wynton Marsalis. Marsalis, already garnering extraordinary acclaim in Art Blakey's Jazz Messengers, had recently completed a world tour with Herbie Hancock. He rejoined the Messengers, but only momentarily, for his brother Branford had assembled the Wynton Marsalis Quintet. The band would feature the brothers on the front line with some of the hottest young rhythm players in New York City: Kenny Kirkland, Jeff "Tain" Watts, and Charles Fambrough.

"Wynton was out on the road with Herbie," remembers Branford, "so he said to me, 'Go get me a band.' It was no big deal. I went to school with Jeff Watts and everybody in New York knew Kenny Kirkland—it was just a matter of whether he'd do the gig or not. So I had a talk with him and said, 'We're gonna rock everybody's world.' And he liked the sound of that. Wynton was writing some real creative shit, and we were playing it in very inventive ways, and Kenny identified with that."

By way of its talent and the determination of its leader, the ensemble would become the most important group of young players in jazz music. Fresh from a highly developmental period under Art Blakey, Wynton was eager to take his own band on the road to perform his own music. But before he would go anywhere, Marsalis resolved one last matter: when a musician leaves Blakey's employ, tradition instructs the departing member to send a replacement. He sent Terence Blanchard.

Terence Blanchard: Wynton had called me and said to come down to Fat Tuesday's [a Manhattan jazz club] for an audition. Me and Donald [Harrison] went together, and I was really nervous because I wanted the gig so bad. [Trumpeter] Wallace Roney was there; he had already played in [Blakey's] big band, so I was worried as hell.

Wynton hipped me to certain tunes from the Messenger songbook. He said, "Learn these tunes! You got to learn them." So I learned them, but when Wallace got up to play the first set, he played them all. We had nothing left to play, so when our turn came, we had to repeat them all!

Donald Harrison: Well, I didn't think I would ever get the chance to play with Art Blakey—even when I was called to the audition. There were quite a few guys down there, like Kenny Garrett. They were all great players, and most of them ended up playing with Art at some time. At the audition I just tried to do the best I could, and I guess it helped with Branford telling Art I was cool.

I wish I could have been at a higher level when I was with Art, but I did the best I could in that situation. And that's all you can ever ask from yourself. I was lucky to be there, and a lot of the lessons I learned are still with me today. I'll always remember what Art told me and how he helped me learn how to play.

Branford Marsalis: This is something that no one, I think, really knows. What actually happened was I recommended Donald Harrison, and Wynton said, "I want to get Terence." You know, Terence and Donald were our boys. But then Wynton [decided] to get Wallace Roney. See, Wynton had a sense of the Jazz Messengers, like a code of honor, and since Wallace had played with the Messenger big band, Wynton figured he was next in line. So when Art Blakey said, "Who do you got for me?" I said, "Donald Harrison is the best cat I know." And it's true. He was and still is. So Art said, "All right, I want to hear him." Then Wynton said, "Yeah, man, I'm thinking of calling Wallace." And Art said, "No, man, I want somebody else." You know, interpret that however you choose, but Art said, "No, I want somebody else." So Wynton said, "Well, hey, Terence." Who's next? Terence, of course. So they came down and auditioned.

Bill Fielder: During that time, Terence was practicing eight and nine hours a day. Art had one of the most significant jazz groups on the scene, and Terence was very intent on becoming a Jazz Messenger.

I was there that night they auditioned at Fat Tuesday's, and after Terence played, Art walked into me and he took his fingers and grabbed me in my stomach and said, [*imitating Art Blakey's gravel-like voice*] "I'm gonna take your boy!"

◆

For decades, Pittsburgh, Pennsylvania, was known as the steel capital of America. Built over a rich bituminous coal seam, the city's concentration on heavy industry secured its notorious reputation as one of the dirtiest places in the country. Born there on October 11, 1919, Arthur Blakey had a childhood that demanded independence and maturation beyond his years.

At thirteen, he considered himself a man. He had been working the coal mines, having grown up without parental support. His father had abandoned his mother after they were married, and she had died while Blakey was an infant. "I never saw my mother or a picture of her. All I know of her is what people told me and from all the information that I could gather. What I understand is she died of a broken heart.

"So, therefore," continued Blakey, "I had grown up—so to speak—in the streets because I'm an orphan. I had a living father, but he couldn't accept me into his family because they were mulatto, and I took complexion after my mother. So they couldn't raise me. We had segregation within segregation."[1] Blakey laughed at the irony with his oft-imitated throaty chuckle.

Blakey's rich storytelling (particularly, his embellished true tales about the heyday of jazz and its greatest players) made him a popular raconteur. He had such a wealth of experience to draw upon that his Messengers were absorbed by his anecdotes and craved his company. "For one thing," recalls saxophonist Billy Pierce, "Art was just a character. He could charm the pants off anybody. But he was so creative that his stories had a way of changing every time he told them. I mean, the story line could be the same, but different characters would pop in and out of them all the time."

At fifteen, while playing piano at the Ritz Club in Pittsburgh, Blakey was supplied with his first piquant tale: "I really wasn't no piano player—I could play a little bit, entirely by ear. But then one day Erroll Garner came into the club while we were rehearsing. He sat in on piano, and that was the end of my piano-playing days. The owner of the club was a real gangster who always carried a big pistol. When he heard Erroll play, he told me to switch to drums. I never studied the drums, but I didn't see any future in arguing with a man who was carrying a gun. I'm self-educated in just about everything in life. I did it because I had to survive. And I had a bad habit of liking to eat."[2]

Survival for Blakey in the "Dirty Thirties" was more than economical. He may have adjusted to growing up without parental care and laboring in the coal mines as an adolescent, but when he was faced with the stress of yet another tragedy, he succumbed to drugs.

"Dope has been around for centuries, and when the pressures and tensions of our society get too much, and people are caught at a weak point, they look for an escape. When I first took drugs," he recalls, "I was a young man and I was married to a young woman I was very much in love with. Then she had a cerebral hemorrhage and died. I couldn't believe it. I'm running down the street with her dead in my arms. I'd never even smoked a cigarette up to that point. But when that happened, I went the full route."[3]

◆

Notwithstanding his tremendous grief, Blakey graduated from Schenley High School (a school that also boasts jazz musicians Earl Hines and Ray Brown as alumni). But after his wife passed, his mind-set reduced him to hard labor at the Carnegie Steel Mill. Ultimately, Blakey's love of music propelled him out of the mills and mines of the Steel City to the clubs and halls of the Big Apple.

In 1942, still only twenty-two, Blakey launched a nearly fifty-year career, first playing drums in Mary Lou Williams's big band. Gigs to follow included a brief stretch with Fletcher Henderson and then a more enduring one with the famous Billy Eckstine orchestra. For three years Blakey played in Eckstine's ensemble, attracting kudos and keeping time for such jazz luminaries as Charlie Parker, Dizzy Gillespie, Dexter Gordon, and Miles Davis.

Curiously, when the band split up in 1947, Blakey was left without work. So out of his desire to study religion and philosophy, he sailed across the Atlantic to West Africa. Raised Christian, Blakey reexamined his faith and ultimately adopted his Muslim name, Abdullah Ibn Buhania, later shortened by his peers to Bu.

Blakey's visit to the African continent did not only produce a spiritual awakening. Upon his return to the States, he introduced a new style of drumming to jazz that gained high regard from fellow musicians. After observing traditional African drummers at work, Blakey began incorporating their rhythms and techniques into his own playing.

In 1949, Bu was back in New York playing in a big band he formed called the 17 Messengers. In spite of a talented ensemble that included Sonny Rollins and Bud Powell, economic factors split the 17 Messengers after a brief run. Then in 1954, Blakey created yet another band, this time a quintet with pianist Horace Silver. The band also featured the young and especially talented Clifford Brown on trumpet. He was only twenty-three at the time but had already played with and earned the high praise of Bird and Diz.

Daring and defiant on stage, Clifford Brown was the epitome of good health and well-being off stage. Reputed for his saintly behavior, Brownie, as musicians called him, was a firm adversary of drugs, aiding many of his contemporaries to resist substance abuse. His vibrant personality was universally loved by his peers and fans alike. Brownie was also a gifted mathematician and championship-class chess player—further evidence of his extraordinary zest for life. So when he died just two years later on June 26, 1956, in a car crash on the Pennsylvania Turnpike, the jazz industry found his death difficult to accept. Clifford Brown was only twenty-five, and despite a recording career that lasted less than three years, he had, remarkably, made an important impact on music. He left behind a legacy of musicianship that inspired scores of ensuing trumpet players, including Terence Blanchard. Still, one must ponder what Brownie would have accomplished both musically and socially if he had been fortunate enough to live a full lifetime.

In 1955, after one year together, Art Blakey had himself his first successful band. It was at this time that Horace Silver suggested the five musicians permanently work together under the name Jazz Messengers.

The name and the band endured for more than a third of a century, but the only uniform Jazz Messenger was its leader—the man behind the drums. Regardless of who suited up, the name stood for a high level of commitment to the art form. From 1955 to 1990, Art Blakey led endless editions of Messengers, most of the musicians green and unknown upon arrival, yet poised and renowned upon departure. The band was something of a traveling academy of learning, establishing Art Blakey's distinguished reputation. As a drummer alone, Blakey would have been remembered as a major figure in jazz history, but for propagating countless generations of young jazz musicians, he is revered as a musical giant.

The list is long: Walter Bishop Jr., Clifford Brown, Donald Byrd, Lou Donaldson, Kenny Dorham, Kenny Drew, Art Farmer, Curtis Fuller, Benny Golson, Johnny Griffin, Bill Hardman, Freddie Hubbard, Keith Jarrett, Chuck Mangione, Branford Marsalis, Wynton Marsalis, Jackie McLean, Hank Mobley, Lee Morgan, Billy Pierce, Valery Ponomarev, Woody Shaw, Wayne Shorter, Horace Silver, Bobby Timmons, Bobby Watson, James Williams, and Cedar Walton.

By 1982, these notable jazzmen all graduated from the "Academy of Art." On March 1 of that year, Terence Blanchard and his New Orleans homeboy, Donald Harrison, joined the prestigious lineage. Included in their Jazz Messenger membership: a future promising musical prosperity and a personal relationship with Art Blakey to cherish for life.

TERENCE BLANCHARD: When I first joined the band, I was like, "What do I do *now*?" I was scared to death. I had a lot of music to learn. And

Art never said too much, which led me to believe all the worst in the beginning. I used to say to myself, "I know I'm bad, but I'll get better." It was that kind of thing.

At our first rehearsal, Art came in and just sat down, pulled out his glasses and starting reading the newspaper. I was really nervous, and here he was just reading the paper!

I remember thinking that I would have to abide by all these guidelines and constantly hear about the trumpet chair that I would have to uphold. All I kept thinking about was Lee Morgan, Freddie Hubbard, Woody Shaw, you know, Bill Hardman and Kenny Dorham. I kept thinking to myself, "Man, Art *played* with all of those cats." Clifford Brown stood right in front of him. And I was putting a lot of pressure on myself. I mean, you don't want the musicianship of the band to drop. So I felt that I had to bring my musicianship up to their level. But I remember Art saying to me, "*You* are a Jazz Messenger now." He said, "Man, I don't want you to give a shit about none of those guys. I just want you to be yourself."

That easy, huh? He was naming all my heroes! But that was one of the things I loved about Art. He never put any pressure on me, or anyone else in the band, and that wasn't what I expected.

But I still remember that first rehearsal for one reason: it was when I learned about humility in terms of Art's personality. The man was so humble it was incredible. I remember we started rehearsing one of my songs, "Oh, by the Way," the title cut of the first album we did, and Art got up on the drums to play the song. Now I just expected him to play, but he said to me, "*How* do you want me to play this?" And I was dumbfounded. "Huh? You're asking me? Yeah, but you're Art Blakey!"

"What do you want me to play? What you hearing, Terence?"

"I-I-I . . . ."

"OK, I got it. I'll hear something."

That was just classic Art Blakey.

Donald Harrison: I was really nervous on that rehearsal, too. But whenever I play with someone of Art's stature, I'm always nervous. I mean, Art had the kinds of experiences, whether it was with Charlie Parker or whoever, that I'll never have. So while you try and get close to his stature, you never do; I've learned to realize that. But I still think about a lot of the lessons he gave me over the years.

I really admired that he took whatever talents he had with his musicians and really developed them to the highest level that he could. He was very sincere and honest about trying to develop a young artist into a human being. That's what I really admired about Art Blakey and the other jazz greats that I've been around. They were sincere in their efforts to develop music and to keep it going, that being one of the great art forms of these times. And that is something of great importance because music on a high level inspires people to do their best and makes the world a better place. So that's what I really keyed into with Art Blakey, and I try to carry that ideal forth.

TERENCE BLANCHARD: The thing I most admired about Art was that he allowed people to be who they are. He would appreciate you as opposed to trying to change you. He didn't run his band by being a taskmaster; that wasn't his thing. His personality, musically, was strong enough to take care of that. He was the kind of guy who let you make mistakes; he let you grow. Art had a way of leading people and making them feel comfortable about being around him, which is the way a musician can really develop. If you're comfortable, you'll want to stretch, you'll want to try certain things, and you might play beyond yourself. That's what Art always used to say. And I try to do that with my own band. I don't know if I am as successful as he was. He had a lot more experience and patience than I do, but, man, he had to have a lot of patience with us. We were so young and naive, full of energy, and out on the road! You know, I think about that and I say, "Damn, my hat goes off to you." I mean, he didn't have to babysit us, but you had to admire his ability to handle us.

BRANFORD MARSALIS: Art and I didn't get along too well. There were certain things that I just had no use for. I mean, there was Art Blakey the musician and Art Blakey the man. And the way he decided to conduct himself in public and in private was just very different from the way that I choose to conduct myself. I guess he was just used to young guys just emulating him and wanting to do everything that he did. But I didn't find his way of life particularly romantic, so, invariably, we were clashing. I was there to learn music from him and to do a gig—and he taught me. He was one of the best teachers I ever had. But there's two sides to every gig: on the stage and off the stage. And the way he was off the stage was not the way I had any particular interest in becoming like or acknowledging. I didn't enjoy it.

TERENCE BLANCHARD: Well, that was Branford's own take on things. I don't see why he didn't admire Art. Maybe he had a problem within himself that didn't allow him to see what was going on with that situation. But frankly, Art did a lot of things that upset everybody. He tried to skim you for your money. You know [*imitating Blakey*], "I got paid in a check; I can't pay you right now." Or, "The check didn't clear." Something like that, which would cause a little friction. But for me, I looked at that and I felt sorry for him; I didn't get upset with him. To me, he was *Art Blakey*! He should have had enough money where it didn't really matter. But the truth of the matter was, he didn't make that kind of money in this business.

BILLY PIERCE: Art deserved ten times more money than he got. But he grew up in the Depression, and for him, playing music was the biggest thrill in the world. So he was never really concerned about the business end of things. And the promoters knew this and they took advantage, always underpaying him. Sometimes we'd even hit the road without a hard contract. The arrangement was loose. He was old-school.

Terence Blanchard: And Art had his vices, too, which led to some problems. But that was his walk in life. Mine is different. I could walk next to him and see all the faults but still appreciate him because I could also see all the virtues. And I try not to focus on the faults, but I know some people do. And when they focus on the faults, they have tunnel vision; they don't see anything else. I try not to be that kind of person. So for the people who didn't admire him, hey, man, let's face some facts, there's a serious track record there. And until we start laying down that kind of level of commitment and contribution to the art form, then maybe we'll have something to say. But up until that point, fuck it. That's the real bottom line.

◆

Post–World War II jazz music was rampant with experimentation and innovation. In a fifteen-year span from the mid-1940s to the late 1950s, the music went through several distinct changes. Generally, jazz welcomed the pursuit of pioneering styles, but the advent of "free jazz" around 1959 turned the industry upside down and split it into separate camps. Also known as the avant-garde, the style abstained from formal structure by using themes as launching pads for free blowing. Purposely out of tune, disregarding chords and organization, this "free" concept captivated several critics and musicians alike. By the early 1960s, its central figure, Ornette Coleman, was inspiring the music of such highly regarded saxophonists as John Coltrane, Sonny Rollins, Roland Kirk, and Joe Henderson.

As the avant-garde dominated much of what jazz was saying in the 1960s, audiences were beginning to feel alienated from such unconventional playing. Consequently, jazz lost its casual follower to the more simplistic value of rock 'n' roll. However, audiences were not alone in their aversion. Many established musicians, including Roy Eldridge, Thelonious Monk, and jazz's most prolific innovator, Miles Davis, resented "the new thing," dismissing it as overbearing and contemptuous of tradition. Davis was particularly candid in his criticism, saying that Coleman's music was just a bunch of notes and hype. Although Miles would suffer a backlash for his comments—interpreted by critics and younger musicians as antiquated notions—he would continue to play straight-ahead jazz, soon assembling one of the most influential quintets in jazz history. (Davis's commitment to the tradition of jazz would later prove as much ironic as incongruous.)

When John Coltrane departed from Miles Davis's band to lead his own, Miles tweaked his lineup for nearly three years, never settling on a group for too long. Then in 1963, he hired a fresh-faced rhythm section of Ron Carter, Tony Williams, and Herbie Hancock. With the subsequent addition of saxophonist Wayne Shorter (who had just completed a lengthy gig as musical director of the Jazz Messengers), Davis found his new quintet. Throughout the next five years, these five artists made illustrious musical statements within the jazz idiom. But by 1968, the stranglehold rock 'n' roll had on the music industry finally began suffocating jazz. Top jazz artists, including Miles, played to half-empty clubs while rock stars packed football stadiums. Columbia Records considered the sixty thousand units sold by Miles's latest albums as diminutive and barely out of the "red zone."

Jazz was no longer viable to record companies and club owners, provoking an argument that it was dead. It was a hard pill to swallow, but if jazz were to persist, the music would have to undergo a commercial makeover. Still, what followed was unthinkable to most of its remaining enthusiasts.

Clive Davis, then president of Columbia Records, suggested to Miles that he consider modifying his music to accommodate the new market. Never the type to wallow in obscurity, the trumpeter complied, immersing himself with rock and pop music to assemble his vision for a new jazz-based music. The result was his 1969 release, *In a Silent Way*—an amalgamation of jazz and rock later coined "fusion." With its repetitive electronic beat, the album appealed to a vast new audience of young rock fans who knew nothing of Miles's body of jazz music. Soon, Davis was playing large venues opening for popular acts like the Grateful Dead, Carlos Santana, and Crosby, Stills, and Nash.

In 1970, Columbia released a double LP from Miles called *Bitches Brew*. It sold over half a million copies in its first year and became the biggest-selling "jazz" album ever. "I had seen the way to the future with my music," stated Miles in his autobiography, "and I was going for it like I had always done."

To some, mixing rock into jazz was ludicrous, but the innovation merited logic. More than providing jazz musicians with a much-needed infusion of popularity, rock and its electronic instruments gave jazz—a music that was forever striving to reach new ground—yet another experimental outlet. However, for traditionalists, these were the dog days. In eschewing rock, many were forced to flea to Europe and Japan for steadier work.

Since its inception, the Jazz Messengers were linked to a dynamic style of playing, though fusion fans judged the ensemble as passé. Blakey struggled to book gigs and retain first-class musicians, and he was unable to land a U.S. recording contract.

In assessing the scene, Blakey said, "Most of the thing with the rock thing now is showing how much energy you can give out on the stage; it isn't a music—it's a show." His scathing criticism was tinged with melancholy when he continued, "The music has gone somewhere else; there's no music, and it's a shame."[4]

By the mid-1970s, many jazz musicians were echoing Blakey's sentiments, declaring that fusion had come to a creative dead end. In the summer of 1975, its leader, Miles Davis, put down his horn for what was said to be a few months; instead, a six-year sabbatical ensued. In 1976, Herbie Hancock formed a cooperative group with Freddie Hubbard, Wayne Shorter, Ron Carter, and Tony Williams called VSOP, dedicated to upright jazz values. VSOP enjoyed relative popularity, but many of its members maintained their careers in pop/rock, so the fusion movement pressed onward.

In the summer of 1979, fresh out of high school, an ambitious Wynton Marsalis arrived at the desolate jazz scene in New York City wondering, "What happened to playing jazz?" That fall he attended the Juilliard School to refine his classical trumpet technique.

The following year, word was out that Miles Davis was preparing a comeback. Rumors spread that he would return to the revered style of his mid-1960s quintet. In 1981, Miles did finally return with an album entitled *Man with the Horn*. But as fast as jazz fans stood in anticipation, they slouched in disappointment, for the piece was produced with an R&B flavor aimed at the pop charts. Actually, a string of such albums followed. His LP *You're Under Arrest* included pop instrumental remakes of "Human Nature" and "Time after Time," songs made famous by Michael Jackson and Cyndi Lauper, respectively. For the first time in his career, the direction Davis chose to take his music elicited little interest from jazz audiences.

About this time, the media was reporting a growing backlash against fusion. Allegations that rock distorted the true meaning of jazz were being seriously evaluated. Then a small but arresting circulation of young and exceptionally talented musicians arrived in New York City. With Wynton Marsalis dubbed their golden boy, these young cats purportedly despised fusion and intended to return to more traditional, acoustic jazz.

> **WYNTON MARSALIS:** Jazz just wasn't getting any publicity—I mean, the real cats that were playing. So me and my generation that desired to play started to bring some media attention back to the music. I was uncompromising in my belief in playing. And all the shit that they wrote, the [golden boy] tag, it didn't make a difference to me. I just wanted to play

because the objective of fusion is very different from jazz. It's not that I had disdain for fusion; I was just wondering what happened to playing jazz. It wasn't so much about fusion at all; that's just something the media picked up on. The only thing about fusion was that that music wasn't really about horns, and we are all horn players. That music is all about synthesizers. The clearest statement of fusion was done with synthesized instruments, electronic instruments.

Terence Blanchard: I enjoyed listening to fusion groups like Weather Report, Return to Forever, and others, but I never envisioned myself becoming a fusion player. Once I started listening to jazz at NOCCA, it grabbed my attention, and I just gravitated toward it. Also, fusion didn't really have any horn players. Wayne Shorter was the only one, but he's a saxophone player, so it just didn't appeal to me at that time. I had a lot of fun listening to the New Orleans traditional bands, which had an influence on the type of music that I wanted to play.

Donald Harrison: I felt that with acoustic music, you could express yourself wholeheartedly, to every aspect of your being. And coming from New Orleans, listening to the parade bands and the traditional style, I felt closer in synch to it. But I love fusion. I have nothing against it. But if you really want to be serious, I think I can do it best with acoustic jazz. So when I got to New York, I was trying to maintain the ideals of acoustic music, which I felt had fallen off to the side. I didn't think—like a lot of the people who played fusion thought—that acoustic jazz was dead.

Indeed, acoustic jazz was not dead, but after slipping into a life-threatening coma for more than ten years, the music and its audience had a lot of catching up to do. During the fusion uproar, pillars of the jazz world—Duke Ellington, John Coltrane, Louis Armstrong, Charles Mingus, Lee Morgan, Coleman Hawkins, Thelonious Monk, Ben Webster, Cannonball Adderley—had passed away. Thus, if the back-to-the-future movement was to flourish, jazz would require new faces to take it back to traditional places. And that is exactly what happened. The 1980s proved to be a decade for "young lions" as musicians under thirty dedicated themselves to furthering the framework established by their musical forefathers.

This was big news, connoting a unique period in the music's history. After endless endeavors into the future, jazz rediscovered its past, using the hard-bop mainstream of Art Blakey and mid-1960s Miles Davis as its conceptual base. This era is known as the 1980s jazz resurgence.

To imply the revival of jazz in the 1980s was indebted solely to the young lions is inaccurate. Groups led by established players such as Dexter Gordon, Woody Shaw, and McCoy Tyner enjoyed their greatest popularity during that decade. And playing with Art Blakey's Jazz Messengers was once again regarded as one of the finest gigs a musician could get.

After surviving the trenches of 1970s jazz, Blakey's hard-bopping was back in the limelight with a lineup of the brightest young musicians in the country. In addition to the Marsalis brothers, Harrison, and Blanchard, such relative unknowns as Kenny Garrett, Wallace Roney, Charles Fambrough, Mulgrew Miller, Jean Toussaint, Lonnie Plaxico, Brian Lynch, Peter Washington, Benny Green, Javon Jackson, and Geoff Keezer were all hired by Blakey in the 1980s and have since become some of the most important players on the scene today. Unjustly, Blakey was not commonly recognized as an integral figure of the resurgence. Most of the attention and acclaim bestowed to jazz's exciting comeback went to his greatest star, Wynton Marsalis.

Mulgrew Miller: I think [the 1980s resurgence] represented a time where young people all over America were finding out about this music. And a lot of that *had* to do with the success of Wynton Marsalis. But if we think about it, Wynton Marsalis was not the first talented musician to come into New York during that period. But when [Columbia Records] took him on and promoted him, Wynton Marsalis—and I can say this without reservation—became the most highly promoted musician in the *history* of jazz. When we think of Duke Ellington and Louis Armstrong, those guys became celebrities because they *endured*. It wasn't until after many years that they became big celebrities. But Wynton received all of this promotion behind his first recording. And so, I don't think that has any precedence in jazz.

Branford Marsalis: Why was Wynton successful? Being good had nothing to do with it. They look for trends. The trend was young, black, well dressed, glib. "So find me a bunch of young black kids who are glib and well dressed. Or we'll dress 'em." You know? Being a good musician, I mean, that's too subjective. How the fuck do they know? They're all accountants. They have to look for things that they can understand. Music is not one of them.[5]

Mulgrew Miller: I think that Wynton's success had almost everything to do with the fact that Art Blakey took him on. I think if Wynton hadn't joined the Messengers, he would have been probably another . . . well, who's to say. But essentially I would credit Art Blakey for having the institution for somebody like Wynton Marsalis, Terence Blanchard, Wallace Roney, or any of these people to come and play and get exposed.

Geoff Keezer: One thing that people misunderstand is that they think Wynton Marsalis brought jazz back in the 1980s, and that's not true at all. The fact is that Art Blakey kept—we're talking about straight-ahead, acoustic jazz—he basically kept it going through the 1970s and made it possible for someone like Wynton Marsalis to basically exist. So Art Blakey is the guy that you really need to credit with the 1980s resurgence because without him there would be no Wynton Marsalis or anybody else.

WYNTON MARSALIS: Art Blakey had been playing the whole time—definitely. He gave everyone an opportunity to play. No matter how sad you were, he would let you play. I'm indebted to him. But I wouldn't concur with that at all. If there wasn't Blakey or if there wasn't Marsalis or any of these younger musicians, there would be some other people because the recorded legacy of jazz would call forth its own people to play—that's how it always is. Who could have predicted Picasso would have come out? I don't think it's predicated on any one person. Not me, not any. The music itself will bring the people forth.

DONALD HARRISON: Art Blakey definitely deserves a lot more credit; so does Herbie Hancock, Milt Jackson, and the other guys who continued to play straight-ahead music. But Art Blakey was very instrumental in hiring Wynton, Branford, Terence, and myself, which sort of gave a spark that young musicians were back playing this music. It gave young musicians the knowledge and confidence to know that you could make a living playing jazz. You didn't have to play rock 'n' roll or fusion.

Wynton was chosen to be at the forefront of the media because he is a great speaker. But he's not the only one—by any long stretch of the imagination—that everybody listens to. He has his voice, and his voice *is* important, but he's only *one* voice. I have my voice, and so do other guys. I definitely know what I want to do with music and where I want to take it. And what's frustrating for me with Wynton is that he thinks he is the only one who knows something about this music. I wish that he would come to the understanding, you know, and say, "OK, that cat is cool—he's doing that. This is what I'm doing." It's not going to take anything away from him. He's still going to be playing what he's playing, and it's still going to be valid. I mean, I love that he's doing well and that he's successful at it; just don't put anyone else down.

TERENCE BLANCHARD: The stupid thing about it is that Wynton gets a lot of the credit because he's like the forerunner; he's the media guy. But if you really think about it, Wynton could play a club what, once or maybe twice a year? Those clubs had to survive the rest of the year. And, of course, he wasn't the only one making them enough money to survive. So, yeah, Art deserves a hell of a lot more credit for that resurgence. But you know, there were a number of bands out there. You talk about keeping jazz alive—to me, I think about Woody Shaw, he had a working band. There was McCoy Tyner and Ron Carter, too. Betty Carter is another name that

> comes to mind with saving jazz. I don't even want to use the term *saving jazz*, because they just kept it alive. In the 1980s, when they were saying jazz is back, Art Blakey said, "Shit, I didn't go nowhere."
>
> But as far as the resurgence of young musicians, I think Wynton did have a lot to do with that because he was the guy that everybody saw. Donald, Branford, and myself played a part in it as well.

◆

In actuality, when Wynton Marsalis began honing his jazz chops under Art Blakey, their alliance proved mutually beneficial. Sure, Blakey provided Marsalis a legitimate platform to express his budding individuality and conservative ideas, but the youngster, with his prodigious command, injected a new shot of vitality into an aggregation that had lost the breadth of its appeal.

Billy Pierce, the tenor ace and jazz educator at Berklee, joined the Messengers shortly before Marsalis and remembers the popular state of the band and its leader. "With the reduction of our music [in the 1970s], Art had kind of fallen from the limelight. It started up again around the time I arrived, but when Wynton came in, it really brought a lot of attention back."

Still a teenager, Marsalis nevertheless wore Brooks Brothers suits, had a sophisticated allure, and had a command of European concert music. He often aired his criticisms about music with the kind of jaunty candor that attracted the media. He denounced popular music and claimed the avant-garde and fusion did not qualify as "jazz," which lodged him at the center of controversy but gained him the public's open ear.

At nineteen, Wynton Marsalis was embarking on stardom. His swift rise within jazz, however, owes a great deal to his affiliation with classical music. "Wynton is so well versed in classical music," says pianist Mulgrew Miller, "that it did a lot for his image and the image of jazz. You know, I think Wynton has as many Grammy Awards for playing classical music as he does for jazz. So essentially the classical thing legitimized him. But that's always been so in jazz. Most of the great players, if they could be aligned on some level with classical technique, you know, they could be glorified a certain way."

With the unprecedented industry adulation given to Wynton Marsalis—arguably the most successful trumpeter ever to play classical music and certainly the most popular jazz musician since 1980—the reputation of succeeding jazz musicians was invariably hinged to Marsalis's. And Terence Blanchard was no exception. "Yeah, you know, it's just the nature of jazz," recognized Terence in a mildly annoyed manner. "It's always been that way, and it's unfortunate because there's a lot of different guys out here who have a lot to say and shouldn't be ignored. But, to me, it doesn't really matter because I didn't get into this business for the recognition. I just want to play this music, and once I started playing with Lionel Hampton and realized I could make a living doing it, I was like, 'Cool.'"

Despite taking comfort in his learned tolerance of the jazz media, Terence would nevertheless fall victim to endless comparisons with Wynton. As a Jazz Messenger, the latter had accomplished so much in such a short period of time. Showered with universal recognition and praise, Marsalis set a new standard of popularity identified with jazz musicians. But for Terence, filling a Messenger trumpet chair with a history of excellence was the intimidating task—not matching the global fame Wynton had garnered.

BILLY PIERCE: The trumpet chair in Art's band has always been a hot seat. It may have been difficult for Terence to succeed Wynton—we were on a pretty good roll—but it didn't seem to me like Terence was too concerned about that. I think some people expected a letdown, but I didn't see it. I stayed with the band about six months after Terence joined, and Art was still getting the same amount of gigs compared to when Wynton was in the band. With Wynton, I think people were coming to see the band because of him at first, but after they realized he wasn't there anymore, they still showed up because they liked the band. Of course, there was always an exception or two.

TERENCE BLANCHARD: The first gig I did with the Messengers was in Chicago. It was a hell of a night, and it was funny because everybody kept coming to the gig, saying, "Yeah, man, is Wynton here?" Yeah, it was definitely comical. Me and Billy Pierce used to laugh about it, too. I remember we were standing around before the gig, and this guy comes up, "Yeah, Billy. Yeah, man. Good to see you again, man. I can't wait to hear the band. Where's Wynton?" So Billy goes, "Wynton's not here, man."

"Oh, he's upstairs?"

"No. Wynton's not here. This is Terence; he's the new trumpet player."

"Oh, yeah, how ya doin', man? So, what, he's in the back some place?"

"No, Wynton is not in Chicago.

"Huh?"

"He's not in *Illinois*!"

That was funny, that cat just didn't get it. But I was fine with all that. I mean, I had the gig now! But a lot of people expected me to be upset about all that stuff. They just didn't realize I never expected to get that far. So by me being in that band, I was like, "Wynton who?"

BILLY PIERCE: I found Terence to be interestingly mature for such a young guy, and I was taken right away by his musicianship. It was remarkable how flexible and versatile Terence was. I mean, he could play piano almost as well as he could play trumpet at the time. Along with

> Wynton, Branford, and Donald, I'd say these guys were so musically far ahead of their peers—and in most cases, equal to many of the older musicians.

◆

Even though Terence now occupied the trumpet chair, many people still thought they were listening to Wynton. Sure, Blanchard's chops rivaled his predecessor's, but the misunderstanding was physical, not musical.

Other than being African Americans of the same age and similar height who both wear glasses, they share no real resemblance. Still, people often mistook them for each other, especially overseas.

While in Tokyo together on an all-star Messengers bill, Terence remembers, "I was at a party, and this guy walked up to me and said, 'I'd love to take your photograph with my mother; she just loves your music.' After he took the picture, he said, 'Thank you, Mr. Marsalis—we'll really treasure this.'

"Wynton and I were there with Benny Golson, Curtis Fuller, Johnny O'Neal, Lonnie Plaxico, and Art. It was a very short tour, three concerts and one television appearance. But I was very glad I did that tour because it gave a lot of people in Japan the chance to see Wynton and myself side by side. When we walked out on stage, you could tell they were saying, 'Wait a minute, there's two of them!'"

At a press conference, to be playful, Terence and Wynton exchanged name tags. But their little prank turned embarrassing after a musician approached Terence and told him how much he liked his father, Ellis. That's when they decided to manage their dilemma more seriously. "I started talking about wearing contact lenses," Terence recalls, "but I couldn't get to the point where I'd want to stick something in my eyes. Then Wynton started wearing them, and I was happy because I didn't have to worry about that anymore."

Until the public took notice of Wynton's new look and realized jazz's newest sensations were individuals, Terence was mostly amused by the mistaken identities. One of his most cherished souvenirs is a clipping he saved from a French newspaper while with the Messengers on his first European tour. It is an article reviewing their concert with a photo of Blakey hugging him. But the caption over the picture reads, "Art Blakey avec Wynton Marsalis."

"People didn't really know who we were," explains Terence. "They just knew about some trumpet players from New Orleans that wore glasses. But I knew that people would catch on eventually, so that stuff never really bothered me." However, when the media began billing Terence as Wynton's disciple, the delusion quickly lost its charm.

Separated by less than five months in age, the two New Orleans natives developed simultaneously under identical instruction. They found support in each other and were motivated by a friendly spirit of competition. Thus, Terence was wronged by the disciple tag, a label potentially disastrous to a jazz musician's career. For among all genres of music, jazz has always demanded individuality. As a musician once said, there is no "greatest" in jazz; there are only the ones who find their own voices.

> **TERENCE BLANCHARD:** I really used to think that people were doing it to help my career. The media has always had a yardstick, and they figured Wynton was the guy. So to get a public who doesn't know anything about me interested in me, they would compare me to him. And that's fine, but after *a while* . . . enough is enough.
>
> **WYNTON MARSALIS:** Nobody knows why the jazz media does what it does. It's not that it's really a respected group anyway. I mean, Terence has his own distinct way of playing. He croons on his horn a certain way. I like that cry that he has in his sound. I also think that he's written some good compositions. He writes things that are unusual—it won't be head-solo-head or some boring format that everything kind of falls into. So who knows why the media write what they write? If I knew the answer to that, I could become a consultant and change the Western world!
>
> **TERENCE BLANCHARD:** The only time that shit became frustrating was when people would try to push it on me. But it doesn't really bother me because I understand how the media work. If you understand that, then it really shouldn't frustrate you. If anything, I would get frustrated by the question, not the issue. I mean, I think it's great that Wynton's as successful as he is. I think it's something that's greatly earned by him, and I think he deserves it, and I think it's great for a young black man to receive the kind of attention that he's receiving for playing jazz. And I remember people didn't like my answer; it was almost as if they wanted to create controversy. I did an interview with this one guy who said, "What do you think of Wynton Marsalis's success?"
>
> "I think it's great."
>
> "It doesn't upset you?"
>
> "Why should it?" I mean, here's a guy who I grew up with, that I know personally. What am I supposed to do? Sit there and go, 'Fuck him!' No. No way. It doesn't go that way for me.
>
> If I was the type of person who set individualistic goals for myself, then maybe it would upset me. I come from a period where we weren't even looking for all of this. So all of this stuff that is happening now is like,

cool. But when I'm asked that kind of ludicrous stuff, it does upset me to a certain degree because it ain't about anything. I told that guy, "I understand that's sensationalism and that's your story."

◆

In joining the Jazz Messengers as Wynton Marsalis's successor, Terence was lured into a compromising situation. But he would not allow the entrapping comparisons to detract from playing with the legendary drummer. In Blakey's band, Terence was complementing the education he received at Rutgers with practical, on-the-job training.

Terence Blanchard: When we were on the road, there were certain things cats would do. If you fell asleep, that was your ass 'cause you might wake up with food all over you. Pictures have been taken. . . . And you couldn't leave your bag around because someone would go inside it, take out your clothes, and hang your underwear off something. The big thing that used to happen a lot in Art's band was that cats would come downstairs to go to the gig wearing your clothes. You'd be like, "Hey, how did you get my hat?"

"It's my hat. I found this hat."

Charles Fambrough used to do that a lot. There was a lot of silly stuff to keep the road light, make it fun.

Mulgrew Miller: I was a bit older than everybody else in the band, so I had like this elder statesman kind of relationship with them. I think they looked up to me in that way because I had played with Woody Shaw, Betty Carter, Mercer Ellington, and Johnny Griffin. But that's not to say I didn't feel like I was very good friends with them. Of course, Terence and Donald were old friends from New Orleans, and they were living together with Jean Toussaint. They had this kind of fraternity, had a lot more energy, and were more spirited about certain activities [*laughing*].

And it was actually very rarely that I got to talk to Art one on one—very rarely. But he would always talk about his days in the Fletcher Henderson band, when he first came to New York. And what was remarkable was that even after all those years, Art remembered those arrangements, note by note, lick by lick.

Art also loved to talk about certain players who had been Messengers like Bobby Timmons, Lee Morgan, Walter Bishop Jr., and he was quite fond of Keith Jarrett. But I know Art was very proud of Terence and very fond of him as well. A lesser trumpet player with Art Blakey would have just been beaten to smithereens because trumpet players really had to be strong. And Terence certainly exhibited that kind of strength; he's strong as a horse. Also, Terence is very charismatic on stage, assertive, and Art placed a lot of confidence in him. Of course, Art soon made him musical director of the band because he saw that quality of leadership in Terence.

BILL FIELDER: Art thought the world of Terence. He'd go around saying, "I got this fella in the band who can play the trumpet, can arrange, play piano, bass, and he can play the drums, but he's not gonna take my gig!" That was Art Blakey.

TERENCE BLANCHARD: Young musicians need experience, and a lot of it. Art was the only bandleader that I ever knew who let the sidemen call the rehearsals, call the tunes, write the tunes. After Billy Pierce left the band—about six months after I joined—Art said to me, "You need the responsibility, so I'm going to make you musical director." It makes me laugh because I remember the first night I counted off a song for the band, and I lost my count because I was so nervous. I had to stop the band: "All right, hold it. OK, one, two . . . ." I didn't freak, though.

BILLY PIERCE: I always really enjoyed my association with Terence, playing with him in the Messengers and on other gigs. He was really creative in a way that some of the other trumpet players weren't. But as much as all of his musical abilities stand out, I think Terence is a wonderful person. He's a good cat, and we're all family. Whenever any Messengers see one another, we start with Art Blakey stories and go from there. It's not the most exclusive of clubs, but it's certainly a family, that's for sure.

TERENCE BLANCHARD: I used to love hanging around Art, just listening to him tell stories. Most of the time he didn't say too much; he would pick his moments to speak up. But when he did, it was like a drum roll.

Some of my favorite stories were about the music, but Art preferred to talk about them as people rather than musicians. He used to always talk about certain cats and the trials and tribulations they had to go through in order to survive and play the music. He'd tell stories about guys who had serious drug problems but came through—you know, cats who had serious behavioral problems and persevered. I think your hat has to go off to those guys because obviously there was something there that made them turn to unhealthy behavior, but they were able to come through it and still be able to play and still be productive and still contribute. See, that's my thing—a contribution to the music. It's what I respect. And if they did that, well, the other negative things don't matter to me.

He talked about Sonny Rollins and J. J. Johnson in terms of that. But, I mean, Art also talked about Billy Eckstine and all the racism and other stuff he had to go through, you know, being a black singer at the time he came along. Art called him a pioneer, and he respected him a lot as a person. And that was the thing that was amazing to me because I wanted to hear the stories about the music. I didn't get it at the time. I was like, "Yeah, that's cool, but what about *Bird*? What was it like *playing* with Bird?"

I remember one time I asked Art about Clifford Brown. He said, "Clifford Brown was an angel, and I knew he wasn't going to last too long because he was too perfect." He said that Clifford had a mind that was amazing and that one time Art went to his house and Clifford was doing like four or five things at one time. He was giving a guy a trumpet lesson in one corner, he was playing a chess game with another guy, he was cooking, and he was having a discussion with some other people, and he would rotate around the room. And Art was just sitting there dumbfounded as he watched this cat do all of this and keep it all in synch.

DONALD HARRISON: Art's stories were inspiring but very funny. Art Blakey was hilarious. He had a real funny thing where we thought he was just joking, but we'd really be learning a lot. When he would tell us those jokes, he was also trying to tell us something. I remember the one he did with our tenor saxophonist, Jean Toussaint. Art wanted Toussaint to realize he wasn't practicing enough, so he told him, "Toussaint, when Wayne Shorter was in the band, he used to record himself every night with a Walkman. Then when he got home he would listen to the Walkman and practice so he could get better." Toussaint was in love with Wayne Shorter—of course, we all were—so he got a Walkman and would tape himself every night from then on. But I think after about six months he carried it a little too far. I mean, some nights he would be holding the band up so he could go and get his Walkman. So Art Blakey came to him and said, "Toussaint, why you taping yourself?" And Toussaint said, "Art, didn't you say that Wayne used to bring his Walkman to the bandstand every night?"

"Toussaint, in the sixties there weren't no Walkmans."

MULGREW MILLER: Art was one of those bandleaders that really didn't like to have confrontations with the sidemen. But he was having some problems with one of the members in the band in terms of what he wanted to hear. I can't reveal this person's name because it might prove embarrassing to him, but because Art didn't want to deal with him directly, he sent Terence, you know, being musical director. So when Terence confronted this person, he said, "Look, man, Art wants to hear so and so . . . ." And this person became very irritated and went back to Art and said, "Well, Art, Terence tells me that you said so-and-so . . . ." And Art said [*imitating Blakey*], "Ah, that's OK—don't worry about it." So he put Terence on the spot, and Terence was pretty pissed at Art for that [*laughing*].

GEOFF KEEZER: It was always my dream to play with Art Blakey since I was fifteen. I had my mind set that when I get to New York, I'm going to play with Art Blakey. It was decided [*laughing*].

Specifically, what I got from Art was a sense of leadership. I observed how he would program his sets—you know, how he would sort of tailor what he played to fit the audience we were playing for. In New York, we played for primarily white and Japanese audiences, and when we played North Philly or something, we played for a primarily black audience. So Art seemed to be able to sense what people would be into. Although he wasn't really into race because he thought jazz was a universal language that everybody could get into. He was just very sensitive as to how the crowd was responding. I don't think anyone would get bored, but if there was a lull or something, he would just like drop one of his bombs or crank it up a few notches.

Wynton Marsalis: Art Blakey was always open to different ideas—he would check out what you were saying. In fact, the reason he could always get good [young] musicians in his band was his talent for being able to listen for what you were doing instead of what you weren't doing.

And the reason I started wearing suits also was because of Art Blakey's band, because we would be playing in overalls, and I was embarrassed, man. I was thinking, "I'm not standing up here with the great Art Blakey playing in overalls." So I said, "Look, man, tomorrow I'm coming to this gig with a suit on." And I went out and got a polyester three-piece deal, a maroon tie, and a derby. I still remember that suit. And after that we started getting clean. For us, it was a statement of seriousness. We come out here, we try to entertain our audience and play, and we want to look good so that they can feel good.

Or maybe, maybe we felt that even if we don't sound good, at least we look good. But it wasn't calculated. I never knew that the response to any of what we were doing was going to be. I was new to all that publicity, man, and I didn't know anything about that. I was just trying to play trumpet. But Art said it was a good idea. He said, "Yes, it's time to get clean again."[6]

Mulgrew Miller: I could go on for hours about him as a musical legend, but Art was one of the most fascinating human beings I've ever known. I think his vitality, his zest for life was fascinating. I mean, by the time I was in the band, Art was quite an elderly person, but he had so much enthusiasm for playing music and for living.

Geoff Keezer: I played with Art for a year, the last year. He was really something. In a way, I wish that I could have been older and more mature when I was in the band; I was only nineteen. But maybe if I hadn't of had that experience, I would have been in a different place with my own development. You know, I feel like I aged five years in my one year in the band! It was like being in the army. It was like being in a rock band; it was wild. We would play for these audiences in Eastern Europe and stuff, and they would just go nuts, crazy. And backstage, there would be all the women and the "extracurricular" activities and things. Art tried to steal my girlfriend. He tried to steal *everybody's* girlfriend.

He was sick most of the year I was in the band. But that showed me the tremendous dedication he had to what he did. He personified the music, really. His whole lifestyle was jazz. He lived jazz music—even when he was sick and dying from cancer. I mean, he couldn't even walk down the stairs at the Blue Note in Tokyo on one of his last gigs. He was like holding on to me and stuff walking down the stairs. But when he got up on the drums, it was like he put whatever reserve, every last ounce of strength he had went into the drums—even on his very last gig in Osaka, Japan, at the Blue Note. You know, we were playing and Art's on the drum stool, and he's playing *OK,* but he's not doing too well. He was really sick, and he was like swaying on his bench. So he motions to the trombone player, Steve Davis; he says, "Steve, come over here and hold me up." So Steve goes over behind him and squats down and is actually propping Art up so he doesn't fall off his drum stool. So Art's playing, and he turns around to Steve and says, "Don't make it *sooo* obvious!"

Terence Blanchard: Whenever we played, Art would tell us, "You got to play like it's your last time. You never know when you'll get a chance to play again." So we used to try and inspire each other up on the bandstand, and it could get hot and heavy up there—oh, yes indeed, especially with *that* band. I remember a couple of nights, man, Art Blakey would catch us completely off guard. One night he kicked off a tempo of "Dr. Jeckyle" that was so fast, we were in shock; no one wanted to take the first solo. And that was challenge: to be able to deal, to go with the storm and strut your stuff. And Art knew he caught us off guard. He was smiling the whole time.

◆

On October 17, 1990, just days after his seventy-first birthday, Art Blakey passed away. His death saddened the musical world and silenced his voluminous sound, but he will not be forgotten. Far and wide, Art Blakey dropped his bomb of virtuosity on adoring fans and musicians alike, leaving behind an alumni of Messengers to carry on his legacy.

Terence Blanchard: Art's death affected me a great deal. I didn't think that I would be *that* affected. When I got the news, I was really depressed. I was on the road in Canada. I was playing at the Top O' the Senator in Toronto, and I got a call from [ex-Messenger pianist] James Williams at my hotel. He told me Art had passed. It was just one of those moments in your life that you know you'll never forget. It's like things are different from that point on. I mean, Art was a father figure to me, and whenever you lose that, there's a serious void in your life that you try to fill, but you really can't. The only thing you can really do is accept the fact that it's no longer in existence and just try to move on. We had a memorial service that we all played in, and that was pretty nice.

If I could say one last thing to Art, it would be "Thank you." That's the first thing that comes to my mind. And it's the only thing I really could say to him. Art gave us such an opportunity, man. When you think about a cat that was as great as he was, who took these young artists and let them really screw up on a nightly basis, it's really an incredible thing. You know, he let us get our feet wet; he helped us grow. And it's incredible because he didn't have to do that. He could have had a band with some really bad cats, you know. So, yeah, I would just say to him, "Thank you."

Notes

1. Mike Hennessey, "Interview with Art Blakey" (recorded on the compact disc *The Art of Jazz*, Nice, France, July 14, 1976), track 9.
2. Hennessey, "Interview with Art Blakey."
3. Hennessey, "Interview with Art Blakey."
4. Hennessey, "Interview with Art Blakey."
5. William Stephenson, "The Many Tongues of Branford," *Jazziz* 9, no. 4 (July 1992): 80.
6. Howard Reich, "Wynton's Decade," *Down Beat* (December 1992): 17.

CHAPTER FOUR
CARRYING ON THE TRADITION

Once you left the band, you had to make a statement—that's what Art wanted.

—*Donald Harrison*

Donald "Duck" Harrison was born June 23, 1960, in New Orleans, Louisiana. He started playing the saxophone at fourteen but never contemplated becoming a musician until he heard Branford Marsalis play. "He was the first young player I heard playing the alto," remembers Harrison, "and he made me realize how much fun it was."

In his junior year of high school, Harrison enrolled at NOCCA, where he received instruction from Ellis Marsalis and Edward "Kidd" Jordan. In 1978, both Duck and Branford graduated high school and decided to further their education at Southern University in Baton Rouge. The pair studied directly under Alvin Batiste, the renowned educator and clarinetist.

After spending just one year at Southern, Batiste spotted the kind of talent and potential that he felt should be nourished in Boston at the esteemed Berklee College of Music. As the legend goes, if they did not transfer, Batiste would have failed them out of Southern.

At Berklee, Donald and Branford mingled with the young jazz elite, sharing a room with drummer Marvin "Smitty" Smith. Branford would also develop a friendship with Jeff "Tain" Watts, who would become his regular drummer.

"Donald and I went to the same colleges at the same time, and he's a great musician," says Branford. "But I mean, cats, you know, come together and we used to be tight, but people have different priorities in life, and we just drifted in different directions."

For Harrison, the direction he chose in Boston had more impact on him than Berklee. In Beantown, Donald was making serious connections.

Roy Haynes, the established drummer, took an immediate liking to the alto player, offering Duck a gig playing in his band on weekends. Thirty years earlier Haynes performed with another "bird" who played alto saxophone: Charlie Parker.

> **Donald Harrison:** I learned a lot of subtle things from Roy, like when to play hard and when to relax. I also worked with [organist] Jack McDuff for a while, which gave me a solid background in playing blues. Like Art Blakey says, "If you can't play the blues, you can't play jazz because blues is the backbone of jazz."[1]
>
> When I came back home from Boston for the first time, I noticed that Terence had really grown a lot. He was still in high school, in his senior year, and he was ready to really start playing. Wynton and Branford, of course, were playing together, and I was actually with them in high school, but since they were brothers, it was like I was on the outside. But when Terence came along, I had somebody I could play with. That was really important for me because I didn't feel like an outsider anymore. I consider Terence like a brother, especially musically.
>
> **Terence Blanchard:** When I was younger, Donald used to push me a lot. See, I was kind of the latecomer of the bunch. By the time I came into the fold, Wynton, Branford, and Donald had already gotten a lot together. I wasn't up on their level, so Donald used to always be like, "Man, you need to practice. Work on this; work on that."

In 1984, while still officially in the Jazz Messengers, Terence and Donald formed a quintet together. It was the brainchild of George Wein, the veteran jazz promoter of the famed Newport Jazz Festivals. In October of that year, the Blanchard/Harrison ensemble made their debut at the now-defunct Manhattan jazz club Lush Life. Borrowing the Messenger rhythm section of Mulgrew Miller on piano and Lonnie Plaxico on bass, with Marvin "Smitty" Smith filling in on drums, the Quintet played to enthusiastic crowds for six nights.

Most of their material was from their debut album, *New York Second Line*. *Second line* is an alternative term for Dixieland, music categorized as part of the New Orleans tradition. Thus, the recording embraces the duo's musical roots while blending the harmonic and melodic sophistication of the New York scene.

New York Second Line was a hit not only in Manhattan jazz clubs but around the world. France awarded Terence and Donald with the Gran Prix du Disque (the French equivalent to the Grammy Award). Despite far-reaching critical acclaim and a recording contract with Concord Jazz

Records (the same label that covered the duo with the Jazz Messengers), there was not enough work to sustain a permanent Blanchard/Harrison collaboration. Forced into moonlighting between gigs with Blakey and minimal performances with their own band, the two did not despair. In fact, they took advantage of their additional time with Blakey, maturing at an accelerated pace.

In February 1985, the Jazz Messengers album *New York Scene* (featuring Terence's composition "Oh, by the Way") won a Grammy Award for Best Jazz Instrumental Performance by a Group. By now, the band had gelled, developing an assured and distinctive sound. In view of the ever-changing Messenger personnel, for one particular edition to establish their own identity was a notable feat, one that did not go unnoticed by their leader. "It's one of the best bands," proclaimed Blakey, "if not *the* best, I've ever had."

The year 1986 proved to be a prolific one for Blanchard/Harrison. *Discernment*, the spectacular follow-up to *New York Second Line*, was released under Concord, and the pair formally announced their departure from Art Blakey's nest. After four enriching years with the Jazz Messengers, Terence and Donald were ready for a new challenge. Now in their midtwenties, they were legitimized as the real deal: polished jazz musicians ready to tackle the performance circuit.

> **MULGREW MILLER:** As a matter of fact, Donald, Terence, and I left Art Blakey together. On the same night we all gave him our resignations. I remember we were playing at the [Manhattan club] Sweet Basil, and afterward we went downstairs to where the so-called dressing rooms are and said, "Art, we want to talk to you." Terence did all the talking, quite naturally; he's the most outspoken of us three. So Art sat down and listened to Terence, who was very tactful about it. Even though Art knew it was only a matter of time, I could see he was disappointed because I don't think he wanted that to happen right then. But he sat there very quietly for a few seconds, and then he said, "I knew something was goin' on 'cause I've been seeing these long looks on your faces for a while."

> **TERENCE BLANCHARD:** The time you spent in Art's band was geared to becoming a leader, having your own band. That's what he wanted us to do—eventually. But the interesting thing about Art was that he knew he had to groom young musicians to become bandleaders because that's what we needed in that particular era.

◆

In the spring of 1986, on the heels of Terence's twenty-fourth birthday, the trumpeter got what he wanted: a recording contract with a major label.

Columbia Records, the same conglomerate the brothers Marsalis called home, signed the newest New Orleans duo to a multialbum pact.

Their debut, appropriately entitled *Nascence*, demonstrates both fire and subtlety, according to the *New York Times*. And critic Hugh Wyatt of the *New York Daily News* wrote, "Donald Harrison is unquestionably one of the finest alto saxophonists to hit the scene in recent years. But the focus here is clearly on trumpeter Blanchard, whose playing is eloquent and the epitome of taste throughout the album's seven tracks."[2]

Three months before its release, on May 13, 1986, the Quintet first previewed the music at Milestones, a San Francisco club Terence and Donald often played with Blakey. Booked for a five-night engagement, the band, featuring Mulgrew Miller, Smitty Smith, and a teenaged virtuoso from New Orleans, bassist Reginald Veal, was well received. Rave reviews appeared throughout the week in the *San Francisco Examiner*, *San Francisco Chronicle,* and even across the bay in the *Oakland Tribune*, where critic Larry Kelp wrote, "Jazz fans are advised to scrape their pennies together and make a pilgrimage to the San Francisco club because this very young band is preaching the truth."[3]

While on the road, the critical praise heated things up, and then Miles Davis started a firestorm, predicting Terence "as the brightest young trumpeter on the scene." Newspaper headlines like "A New Threat to the Trumpet Throne" were spawned, and while these ringing endorsements served Blanchard well, many still regarded him, and now Harrison, in the shadow of the Marsalis brothers.

Terence Blanchard: We didn't expect people to lump us all together, so in the beginning we didn't think about separating ourselves from Wynton and Branford. Maybe that was naive on our part, but we were young. Of course, we wanted to have our own identity, but we were just trying to distinguish ourselves as jazz musicians, period.

Donald Harrison: I know that since we all came from New Orleans, people who really weren't in tune with what jazz is about would categorize us as one in the same. But I didn't feel any competition inside, and it really didn't bother me. I realized there was no sense in beating anyone over the head. I was really starting to express myself in the most natural way I could, and I didn't feel I had to separate myself because I knew that I sounded like myself. My main focus was to follow what was there for *me*. I felt that I should do what was in my heart with my music and just put all those other things aside. But in terms of the press and all of those things, since Wynton and Branford were out here first, I wasn't sure if they'd ever realize that each one of us are individuals who play totally different from each other.

In September 1987, Terence and Donald pressed on with the release of their second album for Columbia, *Crystal Stair*. Named after a poem by Langston Hughes, *Crystal Stair* introduced two new members to the band, pianist Cyrus Chestnut and drummer Carl Allen.

Chestnut and Allen were fresh from long stints with Jon Hendricks and Freddie Hubbard, respectively. With Reginald Veal still on bass, this edition became the quintessence of the Blanchard/Harrison Quintet.

Reginald Veal: I did some gigs with Mulgrew and Smitty, but we didn't have the connection that we had with the group with Cyrus and Carl. Mulgrew is a little older than all of us, and, to be frank, if you don't have a relationship with the people that you're playing with, the music becomes more of a job. But with three of us being from New Orleans, and then with Cyrus and Carl, who are great guys, it was so much fun.

We did a lot of things together: played basketball, socialized with ladies, and just talked about life. There was a real camaraderie, and we all had a love for each other. And that all manifested itself when we got up on the bandstand. It was spiritual; it was uplifting; there was something special in the music. I mean, just listen to *Black Pearl*!

Carl Allen: I met Terence around 1983 while he was playing with Art Blakey. And at that time I was playing with Freddie Hubbard. Being a member of Freddie's band, I was very much aware of the Messenger tradition. I myself always wanted to be a Jazz Messenger, but some other drummer already had the gig!

Freddie and I used to talk about Terence quite a bit. Freddie really liked him a lot. He thought that Terence suited the Messengers' strong tradition of trumpet players and that he was someone who worked well with Art.

Cyrus Chestnut: I remember meeting Terence at Ryles, a club in Cambridge, Massachusetts. I was going to Berklee at the time, and Terence and Donald were there playing with the Messengers. Then after the gig, Terence sat down at the piano and what he was doing was so incredible to me that I went up to him and said, "Say, bruh, can you teach me how to do that?" And he looked at me and laughed, "Man, are you kidding?" I guess he never thought of himself as a piano player, but Terence plays a *whole* bunch of piano! What I heard was just so great that I wanted to learn how to do it.

Reginald Veal: As far as I was concerned, I was definitely not on the same level musically as Terence and Donald; for that matter, I felt I was the lowest man on the totem pole in the whole group. So I was always just striving to be where they were.

Carl Allen: It was quite a thrill playing with Terence and Donald because the concept of the band was very different from my previous experience with Freddie. For instance, with Freddie, you just go on the bandstand and you hit—you just hit hard from start to finish. The arrangements were not very intricate with respect to dynamic time signatures and all of those different things. But with Terence and Donald, I learned a great deal about orchestrating from the drums and about different things. And although I had been a huge admirer of Art Blakey, there were still certain things that Terence and Donald were able to tell me about him, like what he'd do on the bandstand to help establish the groove and help certain situations out. And I was able to incorporate that in my own playing. So by them sharing their knowledge of Art, it made me a better player.

Cyrus Chestnut: There was a period in my life when I thought I wasn't going to play as much music as I had. This was around 1987, and I was just getting ready to leave Jon Hendricks's band. Terence and Donald asked me to audition for their band, but things got turned around, and I wasn't able to make their rehearsal. I remember I went back to Boston and everyone started calling me, saying, "Come on, man, you gotta be out here playing!" So I finally went to a rehearsal and watched Mulgrew play, and I remember looking at him and thinking, "Oh, God, I can't do that!" But I sat down anyway and did my little bit, then did a gig with them in D.C., and we just went on from there. I guess they saw some potential in me.

Carl Allen: One of the things that made the band quite interesting was that Terence and Donald were quite the opposite. Conceptually, the way they wrote music was very, very different from one another. But in most situations that worked well. For instance, if you play one of Terence's tunes and if you play one of Donald's tunes, they're from like two different worlds. But when it was programmed within a set of music, it balanced each other out.

Terence Blanchard: Yeah, a lot of people said that. And a lot of people said it sounded like two bands. I think that helped, but I don't know how to describe the differences. It was kind of weird, though. I mean, since we were so opposite from each other, it kind of brought a wholeness to the situation. You know, he had half and I had half. But it could be frustrating for the band sometimes because the guys didn't know exactly which way to go musically or how to deal with certain situations. But I guess it kind of kept them up on their toes. I didn't realize that until later on when Carl told me. He said, "You wanted it this way, but Donald wanted it the other way." And I was like, "Damn, that must be a trip for the sidemen." It had to be frustrating.

Cyrus Chestnut: I didn't know what the heck I was doing. I mean, sometimes it was like playing in two different bands. Donald would play and we'd be right there, but then Terence would play and the gears would shift—*boom*! I mean, it was all new ground. I remember asking Terence, "How do I play? How do I comp behind you? What do you want to hear?" And he'd say, "Listen to the Miles of the 1960s with Herbie, Ron, and Tony." I listened to that, checked it out, went, and played, but it didn't work. So I ended up finding some way to play by just simply reacting.

But there was a great camaraderie, and we would motivate each other. I mean, once Terence was playing hard, we had to come right on with it. I'll never forget, we were in Amsterdam one time and Terence played, then Donald, and then I just went and played like a chorus or so and said, "That's it." And Terence jumped on me hard afterward: "What's wrong with you, man? You gotta come out here to play. You can't just put it all on us. You better come out here to play."

CARL ALLEN: If you had a bad night, we would have a band meeting and blow up at each other with these heated discussions. If one cat was playing and he missed a form because he was looking at some girl in the audience . . . *man*! The music is very personal, and we take it very personally. Everybody's allowed a bad night, but if you're having a bad night because you're winking at some girl or you think you're too cute with your new suit on, we had to put you in a head lock!

CYRUS CHESTNUT: We all had some stuff to learn, and I learned a lot from Terence. I'm not just talking about musically, either. Terence could be very philosophical about certain subjects in life. He's very warm and a joy to be around. Whatever he can do to help, he does. But he don't take no "stuff" either. Terence is a thinker. He's a quiet person, but I don't know about shy. He's just constantly thinking.

CARL ALLEN: Yeah, instead of saying quiet and shy, I would prefer to say Terence is observant. And there's a difference. For instance, the majority of people, particularly my wife and my mother, will tell you I'm not quiet and shy at all. But there are some people who think I am because if I'm in an environment that I'm not familiar with, I tend to stay in the background, keep quiet, and just observe. And Terence is the type of person who just sits back, observes, and will react not necessarily in a verbal way, but in a subtle way. Actually, he's a lot like Blakey in that way.

Blakey used to have a thing where he would call a band meeting when one of the guys in the band was messing up, like missing rehearsals or showing up late. Hypothetically, let's say it was the saxophone player. Well, Blakey would look at the piano player and say, "And this stuff about showing up late . . . ." So everyone would be looking at the piano player like, "What's going on?" And of course, the piano player is about to get defensive but then realizes the comment is really directed at the saxophone player. It's diversion of attention. And when you think about it,

Blakey is really pulling a deep thing there. And Terence has some of that. I mean, I always used to call Terence sneaky. But Terence is not quiet and shy when he's around people he knows.

Terence Blanchard: There was a video of Kid Creole and the Coconuts and this song about a guy named Endicott. Endicott was this real straight-laced guy, wore a pin-striped suit, carried a briefcase, and was real prim and proper. Since Carl used to talk to us so much about business matters, I started making fun of that side of him by calling him Endicott.

Carl Allen: Yeah, my nickname in the band was Endicott because I've always loved business; I'm into that stuff. But I used to tease Terence about his accent—it was funny. One time Terence and I were driving in the city, in New York, and something happened to my car so I pulled over. So we're both looking under the hood, don't know what we're looking for, then Terence says, "Hey, you got *Earl* in the car?" I said, "Got what?"

"*Earl*."

"Terence, it's just me and you. Whatcha talkin' about?"

"*Earl*, bruh, *Earl*."

He was trying to say *oil*. And, of course, I teased him about it for weeks.

Cyrus Chestnut: A lot of times Terence would go into his New Orleans accent and start talking in that heavy Ninth Ward stuff, and it would have you laughing, boy. He'd look at you sideways and say something, and there was nothing you could do but laugh. It was hilarious! Terence is a fun cat to be around. I remember every time somebody had a birthday, you'd always get jumped, and oh, my gosh, it was practical jokes all the time. Carl did something to me that I'll never forget—see, I love watermelon—and every time we'd go to Italy we'd get good watermelon. So we're going somewhere and I saw this big fruit stand, and I yelled at the top of my voice, "STOP!" So I bought the watermelon, and later on at the hotel Carl goes, "Come on, bruh, we got watermelon here." So they cut up the watermelon and I started eating it, but it tasted funny. So I was like, "Wait a minute, this thing's got something in it." And they were all laughing on the floor. They had poured vodka in it.

Carl Allen: I remember everybody had to have an initiation. And I remember when we were in Munich, Veal had to get his. But you wouldn't know when you were getting initiated until it actually happened. So we all would say, "Let's meet in Veal's room." See, if you met in somebody else's room, the person who got initiated might trash the room, which you obviously don't want to happen. So we just casually sat around talking to Veal, and before you knew it somebody threw a pillow sheet over his head and then we threw him on the bed and just beat him. About an hour later he called me moaning and all sore. But everyone had to have their initiation process!

Reginald Veal: We didn't consider ourselves noble or anything, but there were some limits. We would never do anything like put toothpaste on your face while you were sleeping, but we'd do something crazy like tell some unattractive girl that one of the guys liked her. Then when she'd go up to you, and everybody would be laughing at you.

Cyrus Chestnut: We had some wild times together. One time we were on our way to Japan and our tickets got messed up, so instead of leaving the day before the performance, we left on the day of. We were so late that when we got there we had to dress on the train. There were a lot of great experiences. One time Veal was playing, and all of a sudden his bass goes, "Pow!" and I had to play all the bass lines. It was all good.

Reginald Veal: I think it was that same trip to Japan where I was out roaming around in Tokyo, and then the guys came out and we went across the street to this piano store. So we're sitting at the piano, playing and singing like we were in the Baptist Church of New Orleans or Baltimore. And we had people coming in and stopping on the streets staring at us; none of us are very good singers.

Carl Allen: Now that I think back on that kind of stuff, those were the kind of things that I miss. Those were the kind of things that made us a band. There's a difference between having five cats playing tunes together and having a band. I mean, Terence and Donald played for me at my wedding, and Veal was there, and also Cyrus played for my wedding. I remember on February 28, 1988, Terence's son, T.O., was born, and so he missed our gig in Baltimore and flew to the hospital.

But when we went out on the road, we had a blast. There were two things we would do all the time. Every day, regardless of where we were, we would play basketball. We would travel with a basketball and find a court in Japan or Finland or Yugoslavia, wherever. I mean, we would go to the oddest places where they'd say, "We don't have a basketball court in this country," and we'd still find one. And the other thing we always did was shop. We went shopping a lot. The band itself was kind of a clothes hound at the time, with Terence pretty much winning that award. But for me, there's nothing like that feeling of a band where cats go to the movies and spend time together shopping and hanging out—it's just like an extended family. And it makes such a huge difference because what you play on the bandstand will reflect all of those things.

Donald Harrison: We were great friends and still are. We were doing the things that young guys do: talking to the girls, playing music, and trying to find gigs. But no matter what, we always treated each other like brothers.

Terence Blanchard: We were real close, you know, but we had to be because there weren't too many people who believed in the same things that we did in terms of music, in terms of family, religion, philosophy. So we wound up hanging together, and it was a real nice experience.

Donald Harrison: Terence is a very serious musician with a very personal sound. You know it when you hear it. He has a certain maturity in his phrasing. He's one of the great voices of our generation. I used to tell him, "I don't want to blow anybody down; I just want them to say I found my own voice." That's the highest compliment I could ever get playing jazz.

Terence Blanchard: Donald's not the cat to fool with, and he really hasn't gotten his propers as far as that's concerned. You catch Donald on a night, and he'll put anybody to shame—anybody. I remember there were some nights—one week in particular when we were playing at Fat Tuesday's in New York—he was playing the alto C melody saxophone, and I thought the reed was going to pop off! Him and Carl were really hooking up that week; they always played great together. I remember all week thinking, "Damn, it's going to be like that? All right."

The thing I loved about that band in particular is that we were open to trying new things; we weren't quick to write things off. I remember this one-week tour in Spain playing a song of mine called "Forbidden Dreams." And when we started out with the gig, we were playing the song very much like we played it on the record. But by the end of the week, Cyrus started to play something that would make Donald do something, and then it would make me do something, and then Carl would react. By the end of the week, I looked around and I fell out laughing: Carl had put down his drumsticks and was playing with his hands; Reginald's not playing the bass—he's beating on the body of the bass; Cyrus is reaching into the piano and plucking the strings. It was amazing!

Donald Harrison: Oh, yeah [*laughing*], I mean, when we had the group we were really striving to make a group sound. It was a specific sound, but it was a natural, unspoken thing. There were a lot of things that I loved about that band, but none more than our sound.

Carl Allen: You can play with someone for twenty years and still not really have a group sound. But with that band, we established a sound, which I think came from the writing that Terence and Donald were doing. The type of tunes they wrote forced you to play a certain way, which was good because you had to have great discipline, and you had to listen all the time because there were always twists and turns. I thought it was quite an experience. And for me, that was the overall benefit of playing in that band—developing a group sound even though ours was somewhat steeped in the tradition of Miles's quintet of the mid-1960s with Herbie, Wayne, Tony, and Ron.

Terence Blanchard: We tried not to say so, but it probably was. I think we were definitely steeped in that tradition as far as our approach to being individuals. We all had made a conscious effort to try and develop our own sounds and to have our own personalities; it was something we talked about. I remember Carl talking about using a certain kind of drums because they had a certain sound that was different from some of the other guys'. I think the biggest thing that I liked about that band was that we tried a lot of different stuff. Donald would come in with some crazy tunes, and we would sit down and try it. Sometimes it worked and sometimes it didn't, but we always made the effort. We didn't just say, "Ah, man, this shit ain't gonna work." We didn't do that, and we learned a lot from those situations, which helped us when we played straight-ahead. Because when we played straight-ahead, we didn't sound like a jam session band; we had our own individual sound.

Notes

1. David Yeats, "New Orleans Rhythm Kings," *Blues & Soul* (1984): 45.
2. Hugh Wyatt, "A New Threat to the Trumpet Throne," *New York Daily News*, August 29, 1986, 20.
3. Larry Kelp, "Blanchard-Harrison's Music Is Jazz Milestone," *Oakland Tribune*, May 15, 1986, 3D.

CHAPTER FIVE
FORMING THE JAZZ OF TOMORROW

> It's interesting because a lot of people have made reference to that band as being ahead of its time.
>
> —*Carl Allen*

The twenty-first century has arrived, and the newest disciples of jazz are young, polished, and dedicated to ensuring the music remains vital and creative through the new millennium. Although they hold a reverence for the founding fathers of jazz, they gained palpable inspiration and guidance from their preceding generation.

"When I was a kid," remembers trumpeter Nicholas Payton, a New Orleans native and NOCCA graduate, "there were several musicians in New Orleans that I looked up to, but it was rewarding to see someone like Terence, someone close to my age who was so successful. He was giving young people the confidence to know we could make it as well."

"Terence was a big influence to all of us," proclaims Philadelphia-raised bassist Christian McBride. "He and Wynton were probably the two biggest idols of all the high school jazz musicians in the mid- and late 1980s."

The dramatic ascent to stardom enjoyed by Terence, Donald Harrison, and the brothers Marsalis galvanized an entire generation of high school musicians to become some of the foremost young jazz musicians on the scene today. This distinction adds to the magnitude of the 1980s jazz resurgence.

> **Wynton Marsalis:** When we first came up on the scene, it was real different, man. Jazz wasn't nearly as popular then as it is now. I mean, it's been forty years since there's been a real jazz scene in New Orleans. That's why we all had to move to New York while we were still teenagers. When I went to Juilliard, I still didn't know what I really wanted to do at that

point. Shit, I didn't even know how to shave my mustache properly. But deep down inside, I knew I wanted to play jazz. And in the beginning, we were basically fighting for the survival of it. No one in our generation was playing jazz—it was rough. I was trying to get a band of young musicians on the road to let the world know that there were young musicians who really wanted to play jazz.

Branford Marsalis: It sounds good. But I think that when you're a nineteen-year-old kid, you're not particularly interested in the survival of the music. I was just trying to get gigs and have fun. I was riding on subways, watching people OD and shit. None of that ever happened in New Orleans. I was hanging out in clubs, playing music and shit. I was like, "WOW!" I was nineteen! What the hell does a nineteen-year-old know? I mean, we would come in there with these suits on and these bad haircuts with a lot of attitude. We were always grinning in photos with these big chips on our shoulders. We did a *Down Beat* article once, and we were standing on the cover, and it said, "Why are they smiling?" That's what they put on the cover. I loved that. It had nothing to do with the music. We had a love for music, but being out on the road with Jeff [Watts] and them, making no money, driving to all the gigs—that was happening; that was fun.

I remember Jeff and me, Michael Brecker's old band, Seventh Avenue South, and a drummer, Steve Ferrone, we'd be hanging out until six, seven in the morning playing Pacman. I mean, this is the greatest gig in the world! I wasn't sitting around thinking about revolutionizing the music. I thought we were too young to even be trying to revolutionize anything. I think Wynton was a little more concerned with that. I mean, my attitude has changed a little bit now. Now that I'm older, I'm starting to become more aware of our place in music and what it represents, et cetera.

Terence Blanchard: For me, at the time, it was probably a little bit of both. I felt like most jazz musicians, I guess: that the music had gotten a bad rap and that people really weren't being exposed to our real commitment to the music. So on the one hand I did feel obligated to uphold the tradition, but also, there was a kind of wonderment about it all. I mean, being in New York, meeting a lot of my heroes, and being able to rub elbows with them at the clubs. I remember sitting down and talking to Woody Shaw after he just finished playing. It was an amazing time for me, and when I look back on it, I miss it. I miss that feeling of being able to walk down to a club and see Dizzy [Gillespie] play. All those guys are gone now—Woody, Art, Dizzy—you know, I don't see Freddie [Hubbard] very much anymore. Those were the guys I used to hang around.

Back then, I had a lot of energy, too. I tried to hang out as much I could and listen to a lot of music. I remember hanging out for two or three days at a time without going home. I was just staying up, you know, crashing for a couple of days at somebody's house. I was doing some crazy stuff, and I guess it's all a part of growing up. But my mom's lessons were well learned by me because, while I did have fun, I wasn't extremely wild and crazy.

Branford Marsalis: [The 1980s jazz resurgence] was important because it was the first generation since the 1960s where kids under the age of thirty came into New York armed with certain musical skills and was just playing the shit, man. And we made it possible for a whole crop of other young guys like Joshua [Redman], Ryan Kisor, Roy Hargrove, Geoff Keezer to come out. I mean, a lot of the younger guys who are playing jazz now can attribute that to Wynton's success, Terence's success. We're the reason why a lot of guys who ordinarily wouldn't be playing jazz are playing jazz. They saw that there was a whole other lifestyle there. We were living in New York; the shit was romantic. You know what I mean? We were doing well, we were on TV, and these kids see this. So what happened was, a lot of kids who had a lot of talent in music who ordinarily would try and be in funk bands or try to do something else decided they wanted to put on suits and become jazz musicians. And I mean it's nice they decided to play jazz, but if it weren't for Wynton and Terence, they wouldn't be playing. There were a lot of cats who came in behind us, and we started that shit—definitely.

Terence Blanchard: Well, I don't know. It's hard for me to say that about myself, and I wasn't really aware of it at the time, either. For me, I was still trying to get my own thing together and felt I had so much farther to go. But I do agree with him: because of the success of all of the guys in that generation, especially the three of us plus Donald, it made it easier for some of the younger guys to come out.

Now you see this new wave, and there's a lot of young guys who really want to play. So I feel really optimistic about the future in the sense that there are more players interested in playing jazz.

Carl Allen: Really, the only young bands out there at the time were us and Wynton. It's funny because I never really thought about it, but it was basically just us and Wynton. And Wynton's band had like an elitist kind of vibe, where it had gotten so popular that it was kind of unpopular with the cats. And now thinking about it, I do remember there were always a bunch of kids wherever we played. But at the time you don't acknowledge that stuff; you're just trying to play and struggle along.

Terence Blanchard: I remember Christian McBride when he was still in high school. I used to talk to him on the phone all the time. He would call me when he was worried about some things, but mostly he would be like, "Man, I've been learning this Ron Carter line—check this out!" He'd put down the phone and play it for me over the phone. So I was like, "Yeah, all right, bruh. You got it!"

"Now check out some Jimmy Garrison!"

But I mean with a guy like that, you don't have to do anything—he's already got it. I was just making him believe that he's got it, making him understand that he's got it.

CHRISTIAN MCBRIDE: Terence was really important to me all through high school. He was always supportive, and he made me feel like what I was doing was worth my while—you know, putting the time into learning the craft and listening to the music.

Throughout my whole high school life, I kept in touch with Terence more than anybody. Terence was a huge factor in my formative years. I would call him on the phone all the time and stay on for two, three hours at a time talking about the music. Now that I think back, I was probably bugging him to death because I know if someone called me that much, I might not be as nice. But Terence was always cool.

TERENCE BLANCHARD: I remember Rodney Whitaker used to talk about how Wynton gave him a couple of clinics. There was Geoff Keezer, too. When I did a clinic, Geoff was there and still in school, and he came up and started playing a lot of my songs on the piano. They all had a lot of talent and were eager to play, but Christian: "Hey, man, you gonna call me for a gig? Can I play with the band?" Charnett Moffett, the same way.

RODNEY WHITAKER: I started on violin when I was eight and switched to the bass when I was thirteen. That's when I started listening to jazz records. Paul Chambers, Jimmy Garrison—those were my heroes. The first record I heard Paul play on was John Coltrane's *Soultrane,* and that was it for me. I was in love. So before I ever heard of Wynton or Terence or any of those guys, I already knew I wanted to play jazz even though there weren't a whole lot of signals for me to know it was possible. So when Terence, Donald, Wynton, Branford, Jeff Watts, all of those guys came along, they were indication to me that a person could do this for a living.

ROY HARGROVE: Terence is the man! He's cool; he's one of my favorites. I mean, I always dug him. When I was at Berklee, my roommate, Geoff Keezer, turned me on to him. The thing I love about Terence is that he has his own style, his own voice. It's a very personal sound with great dexterity. And I really hope to get there one day.

GEOFF KEEZER: When I was first getting into jazz, one of my favorite bands was the one Terence had with Donald Harrison. I had like every one of their records. I was in junior high school, maybe high school, when they were making those records for Columbia, and, man, I loved that band. I was actually writing arrangements, trying to get my band to sound like that band—that's how cool I thought they were! And so, the first time I met Terence was at an International Association of Jazz Educators conference in Atlanta in 1986. I was like fifteen years old, so I see him walking down the hall; I'm like, "Hey, Terence! I got all your records." Then I sat down at the piano, and I played all the arrangements off his records.

BENNY GREEN: I don't think it takes long for anyone to realize that Terence is a real special trumpet player. I realized it the very first time I heard him play. When I moved to New York at nineteen—in the late spring of 1982—I heard Terence for the first time. He was with Art Blakey playing at a club called the Jazz Forum. I thought he was great, even way back then. I always put Terence on a pedestal, but he wouldn't have any of it. One time I sat in with Art, and I said to him, "Terence, it's a real honor playing with you." And he looked at me like I was crazy.

What really struck me about Terence was that he was always interested in hearing other people's perspective. After he left Blakey and I became a member, he came back to do a tour in Brazil. We were playing opposite Sarah Vaughn, and there was this great Brazilian pianist who I thought was really harmonizing amazingly, and I told Terence about it, and he wanted my take on it. I couldn't believe he was asking *my* perspective.

TROY DAVIS: I had been hearing about all the [Louisiana] homeboys that went to New York in the early eighties. I remember a lot of guys [in Baton Rouge] were saying, "Man, you gotta see Wynton and Branford, and they got these other cats from New Orleans, Terence and Donald! They all played with Art Blakey!"

I first met Terence in 1984 at the World Fair in New Orleans. He actually came through with Art Blakey, and that same year, Wynton's band came through with Branford and all them guys. And I got the chance to see all these cats because I was attending Southern University and working with Alvin Batiste at the World Fair. So Alvin would introduce me to them back stage and stuff.

But Terence—I'll never forget, man—he was in his dressing room and had on this yellow blazer, yellow shoes, a blue tie—you know, all clean. He was sitting down with his horn warming up before the show, and I just went up to him and said, "Hey, I'm Troy Davis." And the one thing that I was always impressed with Terence was that he always made the person who was talking to him feel as though *they* were the star. I felt so comfortable talking to him because he's so humble. And you would think that his playing would overshadow his personality, but it doesn't. I mean, you forget about the fact that he's such a *bad* cat! So here I was sitting there talking to him, and we were just shooting the breeze like I had known him all my life. And he was like, "Oh, yeah, so you go to Southern? So what are you doing now?" And I was like, "Huh, he's asking me a question?" I was just really blown away.

I think it's all because of what we call his "upbringing." That's what they call it down here in the South. The environment Terence grew up in with his parents—his mother's a real sweet person. They come from a church and a tradition of being nice and respectful. So Terence just made it real easy for me to talk to him. Then he went out there and performed, and it was like my mouth was watering. I was so happy for him; I was so happy to know him; I was happy that he was my homeboy. Man, I was just like, "*That's* what I want to do."

Christian McBride: I started taking acoustic bass lessons privately when I was eleven; that's when I became serious about jazz. By the time I met Terence, when I was fourteen, I knew I would become a musician. All the greats—Miles, Trane, Bird, Dizzy, Freddie Hubbard—they all had a significant impact on me, but Terence was a huge mentor.

The first album I heard Terence on was *New York Scene*, Art Blakey and the Jazz Messengers. Terence's composition "Oh, by the Way" was on there. I was in a band at the time, and we used to love playing that song. Then a few months later I met Terence. He came to Philly for a concert with Donald Harrison, and they did a workshop the day before at a community college. I was really nervous just being around those cats, but they are so warm and cool that they made it easy. Terence was very quiet and very laid-back, but I really didn't know what to say to him.

Afterward, Terence sat down at the piano and started playing, and I thought to myself, "How can I let this guy know how big a fan I am of his without being so blatantly obvious?" So later on, I sat at the piano and started playing one of his songs—I can't remember which one—but Terence came over and said, "Oh, you know that?" Then we started talking, and I said to him, "Terence, I bet I know what street you grew up on in New Orleans." And he said, "What?" And I said, "Odin." "Man, what you know about Odin Street? You from New Orleans?" I had studied his records like *Nascence* and *Discernment* so intensely that I noticed the name of his publishing company was Odin Street Music. So I took a wild guess that that was the street he grew up on. I think at that point he knew I was serious.

Nicholas Payton: I grew up with music from birth. Both my parents are musicians, and being exposed to a wide range of cultures and music in New Orleans had a lasting impression on me. I guess I became serious about music around ten or eleven when I started doing gigs. I was fifteen when I started going to NOCCA, and just being under that roof, I can feel the history. There have been so many great musicians to be turned out of NOCCA that there's a certain feeling I get every time I walk in that building, a certain vibration I feel every time I go in there.

Terence and Donald, Wynton and Branford—I looked up to those guys. I wanted to be the next guy to come out of NOCCA and go to New York and get on the scene. I listened to their records everyday, and then when I'd see them, well, they were like gods to me. The first time I met

Terence, he was playing at Dillard University with Donald Harrison, and I was so nervous. I went up to Terence and said, "*Mister* Blanchard . . . ." I was like fifteen, sixteen, only about ten years younger than him, so he said, "Man, call me Terence." I was just so nervous. From listening to their records and seeing them in videos with Art Blakey, I had created a certain image of those cats. The amount of reverence I had for them was unbelievable. To me, they were comparable to what most kids would think of Michael Jackson and guys like that. They were my heroes. But when I met them, they were so cool. They hung out and played basketball and did things like me. That was really enlightening for me to see that they were just like everyone else, because you tend to put people on such a pedestal without really knowing them. But they were very open about what they were doing, which made me a lot more relaxed and allowed me to see the more personal side of them without the image I saw through the media.

CHRISTIAN MCBRIDE: One thing that Terence always taught me—which I'm sure a lot of other people who know him would say as well—was that he helped me understand the whole process of life, the entire scheme of things. He would talk about the whole process of life for a musician and how music and life relate to each other. So he was a huge mentor to me not only as a musician but as a person.

NICHOLAS PAYTON: I had a very naive concept of what the jazz scene was all about—at least at Terence's level. I knew a lot of local musicians and I traveled a bit, but I had no idea what it took to actually get out there and get a band together. So when I finally met Terence and Wynton, they gave me a lot of encouragement and helped me along. Terence gave me encouragement all the time and still to this day. But we don't see each other much anymore. We're both on the road all the time. Even though we live in the same city—actually, I don't live too far from his house—I probably see him more on the road. One day I was in Philadelphia somewhere, and I passed him on the street! But, yeah, I revered Wynton and Terence—and still do. That really doesn't go away. I'll always have the utmost respect for them.

CHRISTIAN MCBRIDE: Terence was like a big brother to me; he was there for me all the time when I was in high school. He helped me out with this one significant incident that happened to me, which I really appreciated. I did this gig with Delfeayo Marsalis at the Black Caucus Convention in Washington, D.C., and, to be blatantly honest, nobody liked Delfeayo Marsalis. But Delfeayo has mellowed out quite a bit since those days; he's not the person he was ten years ago. He was always telling people how sad they were, that Freddie Hubbard couldn't play—all kinds of crazy things. When I did that gig with him, because he had this big bully personality and I was only fifteen, I was honestly scared of him. But he's *Marsalis*, so I wanted to do my best.

After the gig was over, Delfeayo said we were a little shaky, but since it was just a one-time band, it was a good gig. So here I am thinking I did a good job. A month later I called Delfeayo and told him that I really hoped to work with him again, that I really had a good time in D.C. And Delfeayo said, "Man, I ain't never calling you for any more gigs." I felt like a giant had just stomped on me. I was crushed.

"Well, why not?" I said.

"I don't like your attitude."

Now I always looked up to these cats, so I couldn't understand why he didn't like my attitude. So he said, "Well, you ain't serious. You be grinning and smiling and shit on the bandstand. You're all cocky and confident. I'm not calling you no more." I was like on the brink of tears; I hung up the phone in shock. I didn't know what to do, so I called up Terence. I said, "Terence, I don't know what happened. I just got off the phone with Delfeayo, and he crushed me, man. He called me confident. Is that true, Terence?" So in his very soft-spoken way, Terence didn't exactly say, "Don't listen to Delfeayo," but he consoled me and brought me up out of the gutter of my worst teenage experience.

Nicholas Payton: Terence has always struck me as someone with a very open musical concept. Just from watching him from Blakey's band to now. He's done a bunch of things, everything from playing in straight-ahead bands to fusing a lot of different music together. He was one of the first modern cats out of New Orleans who started incorporating a lot of the New Orleans influences with modern jazz—especially on the first record he did with Donald, *New York Second Line*, and others like *Discernment* and *Black Pearl*. Then, of course, Terence went on to do film scoring. Terence seems like he wants to keep his foot in a lot of different doors. He did a Brazilian record [*The Heart Speaks*] that's really nice. I just think that it's important to be continually evolving. And although Terence has been out here for a while, he's still open to other musical ideas. He's always evolving and still changing. And a lot of people are insecure about that. Once they find a thing that they're good at, they stay within that because no one wants to look like they don't know what they're doing. So I think it takes a bigger person to be able to accept change, and I admire Terence for that.

Christian McBride: You listen to him play, he's very articulate, and if you listen to him speak, he's very articulate. I think Terence is a fantastic artist. And just to give you an example of how cool he is, he did something that no one else has ever done for me since. I was trying to get my high school girlfriend into jazz, so I asked Terence if he could send me a couple of albums so I could give one to her. I meet artists like everyday, and I'll say, "Send me a CD," and it goes in one ear and out the other. But a week later, Terence sent me a box of four LPs of *Crystal Stair*.

Actually, on that same gig—man, I got so many stories to tell about Terence—on that same gig, Terence called me up as soon as they got to town and said that they needed my bass. What happened was, Reginald Veal didn't have his bass for some reason, so they needed mine that night for the gig. Of course, I was more than happy to lend it to them, and I was thinking to myself, "Man, maybe they'll even let me play with them!" So I'm out the door, but my mother's like, "Hold it! Don't you have homework to do?" This was on a weeknight.

"But, Mom, Terence is—"

"I don't give a damn about that. You have to finish your work first. If Terence wants to use your instrument, you have Terence talk to me."

So he did, and my mother agreed. They sent a car for me, but by the time we got to the club, there was a big crowd waiting to get inside. Since they didn't have a bass, they couldn't do a sound check, so everybody had to wait outside. It was nice to know that I was holding up a Terence Blanchard concert!

At the end of the night Terence let me sit in with the band, and I was petrified. I had already sat in with Wynton and Branford, but this was yet another icon that I was going to play with. We played Donald's tune, "Let's Go Off." One thing I remember about sitting in with Terence that night was that I really didn't have a developed conception of harmony. I was playing these random notes, but Cyrus Chestnut was playing these chords that would make them sound right. The song is in F, but at one point I just played a big ol' loud D flat. But Cyrus was right behind me picking me up. That's when I thought these cats could do anything. After the show was over, as always, Terence was giving me lots of encouragement. He was always really cool like that.

NICHOLAS PAYTON: I feel it's very important to share your knowledge with the younger kids. It's not going to take anything away from me to help and enlighten someone else. There's enough room out here for everybody; there's no reason to be selfish or snobbish. The more people on the scene, the more people playing, the wider the arena for playing.

BENNY GOLSON: During my day when musicians like me were coming up, people would put us down. They'd say things like, "Where's the melody? You play like you got a mouth full of hot rice!" Of course, I didn't like them for that. I'm inspired when I see a talented musician, especially a young one, because that's our tomorrow! That's our future of jazz! Why do you want to put them down? If anything, you should try to help them because encouragement can prompt us to try to best ourselves. So as a result, anybody who I see has talent, they're going to get my encouragement. And I know Terence is very much the same way.

TERENCE BLANCHARD: Well, I always felt that if you want the scene to be healthy, you can't have an "I got mine, you get yours" attitude. All the trumpet players that I met when I was younger would help me. Miles Davis, Dizzy Gillespie, Freddie Hubbard, Woody Shaw, all those guys were extremely helpful and extremely nice. And Clark Terry has always been great. He always gives me a music lesson every time I talk to him.

When I was seventeen, Clark came to New Orleans to give a master class, and later I went to his show at the club in the Hyatt Regency Hotel. He remembered me from the school, called me up to play a tune with him, and I played his horn. He was the first guy I saw play who really made me understand what I needed to work on in terms of technique and control.[1]

You know, I don't have any bad stories like some people have of those guys. They were always cool with me.

I remember the first time I met Miles, I was scared to death because I had heard all those stories. When I walked in the room, he said, "Tearrrence!" I didn't even know he knew my name! Actually, I did know because he had made some really flattering comments about my playing a few months earlier. But on that night, I was hanging out with [his drummer] Al Foster, and he said to me, "You haven't met Miles?" I said, "No, man." So he says, "C'mon, let me take you into the back; I'll introduce you." And that's when I met him. He said, "Keep playing, motherfucker. Keep doin' whatcha doin'!" And every time I would see him, it was like, "How's your wife? You OK? Good to see you, man." All the time.

He was funny, though. One night we opened up for Miles—boy, this is funny—this was in Spain. So me and Donald open up for Miles, and the promoter of the concert kept trying to get us off. He was like, "Get off, get off. You guys are playing too long." See, Miles didn't like people opening up for him, so Miles was the one telling the promoter to get us off the bandstand. So we cut our show short by like one song, and then Miles came on and did his show. Now I had spoken to Miles before the show, and I saw him at the airport the next day—see, Miles is a funny cat, man—he said, "Whatcha doin' here?"

"Miles, I played the concert with you last night."

"That was you? Ah, man, I wish somebody would have told me—I would have come down and heard you. Did you tape it?" He was a funny cat. I said, "OK, Miles, all right, sure."

Donald Harrison: I think [the 1980s resurgence] was very important. I mean, jazz is becoming popular again because of the things that the guys of the 1980s did and the older musicians that helped us. There are a lot of jazz clubs opening up, and there are a lot of jazz fans out there now. When we came to New York, there was only one major label signing jazz artists. That was Columbia. Now it's everywhere. All the major labels carry jazz. So the resurgence was definitely important. And since we're all out there now and we're all able to play this music, we really have to think about what we're saying. We have to look at the whole picture, not just at ourselves. We should try to say something that's with love, that would make the music last. Don't put anybody down, pay respect to the elders, and just tell your story.

◆

In 1988, Terence Blanchard and Donald Harrison added a few more chapters to their story. In January, they concluded recording what many consider their finest album, *Black Pearl*. Named for the trumpeter's newborn son, Terence Oliver II, the piece captured another Gran Prix du Disque from France.

Later that March, Terence and Donald were presented with the first annual Sony Innovators Award, an honor designed to celebrate musical excellence, cultural and innovative sound, and ideals of young talent who, the company feels, will provide the artistic direction of tomorrow. A panel of judges led by Herbie Hancock and Quincy Jones selected the duo. Said Hancock, "Donald Harrison and Terence Blanchard are true innovators on trumpet and saxophone. . . . Their work recognizes the value of great jazz from the understanding of its tradition. They have an emotional style and technique that defines the image of jazz. Harrison and Blanchard are forming the jazz of tomorrow."

Branford Marsalis: It was different because all of us, with the exception of Art Blakey and a few others, were out there by ourselves. Terence was twenty-two when he did his first record. Wynton was twenty; I was twenty-three; Donald was twenty-four. We were all a bunch of kids. We shouldn't have been making records! It was amazing that we made these records. And the Donald Harrison/Terence Blanchard records are so incredibly underappreciated. They made some very, very good records.

Carl Allen: Looking back now, a lot of people feel—including myself—that the band really didn't get the recognition and the amount of worth that it should have.

Cyrus Chestnut: Yeah, looking at it in retrospect, it would have been great to have done more with the band, but this industry is too funny. I mean, I remember at the time they were trying to do the competition thing between Terence and Wynton. And there was no competition. There was *no* comparison because they both had their own various sounds. But I think we had poor record company support. They tried, but they only went so far. This may be a thing in which ten, twenty, thirty years from now, people will look back and realize just what was going on.

Carl Allen: It's interesting because a lot of people have made reference to that band as being ahead of its time. I mean, the last record we did was

Black Pearl, and when it came out in '88, a lot of younger musicians told me that they thought it was revolutionary. But, you know, that was just the kind of stuff we would be doing on a nightly basis without arrangements.

TERENCE BLANCHARD: Well, I don't know about being ahead of its time, but I know we didn't get the recognition we deserved. But that was because we were on Columbia Records.

REGINALD VEAL: To be successful out here, you must have your record company behind you and then the booking agent and management, too. And I got the feeling that Terence and Donald were not being treated fairly by Columbia, and it's sad because they should have.

BRANFORD MARSALIS: I think that it was a mistake for Terence and Donald to sign with Columbia. They thought they were going to get the same kind of success that Wynton had. A lot of people thought that when Wynton became successful, Columbia was working this wonderful magic. And Miles was on Columbia. And I mean, I was on Columbia, too, but I knew for a fact that when it came to jazz, it was not a priority there. Wynton was a priority because he had done so well. So they were going to prioritize the jazz roster. And when it came time for the funds to trickle down, most of it went to Wynton, a little of it went to me, and none of it went to them. I knew that. But I think they thought that a lot of the success had less to do with Wynton and more to do with Columbia. And I think it was a big mistake on their part.

TERENCE BLANCHARD: Well, it *was* a mistake for us to sign there, but the thing that you have to understand is that where else were we going to go? Who else was signing jazz artists at that time? I mean, the smaller labels were, but we were already on one. Columbia was really the only big label signing young talent.

Columbia had Wynton, and they didn't really know how to market more than one jazz artist—and still don't. I mean, that's sad, and it was a big problem for us.

REGINALD VEAL: When Columbia was putting a lot of money into Wynton and he was considered the best band by the public, I remember our band and his were both in New Orleans doing the same workshop. And despite all the attention Wynton was getting, I was *proud* to be on the bandstand with Terence and Donald. Still to this day, I think the Blanchard/Harrison band was one of the greatest ever—I mean, in the history of music. And I can say that with ease, without biting my tongue.

DONALD HARRISON: Well, you never know what kind of recognition something is going to get later on, and I've learned to take things as they come, especially if that's the way they're supposed to be. But I've realized that there have been some musicians at the highest caliber who died penniless and underappreciated. Whether you're an artist or a great genius, that's just the way it is sometimes. You know, I'm making a living, and things could obviously be a lot worse. I *know* people who are going through a lot worse than me.

But actually, you know, I really wanted to go with Atlantic, but I followed Terence. He really wanted to go to Columbia, so I said, "OK, bro." I mean, Columbia is a big company—they're the big boys! So I think it's hard to say whether it was a mistake or not. We could have gone to Atlantic, made one record, and it could have been over.

◆

By the end of 1988, it was over. Following a Christmas gig, Terence Blanchard declared he would be leaving the band after all commitments were concluded in May 1989. The announcement surprised everyone, but none more than his partner.

Donald Harrison: Yeah, I was surprised at that point because I felt we were really on the brink of something great. But Terence felt he had to go on and do something else. I guess he wasn't hearing my sound and was searching for another way.

There's a lot of pressure in the music business, and I felt there may have been outside forces telling Terence certain things, but I never discussed this with him, so I don't really know what he was feeling or what really happened. But I was definitely surprised and disappointed, too. But I had to move on.

Cyrus Chestnut: Surprised? I didn't know what was going on. I found out secondhand that the band was breaking up. Then about two weeks later, Terence told me. At that point in time, there was a lot of distance between Terence and Donald. Carl had left the band before the last couple of gigs, and Gene Jackson came in. Terence was *here*, and Donald was *there*. They just had another agenda, and it wasn't together. It was interesting because we still continued to play anyway.

When the band broke up, Donald and Terence went their separate ways, and I started working with Donald. I don't know all the details of the breakup, even to this day. But you know, people are in each other's lives for a long while, and then you grow, and sometimes you grow apart. I think that's what happened.

Carl Allen: I just think the band had to split. And one of the reasons was just because Terence and Donald are very strong-willed individuals who had their own ideas about being a bandleader. You have to understand that being a coleader is very tough. When you talk about being a leader, period, it's due in part to the fact that you have your own ideas about music and about the way your band should be run. So when you talk about being a coleader, then that vision has to be split. And when you talk about that, for some people, they feel like they might as well be a sideman. But I think in most instances Terence and Donald handled it very, very well. There just became a point where they were growing in different directions, at different paces, so I think it was necessary for them to move on to something different. You have to understand, too, by that time they had been playing for so long, you know, with the time they had spent together with Blakey, from the time they knew each other from New Orleans. I mean, other than in a husband-and-wife situation—and even sometimes in that situation, too—you just need a break.

DONALD HARRISON: I was in a situation where I had to regroup and was either going to sink or swim. I was all alone for a while, but it made me a stronger person. And I guess, looking at it from the most positive side, the end result was that we both grew into our own men. Over these past years, I've developed another thing that I deal with outside of playing with Terence. So in hindsight, it was good for him and it was good for me because I needed to develop a state of Donald Harrison without Terence Blanchard, which I've done. But I still remember how to play that sound Terence and I created!

RODNEY WHITAKER: I caught the tail end of that band, the last year, but we were all pretty close. We used to do a lot of things together. We used to go and shoot basketball together, go shopping, and just hang out. We were like brothers in that sense, and it was just a great experience. And I don't really know of any specific reasons as to why the group broke up; I just know that Terence one day decided that he wanted to move on.

I remember the last gig because it was a terrible day. We played outside on a Sunday afternoon in Tucson, Arizona, and it was 108 degrees. Everybody was too physically exhausted to play. The energy was different, too. I've heard of situations where bands broke up and went out with a bang, but this wasn't a bang. We had dinner later on that night, and by that time, there was just a lot of distance between Terence and Donald. It was really awkward. I don't know a lot of the intimate details that went on between those two, but I definitely felt that there was distance between them and that they had pretty much stopped communicating with one another.

TERENCE BLANCHARD: It *was* an awkward time for me and everybody else. My whole thing about that period is that we were in a sense inexperienced. You don't go to school to learn how to run a band. You go to school to learn how to *play* in a band, how to compose, arrange, and all of that stuff. But the daily trials and tribulations of being on the road, dealing with promoters, agents, and all of that stuff—nobody can really prepare you for.

But ultimately, I think the band split because it was just time. And that's the only thing I can say. It was just time for everybody to do their own thing. I really believe we were just at the end of that run.

Note

1. Ted Panken, "Sincere Sounds," *Down Beat* (December 2000): 45.

CHAPTER SIX
MO' BETTER MAKES IT MO' BETTER

> Terence has been a part of music for so long that if you took it away from him, he wouldn't know what to do—he'd be lost.
>
> —*Mrs. Blanchard*

The year was 1986. The movie was *She's Gotta Have It*. The auteur was Spike Lee. For some, it had been years; for others, it had been a lifetime since they were captivated by such a natural, realistic portrayal of African Americans on the silver screen. The film's uncompromising look at the everyday African American experience marked the emergence of an artist destined to revolutionize the depiction of blacks in cinema.

Eight years later, that destiny had developed into reality. By 1994, Spike Lee had made seven diverse and challenging films, becoming a respected social commentator and one of the most influential filmmakers in the United States.

That year he was honored at the Essence Awards, where the venerable actor Ossie Davis credited him for "demanding action not only from the whites in the industry, but also from the blacks. He has opened up the can of worms no matter what."

Martin Scorsese also applauded Lee that evening for "taking Hollywood to task, not only for its reluctance to bring positive images of African Americans to screen, but also for its dismal hiring practices."

Spike, outfitted in a formal but flamboyant ensemble, sat in the audience trying to keep his composure as his film mentor continued. "He was born Shelton Jackson Lee and is one of America's most gifted filmmakers," said Scorsese. "Spike is a visionary, a disturber, and an artist. He's a terrific storyteller who knows how to use words and pictures to tell those stories.

That in itself is quite an achievement. But to be blessed enough to use his gift to truly say something, to truly have a voice, an original voice, then you have one powerful filmmaker."

From the beginning of his career, Spike followed his own heart, determined to make films with complete creative control. He would not be corrupted or shackled by Hollywood's interpretation of commercial viability. "For me," he said, "it has to be black actors and black directors deciding what we put on screen. And so, the subject matter of my films will not be determined by studios or critics or whoever."

In October 1981, during his final year at New York University film school, Spike Lee began shooting his thesis film, *Joe's Bedstuy Barbershop: We Cut Heads*. The hour-long drama about a barber torn between right and wrong garnered him a student Academy Award. But in spite of its success, *Joe's Bedstuy* did not generate him a single job offer from Hollywood. "I never got one offer, not even an 'after-school special,'" lamented the filmmaker in his book *Spike Lee's Gotta Have It*. "So that just cemented in my mind what I thought all along: that I would have to go out and do it alone, not rely on anyone else."

In 1984, his ambitious attempt to make an independent feature film called *Messenger* resulted in the most devastating period of his young career. After eight drawn-out weeks of preproduction, Lee ultimately pulled the plug on his own project, squandering $20,000 of his beloved grandmother's savings and landing him "on everybody's shit list."

Although inauspicious beginnings wounded his reputation and disheartened his spirit, Lee was back on his feet less than a year later with newfound determination. After writing a new script, he managed to raise $175,000 to complete his feature film debut, *She's Gotta Have It*. In the end, the picture made $8 million and established Spike Lee as an overnight success.

The trials and tribulations of making the groundbreaking *She's Gotta Have It* are well documented. Made on a shoestring budget, Spike eradicated the disastrous experience of *Messenger* with one of the most original and compelling independent films of its year. And while *She's Gotta Have It* is remembered for launching Lee's career and revered for changing the face of black film forever, it was also responsible for inspiring a spirit of possibility among African American artists of all types.

> **TERENCE BLANCHARD:** After I saw *She's Gotta Have It*, I remember thinking that I wanted to work with a cat like Spike Lee. But it's funny because I didn't think about it in terms of scoring his films or anything like that. I just appreciated seeing another young African American as serious about his art form as I was about mine.

For years people had always told me to forget about jazz because there's no money in it. They'd say play funk, make some money, then go into jazz. But I never believed in that. That's one of the reasons why I could relate to a cat like Spike. He never waited for some big studio to sign him up; he just went about doing what he believed in. He went around scraping every cent he could get his hands on to make his film. And I really respect him for that. That's the main reason I wanted to work with him. I just wanted to be around that kind of environment. Then the next thing I knew I got called to play on the soundtrack for his next film, *School Daze*. It was so ironic that I was taken a little by surprise.

I was called by [contractor/saxophonist] Harold Vick; he wanted me to be in a big-band session for a scene in the movie. It was called "Straight and Nappy: The Jigaboos & Wannabees Chorus." There was this trumpet and tenor trading off that me and Branford played. I was supposed to be the "jigaboo," and Branford was supposed to be the "wannabe." It was a lot of fun. I also played a trumpet solo in the movie, and at the premiere I overheard some people talking about my scene. Since I used a mute and it was expressive, a lot of people mistook it for Miles Davis. Some cat said, "Man, Miles sounds good tonight!" I didn't say anything; I just took it as a compliment.

A year later, I got called back to work on the soundtrack for Spike's next film, *Do the Right Thing*. I was just happy to get a call-back!

New York City's hostile social climate in the 1980s—particularly the incident in Howard Beach—gave impetus to *Do the Right Thing*, Lee's politically charged film that induces laughter about interracial strife until its sobering denouement. It became an important part of the American film canon and propelled Lee from an independent filmmaker to a major player in Hollywood.

For composer Bill Lee (Spike's father), Terence's trumpet was summoned once again to play over the jazzy soundtrack. Then, in the words of Terence, "A year later, Spike contacted me himself."

Continuing his prolific pace of making motion pictures, Spike returned to the preproduction scene in the summer of 1989 with an original screenplay called *Love Supreme*. Later renamed *Mo' Better Blues*, Spike's fourth film in five years centers on Bleek Gilliam, a fictional character driven by his selfish, obsessive devotion to being a jazz trumpeter. To play the role, Spike cast Academy Award–winning actor Denzel Washington.

The son of a jazz musician, Spike regularly envisioned making a movie about the music closest to his heart. As a youngster, he took piano, violin, and guitar lessons and vividly recalls watching his father perform annually at the Newport Jazz Festival in Rhode Island.

Bill Lee, an established bassist who has played alongside such musical giants as Duke Ellington, Joe Henderson, and Sarah Vaughn, is also a superb composer. In the early 1980s, he wrote and performed the scores for his son's NYU student films. And despite the growing popularity of rap music among young people in the mid-1980s, Spike continued to use his father's jazz-based scores for his feature films. For *Mo' Better Blues*, Bill Lee wrote his fourth feature score and contributed two compositions to the stellar soundtrack.

"I often think that if my father weren't a jazz musician, I would never have been exposed to the music," admitted Spike Lee in his companion book to *Mo' Better Blues*. "I wouldn't have heard it on the radio, that's for sure. If you don't hear stuff, you'll never develop a taste for it. So much good jazz music just goes unheard.

"Jazz has been an integral part of all my movies. Back in '85, the writer Nelson George, who invested in *She's Gotta Have It*, begged me to reconsider the film's jazz score. He thought that young people into hip-hop wouldn't be able to relate to jazz and the film would suffer at the box office. Certainly jazz has never detracted from the appeal of my films. If anything, it's made them better films."[1]

For *Mo' Better Blues*, the Branford Marsalis Quartet was hired to record the featured music and tutor the actors on their respective instruments. Everything was set, apart from one major detail: there was no trumpeter in Branford's band, and since the film's main character plays trumpet, someone had to be hired.

> **Spike Lee:** In the mid-1980s, I became aware of a bunch of guys from New Orleans that were young and talented jazz players. My uncle, Cliff Lee, turned me on to Wynton, and through him I met Branford, [whom I became friends with]. Then through Branford I met Terence. Terence lived in Brooklyn—everybody lived in Brooklyn—so that was [how we all met].
>
> When I came up with the idea that Branford should play saxophone for a character, he suggested that Terence should play trumpet for Denzel Washington's character. Terence also tutored Denzel and did a great job.
>
> **Terence Blanchard:** Spike called me and said, "I want you to teach Denzel how to play the trumpet!"
>
> "Yeah, in three easy lessons for $19.95!"
>
> Spike's funny. But I agreed because I figured it was a way for me to make money, stay home, and practice and get my embouchure [the formation of his lips on the trumpet mouthpiece] together.

◆

After becoming an integral part of the 1980s jazz resurgence with four highly successful years as musical director for Art Blakey's Jazz Messengers, a subsequent gig as coleader of the award-winning Blanchard/Harrison Quintet, and work on three Spike Lee films, the trumpeter's accelerating career suddenly crashed into a technical barricade.

In 1989, Terence was forced into an extended hiatus from the performance circuit, for his embouchure had become so problematic that is was frequently cutting his lips. Along with the pain came the realization that his embouchure was limiting his compositional range and that he could never develop technically to the extent he desired. Therefore, he took a year-long sabbatical to reconstruct the entire formation from scratch.

Although this visit to the woodshed proved invaluable, such an intricate procedure generally indicates the end for many less driven musicians. In fact, during the rebuilding process, rumors began to circulate around the world that Blanchard's career was indeed over. He was dismissed as washed up; he was written off as a has-been. Realistically, he could strive to come back as a studio musician, but any aspiration of returning to the jazz performance circuit was an impractical fantasy.

> **TERENCE BLANCHARD:** I got depressed. I kept hearing, "Blanchard can't play anymore." There were certain gigs I wasn't getting. A promoter in Japan wouldn't pick me up for a tour because he heard I had lost it. It was a hurtful thing because *I* knew that it was just a matter of time until I would be able to come back—but better. But it's not about the process; a lot of people want it *right now*. It's the "What have you done for me lately?" attitude. So my optimism would fluctuate, but I tried to remain as optimistic as I could. The only thing that would keep my spirits up was the development. But once I got better at one thing, it would uncover like ten other things! It was a crazy experience.
>
> And that was another part of my reason for leaving the band [with Donald]. My playing had deteriorated greatly, and I remember I was trying to practice with the new embouchure but still play with the old one, and the shit wasn't working. And I remember that week we were at Fat Tuesday's in particular because Donald and Carl were hooking up like gangbusters. I'll never forget that. That's when I said, "I got to stop. I gotta stop and practice. I can't continue to go on like this." So that's why I decided to leave the band—well, it was one of the things that really helped me make the decision.
>
> I went back to the basics because the artistic side demanded that. It wasn't like an injury, but I got knocked back ten years. Before, when I was playing, it was a mystery to me because I would do all the exercises, but some aspects were inconsistent, and I didn't know what was going on.
>
> **BRANFORD MARSALIS:** It's a real serious procedure, particularly for trumpet players. I mean, you're unlearning something that you've learned to do

for years. It's a muscle thing; it's terrible. I've never had to go through it, but I can imagine how terrible it must be.

Terence Blanchard: Yeah, it was terrible having to re-form my lips, but it was something I had to do. I started playing the trumpet before I ever had a teacher, so when I eventually got one, he didn't recognize my problem because I was continually progressing. My teachers never realized exactly what I was doing; they didn't know that I was getting cut all the time because my bottom lip was tucked over my bottom teeth. But finally, technically, I hit a brick wall. It came to a point where I found that my limitations in trumpet technique were interfering with the articulation of my melodic ideas.

Bill Fielder: Terence is very level-headed; he's the type of person that was never satisfied, only gratified. He was trying to go onward and upward; he could never stand still. So one day he called me and said, "I can't keep playing like this." So I said, "Why don't you come out to the school and we'll work on it." We had about seven sessions on that, and I would talk to him on the phone all the time. He needed a lot of encouragement at the time. I mean, he couldn't even make a sound.

◆

In July 1989, in the midst of his performance hiatus, Terence began work on Spike Lee's *Mo' Better Blues* as a technical consultant to the director and as trumpet instructor to Denzel Washington. While devoting most of his day toward familiarizing Washington with the trumpet and the idiosyncrasies of a jazz musician, Terence spent the remainder pouring everything he had into making a comeback. As dismal as the process may sound, he was fortunate enough to be surrounded by several friends who encouraged him to find his way through the fog.

Branford Marsalis: I did what friends are supposed to do—I just teased him. I just teased him in a way that let him know that it was all right. But he was doing the right thing, and it was a courageous thing. I mean, he sounded like shit, but he was *supposed* to sound like shit—deal with it. Let's face it, Terence is a smart person; he knew he had to make the change; that's why he made it. I'm not a trumpet player; I wasn't staring under his lip one day and said, "Man, you need to change that embouchure." He said, "Man, I'm thinking about changing my embouchure." And I said, "You should. You're going to sound like shit for a year, but so what? What's the big deal? If it makes you a better trumpet player, no one will remember what you sounded like three years from now."

TERENCE BLANCHARD: During that year, I would work a lot less. I was taking two or three gigs a month, playing in all-star bands and recording on other people's records. I was also starting to put my own band together, so a lot of things were going on in my life at that time. I learned a lot about people's personalities and about people who were really serious about the music. There were some people who really understood what I was going through and were very supportive. Branford was supportive, but actually, a lot of people didn't talk to me about it. The guys in the new band—Rodney Whitaker, Bruce Barth, Sam Newsome, and Troy Davis—they understood what was going on.

TROY DAVIS: Terence was really weak at that time. Yeah, he was like a baby. He had to start all over, and it was very frustrating for him. At first, he couldn't hold long musical phrases, so he would tell me, "When I come out of that, fill in all of that." So I got a chance to really *play,* and it just carried itself over. The stronger he got, the more we connected musically.

◆

Paying homage to "the music," Spike Lee's *Mo' Better Blues* contains a collection of jazz classics: "Footprints" by Wayne Shorter; "Mercy, Mercy, Mercy" by Cannonball Adderley; "All Blues" by Miles Davis; and Ornette Coleman's "Lonely Woman," performed by Branford Marsalis.

The final sequence of the film, a montage spanning eight years, features John Coltrane's "Part One—Acknowledgment" from his landmark recording *A Love Supreme.* The composition underscores the montage, as Bleek Gilliam finds redemption through marriage and fatherhood.

The soundtrack also includes an eclectic array of original jazz from Bill Lee and Branford Marsalis, showcasing Terence's trumpet throughout. There's a vocal rendition of W. C. Handy's "Harlem Blues" by actor Cynda Williams and rap work by Wesley Snipes and Denzel Washington on "Pop Top 40," as well as Gangstarr's "Jazz Thing."

Bill Lee's "Again Never" received a Grammy nomination, as did the Branford Marsalis Quartet featuring Terence Blanchard for Best Jazz Instrumental Group.

"I didn't make this film out of some lofty mission to bring jazz to the masses," insists Spike, "but if people are exposed to jazz, that's wonderful."

Spurred on by his disdain for Clint Eastwood's *Bird*, the grim and humorless portrayal of Charlie Parker, Spike made an antidote for it and others, such as *'Round Midnight. Mo' Better Blues* is a jazz picture free from antiquated clichés common to the genre, offering audiences a fresh and authentic perspective of contemporary jazz musicians.

"Period pieces about jazz have been done before," said Spike. "I wanted to show that there are young jazz musicians out there today who are carrying on a tradition. At the same time, I didn't want to do a film that was about jazz exclusively, though I knew the script would center around characters who were jazz musicians."[2]

Marking the first in a series of several Spike Lee/Denzel Washington collaborations, *Mo' Better Blues* focuses mostly on the Washington character, Bleek Gilliam, a successful, charismatic musician, absorbed by his ego and love for his art. In fact, he's especially forthright about how everything and everyone is secondary to his music.

Bleek performs nightly with his band at New York City's grandiose jazz club, Beneath the Underdog. The Bleek Quintet consists of Shadow Henderson (Wesley Snipes) on saxophone, Left Hand Lacey (Giancarlo Esposito) on piano, Bottom Hammer (Bill Nunn) on bass, Rhythm Jones (Jeff Watts) on drums, and Giant (Spike Lee) as their manager.

Bleek and Giant are best friends, but the latter's gambling addiction puts a strain on their relationship. One night during a gig, a couple of thugs drag Giant through the club, past Bleek as he's performing, and into the back alley. Well overdue on his gambling debt, Giant pays a hefty fine: a vicious, bone-breaking beating that renders him unconscious.

Leaving his audience, Bleek rushes outside to the alley to save his best friend from being killed. In frustration and anger, Bleek starts swinging punches at the thugs but is ultimately smashed in the mouth with his own trumpet. It's a symbolic incident that forces him to confront and amend the damage his selfish obsession with music has caused to loved ones.

Bleek Gilliam is one of the more complex and intriguing characters to emerge from Lee's pen. Though Lee cites the young generation of jazz artists as his inspiration, Terence believes his vision for the character comes closer than his musician friends. "Bleek is Spike," laughs Terence. "I don't know if he acknowledges it, but I know it's him. Like Bleek, Spike is a really determined guy when it comes to his craft—so much so that it had a great effect on his relationships with women."

"All I can say," responded Lee, "is I love film more than Bleek loves his music. All artists are driven by love for their art, and great artists are selfish in their devotion to it."[3]

"I think there's a good bit of him in me, too," admitted Terence, "but I'm not as blindly devoted and selfish as Bleek was. I'm committed to the music, but the thing that I've learned after having four kids is that music, while it's very important to me, is not the most important thing in life. I mean, if it came down to the jazz industry or my family, the jazz industry can kiss my ass. I'll work; I'll do something. When I hang out with my kids, they make it hard for me to go out on the road. But, yeah [*laughing*], before the kids, I was more like Bleek."

If nothing else, *Mo' Better Blues*, like *She's Gotta Have It*, is an authentic movie about African Americans and, more specifically, contemporary jazz musicians. The characters, all so fully realized by nuanced performances, actually look, behave, and speak like real jazz artists. The director openly credits Terence for much of his film's authenticity, as he was on set day and night lending his expertise.

SPIKE LEE: Terence made it his personal crusade to see that Denzel looked real on screen—his trumpet techniques, mannerisms, attitude. He wanted Denzel to come across nothing short of a real-life jazz musician.[4]

We were all tired of seeing not only jazz films, but music films in general, where you just knew the actors were not playing the instrument. And so Terence, Branford, my father, [bassist] Bob Hurst, everybody, was committed to make it seem as though the actors were playing the instrument. The actors were committed, too. They were hanging on their tutor's every word. Denzel and Terence got along great, and they're still friends. We had a lot of fun making that one.

TERENCE BLANCHARD: I had never done anything like trying to show someone how to act the part. I didn't even know how to approach doing it. How do you teach someone to act like they're playing an instrument? When Spike called me to do this, it seemed like a tough assignment. I thought about some of the other movies like *A Man Called Adam* with Sammy Davis as a trumpeter and *Paris Blues* in which Paul Newman looked pretty good as a trombonist, but Sidney Poitier was kind of questionable on saxophone. It was unusual for me, but it turned out well.

SPIKE LEE: I asked him how difficult a task that was, and Terence took the opportunity to tell me what I already speculated: "Denzel's the type of actor that whatever information you give him, he's gonna run with it; he's going to give it a lot of work."

TERENCE BLANCHARD: Since I was working directly with Denzel, Spike was watching closely, which really gave him the first opportunity to see what I was all about. It could have been easy for me to go on that set, as a professional musician, and condescend the actors who were playing jazz musicians. But I wasn't about to disrespect the actors, the crew, or Spike himself. I was just happy to be a part of it all. Spike took note of that, and he soon began to parallel his work ethic with mine.

Spike and I never really got a chance to get to know each other during my involvement in his two previous films. He was always—and still is—very busy. I'd see him in the studio talking with his father about the music. He seemed quiet, very much to the point. He basically stayed in the booth with the engineers.

On *Mo' Better* we got to know each other, and he understood what I was going through with my embouchure. He always showed a lot of confidence in me, but he would always joke with me about it, too. He'd say, "The way you write for film, you should put that trumpet down!"

SPIKE LEE: I don't remember saying that! Terence was a great, young trumpeter, and when we witnessed his embouchure change, when he had to shed and change his whole style, it showed that he had a tremendous work ethic. He put in a lot of work in order to improve. But that's Terence: he's never run away from hard work.

Any day that Denzel was shooting a scene with music, Terence, as his tutor, was on the set lending technical and moral support. And any evening we screened dailies from one of Denzel's music scenes, Terence would be sitting right next to me, hipping me to what was good and bad. It was 100 percent dedication.

TERENCE BLANCHARD: I said to Denzel, "When you're at the piano, it's like you're in a trance. The music is just coming at you like an explosion, and you got to get it out before you lose it. If you're really into it and you're hitting the right notes on the piano, you might not notice people around you." Actually there's a scene like that in the movie when [his girlfriend] Clarke was talking to Bleek, but you couldn't hear her voice—it was muted. To some that scene may look silly, but it's the truth. It's happened to all of us at one time or another.

SPIKE LEE: There were some things Denzel did at first that I didn't feel were appropriate. He seemed too flamboyant, holding the trumpet with one hand like a fusion all-star and not like a jazz traditionalist. Before I had a chance to mention it to Denzel, Terence was on the case. Anyway, it was best that Terence talk to him about trumpet technique. Terence had the expertise, and Denzel respected his opinion.[5]

TERENCE BLANCHARD: Sometimes Spike would ask me certain things about Denzel's mannerisms, like the way he held his horn or something like that. I remember this one time during filming, Denzel was doing something with his hands and Spike turned to me and said, "You wouldn't do that, would you?" I said no, and Spike yelled, "Cut!" So after I told him—Denzel's funny, man—after I told Denzel about it, he said, "*Oh* . . . that ain't hip, huh?"

Denzel, Spike, and I went to see a Mike Tyson fight in Atlantic City about four months before the shoot. This was the first time I met Denzel. On the drive down, I let him hold my horn so he could get familiar with it.

I said, "It has to become a part of you; you can't look like you're afraid of the instrument." He took it out of the case and held it all the way down.

SPIKE LEE: The trumpet never left his hands for two months before we started to shoot. Denzel was great.

TERENCE BLANCHARD: I suggested to Denzel that he listen to as much music as he could get his hands on. I directed him specifically to musicians whose work related to Bleek, the character, his one-sidedness—Miles Davis, Thelonious Monk, and John Coltrane.

DENZEL WASHINGTON: Hanging out with Terence and the musicians, checking out their lifestyle, was an education for me. And the trumpet? Well, it was enjoyable, it was painful, it was humbling, it was hard, and hopefully it was rewarding. Just try to make a sound out of the damn thing! It's got to be one of the most, if not the most, difficult instruments to play. I tinkle on the piano, now and again, but the trumpet is unforgiving.[6]

TERENCE BLANCHARD: I made a videotape of myself playing Bleek's trumpet parts and sent it to Denzel in California so he'd have something to work with before he came to New York to begin rehearsals. During rehearsals, Denzel carried around a Walkman with a tape of the music we were using for the film.

SPIKE LEE: The band members and tutors received a cassette tape of each song. On these tapes, each actor had his instrumental part mixed higher than the others. So if you were the bass player, in your right ear you'd hear your part loud and clear, and in your left ear you'd hear the rest of the ensemble at a lower volume.[7]

TERENCE BLANCHARD: In the beginning, Denzel was having a little difficulty with the fingering of the notes. He's such a perfectionist that he wanted to be precise in each fingering, trying to play the music perfectly. But when he missed a fingering, his natural inclination was to go back and correct it. And when he did that, the playback track of the music would get ahead of him, which was no good. So I assured him that it wasn't necessary to be so precise. I said, "Don't worry about it; most musicians aren't even going to know what you're playing."

I thought he should just listen to the music all day long. By listening to the music backward and forward, he would eventually be able to sing the melodies. So when it came time to film, by singing [in his head], he would always know where he was. He didn't have to press the right valve; he just had to press something in time with the music. And that really helped him a great deal.

Denzel has a good ear and such a serious work ethic that it wasn't long before I was able to sit back and just watch him perform. He had a really good feel for the character, and he never really had to ask how to do

> things. I mean, he would ask me how to hold the horn in certain situations, but he didn't go around saying, "What about this? How do I do that?" He didn't need to ask questions; he observed. Wesley [Snipes], too. They just sat back and watched us. We'd go out to jazz clubs and just hang out until they got a feel for it.

◆

Ironically, just one month after their quintet disbanded, Terence and Donald were working alongside each other again. Harrison, who had also performed on the musical soundtrack for *School Daze* and *Do the Right Thing*, was hired to fill in for a touring Branford Marsalis as Wesley Snipes's saxophone instructor.

Everyone on set, including the director, thought the actors were effectively assuming their roles. "I was struck by the believability of the band members," wrote Lee in his companion book to the film. "Denzel and Wesley had the fingering down, and so did the other guys. They looked like real musicians."

Donald Harrison downplayed his contribution, crediting Snipes for being a brilliant actor. "Basically, all I told Wesley was, 'This is how you hold the saxophone, and these are the notes.' Nothing too complex as far as playing. But I would tell him about the music, that it was very serious but we play it with a lot of love. And you know, just try to be as dignified as possible, and he carried himself in that manner. Wesley is a very intelligent person; he grasps stuff very quickly and has a serious work ethic."

"One night after rehearsal," remembered Snipes, "Bill [Lee] had passes to the Paradise Club, so we all went there. I had both saxophones, soprano and tenor, and Denzel had his trumpet. We hung out in the back of the club playing our horns and carrying on. We were seriously off-key. It was a riot. I went to the bathroom, and when I came back, the fellas were surrounded by a posse of women saying things like, "Are you guys really musicians?"[8]

Bill Nunn, a versatile actor in his own right, who portrayed Bleek's bassist, thought, "Denzel and Wesley were interesting to watch. They're both extremely talented, but they come at it in a different way. Denzel is like a surgeon: precise, thought-out, meticulous. Wesley is more of a raw talent, but he still works at his craft."[9]

"Denzel's a method actor," explained Robi Reed, the film's casting director. "What 'method acting' means to me is when an actor just becomes a character, whether it's in rehearsal or on the set. Denzel, I would notice, would go off alone and go through whatever process he had to go through to become Bleek. Then he would be Bleek for the rest of the day and would answer you like Bleek would answer you."[10]

"The costume department was two floors below the rehearsal space," remembered designer Ruth Carter, "and each time Denzel came down for a fitting, he had his trumpet and he was in character. I'd get a shirt on him, and he'd sit down with that trumpet and start blowing. And I'd say, "OK, let's get the pants on." He'd put the pants on, and he'd sit down and blow some more. It would take twenty minutes for him to try a suit on."[11]

After principal photography wrapped, Denzel Washington explained his eccentricities to *American Film* magazine. "It was difficult to separate myself from the group and stay in my own head, to stay concentrated. Working with an African American director means a more relaxed set, more camaraderie, which is good and bad. It was tough for me to keep up my wall of concentration.

"I learned early on, when you do a film and people go to see the film, they don't go, 'Whoa, he stunk but I bet he was nice to everybody.' I've learned a balance. Now, I stay in my room. I learned how to shut the door. But I heard some of the stuff on Spike's sets, people saying, 'Oh, he's so Hollywood.' That's 'cause when I come out of the room, I'm making a bee line for the set. It's almost like a boxing match. I've got my head—I've psyched myself up."[12]

> **Terence Blanchard:** We were shooting a scene one day, and I, as usual, was at the video monitor watching Denzel. The camera started rolling, and I must have had a worried look on my face because Denzel stopped in the middle of the take. "What's the matter with you, man?" he said. "You look like a nervous mother. Get away from me, man, you're making me nervous!" But everything was cool, and a couple of years later he got me back when we did *Malcolm X*. I had a little cameo in the film, and shooting that scene was hilarious because Denzel was messing with me, saying, "How does it feel now? How does it feel to be on the other side of the camera?"

◆

During a break one evening in the studio, Terence began tinkering with a melody on a piano. He was preparing for his "comeback" album, his self-titled debut as a leader for Columbia Records. Spike overheard him and approached.

"I really like that melody! What is that?" asked Lee.

"Oh, just something I wrote," replied Terence with his usual humility.

"What's the name?"

"'Sing Soweto.'"

"Bet, man, we gotta use this in the film!"

Terence wrote the stirring ballad in memory of the sixty-nine people who were killed when South African police opened fire on blacks protesting apartheid in 1960. The tragedy is known as the Sharpeville massacre.

"I told my father," explains Spike, "that I wanted Terence to incorporate his song into the score. Terence agreed to let us use it, and that same night we recorded him playing the song as a solo for muted trumpet. Then he arranged it for a string orchestra. We ended up using it when Denzel is playing alone on the Brooklyn Bridge. We had this great crane, this large shot that sweeps down from out of the sky to this lone trumpet player on the Brooklyn Bridge. I love that scene, and it's such a beautiful song.

"Terence was on the set that night and he kept saying, 'Spike, when women see these shots, they'll go crazy.' He was right. Denzel Washington in a suit playing trumpet alone on the Brooklyn Bridge, with the Manhattan skyline in the background. You can't get much sexier than that!"

With its sex appeal, authenticity, and wonderful music, the finished product became another successful Spike Lee Joint. *Mo' Better Blues* generated over $20 million at the box office, more than twice its budget. Such a financial surplus is a particularly important feat in the precarious film industry, for Hollywood considers filmmakers as marketable as their last movie. Thus, Spike was approved financing for his most costly film to date: a $14 million picture called *Jungle Fever*. The peculiar title was suggested by a friend of Spike's, which prompted him to declare, "Based on the title, I wouldn't mind paying $7.50 to see the film myself."

Notes

1. Spike Lee and Lisa Jones, *Mo' Better Blues* (New York: Simon & Schuster, 1990), 155.
2. Lee and Jones, *Mo' Better Blues*, 40.
3. Lee and Jones, *Mo' Better Blues*, 31.
4. Lee and Jones, *Mo' Better Blues*, 158.
5. Lee and Jones, *Mo' Better Blues*, 161.
6. Lee and Jones, *Mo' Better Blues*, 208.
7. Lee and Jones, *Mo' Better Blues*, 159.
8. Lee and Jones, *Mo' Better Blues*, 77.
9. Lee and Jones, *Mo' Better Blues*, 60.
10. Lee and Jones, *Mo' Better Blues*, 67.
11. Lee and Jones, *Mo' Better Blues*, 64.
12. Thulani Davis, "Denzel in the Swing," *American Film* (August 1990): 29.

CHAPTER SEVEN
TERENCE GETS THE FEVER

> I really enjoy writing film scores because it's a separate thing away from jazz. It's a different outlet for creative expression without pimping myself.
>
> —*Terence Blanchard*

To this day, Terence Blanchard vividly remembers his first film experience: the call by Harold Vick, the studio full of musicians, observing composer Bill Lee at work, and thinking, "Man, that must be a great opportunity, a great feeling to be able to write for those situations." Even though Terence dreamt about writing music for movies, conducting an orchestra, and collaborating with talented directors, he set practical expectations for himself: "I thought I'd be in my sixties by the time that happened to me, after I had done two hundred recordings and was on my deathbed."

Terence wasn't even thirty when Spike Lee looked to him to compose, arrange, and conduct an orchestra for his next picture, *Jungle Fever*. Terence's hard work and creativity so enhanced *Mo' Better Blues* that he had found himself a new fan in the director.

Jungle Fever marked both Terence's coming out party in the film scoring industry and the birth of his long-standing designation as Spike's music director of choice.

> **Spike Lee:** After Terence wrote that piece for *Mo' Better*, I really began to think about [hiring him to score my next film]. I knew that he was gifted and even though that doesn't mean he could score a film, I decided to give him a shot. He wrote the score for *Jungle Fever*, and, in fact, "Sing Soweto" became its main theme.
>
> My father and I both agreed that we had come to the end of the line as far as our working relationship was concerned. So Terence stepped in, and

we didn't miss a beat. I've always believed in giving people opportunities, and I thought Terence deserved the shot. I was very confident that he could do it. I didn't think I was gambling or anything. He was probably more nervous than I was.

Terence Blanchard: When Spike asked me to score *Jungle Fever*, well, I was just amazed. I was really nervous but also real excited. When I first started playing [on the soundtrack] for his films, I loved just going to the sessions to watch them record the music. And it was really cool to be in an orchestra where we were playing somebody's music who was right there and had just composed it.

I don't know what convinced Spike I was capable of scoring a film and I don't care; I'm just happy he did. I guess it must have been that one scene I wrote for *Mo' Better Blues*. That project was a rare opportunity for me. I had never even had a chance to write for strings before, let alone a full orchestra. The whole experience was a threefold break for me—as a player, a teacher, and a writer.

I will always be grateful to Spike because scoring music for films is a rough business to break in to. At clinics students ask me, "How do I become a film composer?" And I feel sorry for them because my only response is "Prayer!" I mean, there's no finishing school for it. You can't go to a school and then submit your résumé. Most of the people who I know in the business kind of fell backward into it. If you have the fortune of getting into the business, it can be a great thing for you in terms of creativity. I've written all different types of scores and have had a chance to conduct large orchestras.

But with *Jungle Fever*, I remember when I stepped in front of that orchestra to conduct for the first time. I was doing everything I could to hold back the tears in my eyes. It was amazing—one of the most incredible moments of my life. Hearing the orchestra play the music that I had written was an indescribable type of feeling. Actually, it kind of brought me back to the rush I got when I played with Art Blakey for the first time.

◆

The term *jungle fever* is a colloquialism for interracial sexual attraction. In the film, when characters played by Wesley Snipes and Annabella Sciorra get hit with the bug, it gives birth to yet another provocative and politically charged Spike Lee Joint. As always, Lee blends the dynamic conflict with a colorful soundtrack full of soul and jazz. Famous for the wall-to-wall music in his films, *Jungle Fever* is no exception. Spike commissioned Stevie Wonder to write and perform a dozen songs to accompany Terence's jazz-orchestral score.

"One of the things I love most about filmmaking," gushed Lee, "is gathering together talented people. That's the best thing I'm able to do: to tap into great black artists like Terence, Branford, Stevie."

Terence as a boy in an undated photograph. (Courtesy of Wilhelmina Blanchard.)

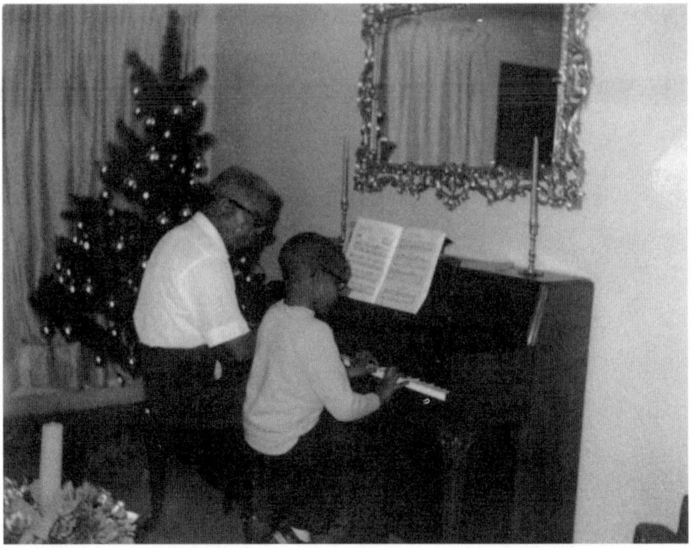

Terence gets a piano lesson from his father, 1968. (Courtesy of Wilhelmina Blanchard.)

Sitting at the piano with his new instrument, January 1972. (Courtesy of Wilhelmina Blanchard.)

Dancing with his mother at a carnival ballroom celebration, 1973. (Courtesy of Wilhelmina Blanchard.)

Outside Terence's church, where he was honored that day for his musical involvement and attendance, 1978. Left to right: Mr. Blanchard, Mrs. Blanchard, Terence's grandmother Susie Ray, the Honorable Andrew Young, and Terence. (Courtesy of Wilhelmina Blanchard.)

At Rutgers University, 1981. (Courtesy of Terence Blanchard.)

With Lionel Hampton at a jazz festival in Holland a decade after playing in his famed orchestra, 1992. (Courtesy of Loes Hento v.d. Kraats.)

With Dizzy Gillespie in an undated photograph. (Courtesy of Terence Blanchard.)

With Art Blakey at a Jazz Messengers gig in Geneva, 1983. (Courtesy of Berinda Pizurki.)

In Tolentino, Italy, with the Jazz Messengers during his first European concert tour, 1982. Left to right: Billy Pierce, Terence, and Donald Harrison. (Courtesy of Carlo Pieroni.)

Chatting with Billy Pierce during the Tolentino gig. (Courtesy of Carlo Pieroni.)

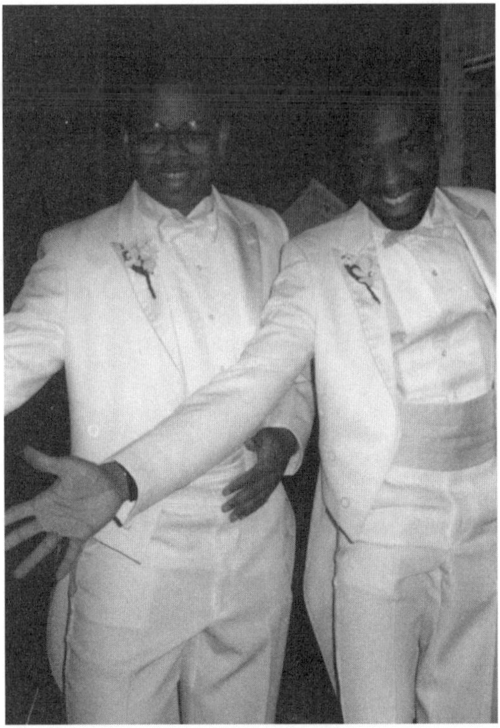

Terence with his best man, Donald Harrison, at his wedding to Jackie DeMagnus, 1985. (Courtesy of Terence Blanchard.)

With Wynton Marsalis, 1987.

The last edition of the Blanchard/Harrison Quintet, 1988. Left to right: Cyrus Chestnut, Rodney Whitaker, Carl Allen, Donald Harrison, and Terence. (Courtesy of Pierre Blanchet.)

Spike Lee, Denzel Washington, and Terence during rehearsals for Mo' Better Blues, *1989.* (Courtesy of David Lee.)

Denzel Washington with his tutor on the set of Mo' Better Blues, *1989.* (Courtesy of David Lee.)

Collaborating with Branford Marsalis on the soundtrack for Mo' Better Blues, *1989.* (Courtesy of David Lee.)

Conducting his score to Malcolm X *for a seventy-piece orchestra at the BMG Studios in New York City, 1992.* (Courtesy of David Lee.)

The Terence Blanchard Quintet performing music from The Malcolm X Jazz Suite, *1993. Left to right: Bruce Barth, Terence, Tarus Mateen, Sam Newsome, and Troy Davis.* (Courtesy of Terence Blanchard.)

Performing with Sonny Rollins at New York City's famous Carnegie Hall, 1993. (Courtesy of Jack Vartoogian/Front Row Photos, NYC.)

In Germany on a European tour with Benny Golson, 1993. (Courtesy of Hans Harzheim.)

Chatting with Clark Terry at his idol's home in Glen Cove, New York, before their Down Beat *cover shoot, October 2000.* (Courtesy of David Bartolomi.)

Going over the charts to Jazz in Film *with Joe Henderson, March 1998.* (Courtesy of Dana Ross.)

Spike Lee poses for author Anthony Magro at Studio One in New York City, March 2001.

Cassandra Wilson recorded and toured the music of Jimmy McHugh with Terence's band. She is seen here with Terence and pianist Edward Simon at the Toronto Jazz Festival, June 2001. (Courtesy of David Tak-Wai Leung.)

Let's Get Lost. *In performance at the Toronto Jazz Festival, June 2001*. (Courtesy of David Tak-Wai Leung.)

Alex Steyermark, Spike's longtime music supervisor, says the director is "incredibly knowledgeable about music. I think music is very important to Spike generally, but a score is able to convey certain emotional truths that songs can't always do. So to him, scores are a very important part of his films. He devotes a lot of time to it and a lot of resources—the scores on his films are usually very well budgeted."

Although Terence's debut score garnered warm reviews from critics (the *Washington Post* called the film "delirious with good music," singling out Blanchard's score as "memorable"), simply completing it was a triumph for him, considering that just a year earlier he bluffed his way into scoring the one scene for *Mo' Better Blues*. When Spike asked him whether he knew how to arrange "Sing Soweto" for strings, Terence responded with confidence despite his utter lack of experience.

> **CARL ALLEN:** When Terence first started writing for movies, he didn't know—and this is not a criticism—he didn't understand too much about orchestration in respect to a range of instruments. Actually, it's a very high compliment because Terence studied very hard and became very intent on learning. In fact, he came to my house to get a book on how to write for percussion instruments, and I've yet to get that book back!
>
> **TERENCE BLANCHARD:** Oh, yeah, in the beginning I knew nothing, zero. I learned from talking to [composers] like Miles [Goodman] and listening to CDs—you know, breaking stuff down. And that was another great thing about going to NOCCA because it really helped me learn how to analyze. I remember when I did *Malcolm X*, I was listening to the score to *Glory*—that movie was great. Denzel took me to the premiere (we were working together on *Mo' Better* at the time), and, man, that movie made me cry! And James Horner's music . . . *wow*! Especially at the premiere, you know, they have it pumped up.
>
> So I was listening to James Horner's score and started to learn that it's all about orchestration. See, a lot of the stuff he was writing was in three parts, but the orchestration made it sound so much fuller, so much larger. I kept saying, "Oh, yes, the melody, the bass, the bottom . . . ." So when you bring it all together, it has a big effect. But if you break it down to its core, it's simple; that's when I started to learn orchestration.

◆

While theater is an actor's medium and television is a producer's, film is unquestionably the director's vehicle. Everything from the visual and sound design to the performances and story structure typically derive from the director's vision. In addition to toiling with all things artistically pertinent to the filmmaking process, directors oversee hundreds of cast and crew members and carry the burden of delivering the film on schedule and under budget. It can be an awesome undertaking that proves daunting to the most adept. As Spike Lee once affirmed, "Making a film has to be one of the hardest endeavors known to man."[1]

One of the more trying areas for directors is a film's musical score. Music is an indispensable tool in aiding an audience's capacity to comprehend plot and tone. At its best, the score will address the heart and soul of the film, providing its viewer with emotional insight into the characters' thoughts and feelings. Since most directors do not study music, they have a difficult time translating their creative vision into words that make musical sense. As a result, they are compelled to place a great deal of trust in their composer to conceive the most effective music possible. Their relationship is a delicate collaboration, one of creative intimacy and duration. Some of the more famous partnerships have been Alfred Hitchcock and Bernard Herrmann, Federico Fellini and Nino Rota, Blake Edwards and Henry Mancini, Steven Spielberg and John Williams, and Martin Scorsese and Elmer Bernstein.

Terence Blanchard: As artists, there are a lot of things that correlate from one art form to another, but one of the things that makes me and Spike work is that I've come to learn exactly what it is that he wants when he says certain things; that's always the hardest part about working with a director. When you start talking about music, there has to be some kind of language that gets you on the same wavelength, which can be really difficult. Fortunately, me and Spike have come upon a language that works for us, and we're constantly working to get better and try different things.

Of course, in the beginning we had our difficulties communicating, but now, over the long period of time that we've worked together, we've come to a point where I can actually recognize and understand exactly what kind of music Spike wants just by the tone in his voice when he describes it. I also can sense how much latitude I'll have on a certain piece or if I'm able to experiment and take new chances. On *Clockers* I did something real different on a particular cue. Actually, I took a chance because it was something Spike didn't like in the past, but I insisted on it and he loved it—and wanted more. He said, "Do you have another one like that?"

Alex Steyermark: I started out with Spike as a music editor, and the first time I met Terence, he was playing trumpet in the orchestra on Spike's *School Daze*, so that was the first time I actually worked with Terence. The thing about him that has always stood out to me is how congenial he is. Terence is just a genuinely open person—and a very curious person, too. He has this great curiosity about the world around him.

TERENCE BLANCHARD: The first thing that comes to mind about Alex is anal-retentive [*laughing*], but I shouldn't say that because he's a great guy; he's just very precise in his work. He's very knowledgeable and has a very good ear. But Alex is detailed to a point where it can actually become a pain. Then again, if you think about it, sometimes you need that. You know, there are times where you can be so fatigued working on a score and he'll be there pushing me to do my best.

ALEX STEYERMARK: As the years have gone by, Terence, Spike, and I have all grown together and developed a real intuitive thing. You know, we get down in a room and go through the film, exchange ideas, and we'll talk about the scenes where there should be music. Spike's a very musical person and often has strong ideas, but it's almost like Terence can read his mind musically, which is really great emotionally. And I know Spike relies on me to help put it all together. It's just like a nice team—it really is. And I think that with each one that we do, it just gets easier.

SPIKE LEE: Our familiarity with each other obviously comes from working together for so long, but it's a unique dynamic. We have a really great trio that understands how music can best serve a film. We share our ideas; if there's a score that someone likes or a certain phrase or a certain instrument, we'll see the movie or listen to the CD. Terence and I really liked the soundtrack to *The Shawshank Redemption*, and we talked about it a lot. There were some things in that score that influenced the music of *Summer of Sam*.

TERENCE BLANCHARD: When I'm dealing with Spike's films, I really deal with his subject matter. It's hard to make a big statement because the music takes a back seat. The music is just the window dressing; it can be a helluva window dressing, but it's still not the primary focus.[2]

Probably the hardest thing about working with Spike is coming up with the melodies for his characters. Spike loves melody. Don't give him anything emotional without a melody. He doesn't like underscoring. He wants to hear a theme. "What's the theme for this character?" Sometimes it's rough because music can get in the way of the dialogue, so you really have to choose your points.[3]

SPIKE LEE: Yes, I'm very big on themes. Personally, I don't really like atmospheric scores—I like to hear a melody. So the first thing we begin with is the main theme. That's very important to me. So in those initial meetings, I like Terence to start thinking about it. In fact, even before that, when I'm still writing the script, I let him know what it's about and give him a copy as soon as I'm done. After he reads it, he might come up to New York for a couple of days and visit the set or we'll send him dailies and some cut scenes. Then Terence will send me a CD with some sketches of the themes. That's where we have to start from: "What is going to be the theme of this film?"

Terence Blanchard: Spike's very up-front about what he likes and what he doesn't. He'll come right out and say it: "Yes, I like it." Or, "No, that's not it." He's not the type of guy to say, "That's good but could it be a little different." A lot of directors say, "That's good! But could it *beee* . . . ."

Branford Marsalis: Spike's anal; he loves having control. But he's my boy because I can separate the business from the personal. When we work together, though, I drive him crazy because I do what I want to do, and that drives him up the wall. I really fervently believe that I know more about music than directors. And when I'm forced to deal with people that are not musicians, it can become irritating sometimes. You know, I let directors tell me what kind of music they want, and they can even give me a song that they want the shit to sound like, and then I go about the task of writing it. You just like kiss their ass: "How do you want it to sound? Is this good? Is this bad?"

"Well, I-I-I don't know. I'm not *sure* about that."

And then sometimes you'll have directors where you'll write something in verbatim to what he wanted and then he'll say, "That's not what I want." And I'm like, "Hey, too bad, that's what you told me to write."

Terence Blanchard: For me, that's the challenge: to sit down and try to figure out what they're saying and then convey that into a musical form for the film. That's really interesting to me because it gives me an insight into how laymen perceive music. I mean, it can be frustrating sometimes, but it's not a big deal for me. Usually, it's more of a problem for them. They tend to have a hard time articulating their ideas because they're insecure about some of them and don't want to come off as ignorant or whatever.

When you're working with a director, the thing that you have to remember as a film composer is that he's been with the film a lot longer than you and really has an intimate understanding of the story that he's trying to tell. So it may take a while to get the direction that he's going in. I've yet to have that experience, but I could foresee it happening where I'd be like, "C'mon, this would be good for the scene." And it probably would be, but it may not have anything to do with the totality of the story.

Writing for my band, I do write from my experiences in life, so there may be some sort of visual interpretation. But the big difference is those are my reflections, so the expressions can change and they're malleable, and the music is basically my impression of it, so it can take on any kind of color. Writing for film is limited in that regard, but it's liberating for me because the limitations bring about a certain kind of creativity—you have to be creative because you only have a certain amount of space to work with.

Wynton Marsalis: It's great. I think Terence brings another sensibility to that field, and I think he does a great job. He's very serious. I don't really know it well enough. I get a lot of different scripts, but I'm not really a *great* moviegoer and have a lot to learn. I've wanted to do it for a while though, but I've either been working on something else of haven't found the film I liked. I did one film in 1990 called *Tune in Tomorrow,* and after that, I've been getting a lot of scripts but never really got involved. I did a Charlie Brown cartoon in 1987, and I did a television movie in the late 1980s.

◆

In 1997, Wynton Marsalis would find the time to become more involved in the film industry. His prestigious commission as artistic director of Jazz at Lincoln Center had indeed kept him active, but two major motion pictures released that year hired Marsalis to write the music. *Rosewood*, the John Singleton film based on the true-story genocide of an Afro-American town in Florida during the 1920s, and Sidney Lumet's *Night Falls on Manhattan* both rejected Marsalis's work and hired replacements to rescore their pictures.

WYNTON MARSALIS: My music didn't work on any of those films. It just wasn't good for those films. They didn't want to use a lot of it, yeah. I guess they thought I was going to do something different from what I did. They're not obligated to like it, and they didn't.

TERENCE BLANCHARD: Oh, it happens quite a bit in Hollywood. It's frustrating, but you can't take it personal. It happened to me once on the HBO movie *Soul of the Game.* Even though they didn't reject the entire score, I was still upset because it was just unfair how they handled me. They gave me a small budget, so we went ahead and did it with a small group. The director loved the score, but the executives came in and overrode his decision and went out and got [Lee Holdridge] and gave him enough money to get an orchestra! So I'm sitting there, "OK, that's the way the game is played?" That was definitely a learning experience. I guess it's all part of the business. And that's cool; it is what it is. I didn't even have time to be bitter about it because right after that, I got really busy working on the next project.

When I'm hired to score a movie, I always start with the script. Once I get a sense of the story, I talk to the director about what he wants to do, which gives me a chance to come up with some ideas. At that point we'll sit down and go through the film so I can really get a sense of how it plays visually because the transition from script to film is a large leap—it's really amazing; that's why I have a lot of respect for directors. Once that's done, we start to get an idea of what the melodic material is going to be, and then we'll have the spotting session.

SPIKE LEE: The big, big meeting is when Terence comes up from New Orleans to see the entire film for the first time in the screening room.

He'll watch it straight through without any stopping. Then we have our spotting session. That's when I sit down with Terence, the editor, music editor, and go through the film and tell him where we want music, how long the cues should be and where they should enter and exit. Also, we discuss instrumentation, color, and the feel that we're going for.

One of my favorite parts of the filmmaking process is when we're scoring the film. Up to that point, I've only heard sketches on a synthesizer, so when I get to hear the full arrangement with an orchestra, I just love it. For me, it's not really a movie until we put Terence's score to it—*that's* when it becomes a film. And just being there and having the musicians there give me a real joy.

Alex Steyermark: There are composers that I've worked with where there's sort of this weird filter that they have to go through because they can't perform the music themselves. So they end up sort of having to translate to the orchestra that's performing. But because Terence is a performer and a conductor, he has this ability to impart to people very specifically what it is that he wants and needs. And when it comes to writing music, the fact that Terence is a jazz musician—and because of what that requires—he's particularly suited to creating ideas on the spot. And that is really an interesting and pretty unique thing to watch.

Terence Blanchard: Though when you're developing a film score, it's not always necessarily like divine intervention. Sometimes it's just a nuts-and-bolts thing. Like, when the film is moving a little slow, the music can push it along or if the film is jerky, the music can even it out. Music is such an emotional, artistic thing, but you don't always have to think about it in abstract terms.

So during the spotting session, I'll apply some of that pragmatism. I'll figure out how many cues I'll have on each reel and also keep notes on what the director is looking for as far as timings, where the music needs to start and stop, stuff like that. Then after you spot a film, it really changes from director to director at that point. Once I spot a film with Spike, I'm cool; I'm good to go. Some directors may want to hear specific cues before you go into the studio so they can make sure that the turning points of their film are handled the way they want it. Spike is different. Spike's like, "Hey, man, see ya." He trusts me.

Their mutual trust and admiration has transmitted to screen so often that the *Chicago Tribune* asserted, "Lee and Blanchard forged a partnership for the nineties worthy of any of the great director–composer collaborations from Hollywood's fabled past."

While they have formed a celebrated union, Terence is often interviewed and sometimes hired to compose scores for other directors' films.

Like movie stars, there are a handful of film composers in Hollywood on every director's wish list. James Horner, Hans Zimmer, John Williams, Elmer Bernstein, Ennio Morricone, among them, call for lucrative contracts and accommodating work schedules.

Although jazz musicians have been composing film scores since the days of Duke Ellington, producers and directors still wonder whether they can adhere to the rigid constraints of writing for each specifically timed scene, or worse, if the score will just consist of long-winded improvisation.

Today, despite a growing reputation and over thirty spectacular scores under his belt, Terence's interviews with filmmakers are heavily scrutinized: "Can a jazz musician *really* score movies?"

TERENCE BLANCHARD: I get tired of the stereotypes, so it's important for me to establish myself as a legitimate film composer rather than just a jazz musician scoring films. I was up for this one film, and the producer told [my manager] Robin [Burgess] this would be the most different thing I've ever done because I've probably never worked with an orchestra.

SPIKE LEE: I can't believe the stories Terence tells me about going to interview for film jobs and having to endure such idiotic questions. First and foremost, Terence *is* a jazz musician, but it's his knowledge of jazz music that enables him to do everything else so well. He's a great composer who has the ability to write for any kind of film. I'm telling you, these guys who have a jazz background can do anything!

TERENCE BLANCHARD: Not all filmmakers are that ignorant because I've had some very interesting interviews. In this one film, *Copland*, I thought I bombed in the meeting with the director [James Mangold]. I told him, "I see the character development at four different stages and that there's a couple of things that you can do to help develop those stages by using different moods and different timbres." And he was looking at me like I was crazy. That's the vibe I got from him, but as it turned out, he talked to my film agent and said, "Terence had an insight into the movie that I didn't even know." So that's when he became my biggest proponent for getting the film. If the decision was up to him, I would have had the gig. But sometimes it's not up to the director, especially since Jim was just a second-time director on that project; it's up to the producers—they sign the check.

ROBIN BURGESS: Yeah, it was the same thing with *Rosewood*. John Singleton called us and said, "I've got a movie for us to work on." We had lots of dialogue with John at the time, but when it came down to it, [producer] Jon Peters wanted a more visible name, which of course was Wynton. But the funny thing is, it then got tossed up to John Williams.

Michael Cristofer: It's a mistake to categorize Terence as a jazz artist because there's an incredible versatility there. Not everything he does is, strictly speaking, jazz. He writes across the genres, whatever is needed for the particular project.

We've worked together twice now [on *Gia* and *Original Sin*], and I really enjoyed both experiences. The more I get to know him, the more I realize he is not limited by being a New Orleans jazz performing artist. Listen to the score he did for *Original Sin*; it's straight composing for the specifics of the genre.

I can't imagine too many films he'd be wrong for; maybe if I directed a film and needed a Chinese score—but even then, I think he still could do it.

Terence Blanchard: The bottom line is that directors want to have the feeling that you really "get it." They want to ensure that when they hand their baby over to you, you're going to take care of it. So in meetings, they ask my ideas about the film, something like, "What do you suggest when the film takes a turn here?" They'll ask about certain characters, too.

As filmmakers go, I like Oliver Stone. He may not have the facts right all the time, especially with the Kennedy movie, but I like his cinematic vision. I didn't like that crazy movie he did *Natural Born Killers,* but I like the pace of his movies, and I think they look great. He would be interesting to work with. I'm not a big Scorsese fan, but Spike loves him. I'd love to work with a lot of them. Brian De Palma is cool. I'd like to work with Robert Altman just because he's a big fan of the music. I'd like to work with Rob Reiner; I know that's a different type of filmmaker than most people would associate me with, but I think he makes good films. I like Ron Howard's work for the type of stuff that he does. I like those guys because they have their own voice and their own style.

To date, talented filmmakers with whom Terence has worked include Ron Shelton, Michael Cristofer, Peter Bogdanovich, Kasi Lemmons, and Matty Rich. Rich is a filmmaker with a unique claim to fame.

While most teenagers squander their weekends by hanging out late and sleeping in even later, seventeen-year-old Matty Rich began shooting his feature filmmaking debut, *Straight Out of Brooklyn*. His actors worked for free, he paid his crew what little he could, and he shot on weekends for two years. Born and raised in the Red Hook housing projects of Brooklyn, Rich financed the picture as he filmed from small investments but most notably through a fund-raising campaign on WLIB, a black radio station in New York City. When $77,000 came pouring in, the money enabled Rich to finish his movie. Upon its release in 1991, Rich was merely nineteen, and his gritty film made him a hot commodity in Hollywood. That year, in fact,

Straight Out of Brooklyn received comparable hype to more major African American films like Spike Lee's *Jungle Fever* and John Singleton's *Boyz N the Hood*.

Interestingly enough, *Straight Out of Brooklyn* and *Jungle Fever* opened on the same day that summer, prompting a New York media war between its directors. When Rich informed Lee that his distributor planned the identical release, Spike, out of his concern for the newcomer, suggested that he get it rescheduled because the films would be splitting the market. Certainly, it would hurt the low-budget, independent film more than a studio-financed film with major stars from a hot director. "The next thing I know," recalled Lee, "I'm [a headline] in the *New York Post*: 'Matty Rich Steals Spike Lee's Thunder.' I couldn't believe it. [Rich] was quoted as saying I had a big fight with him and was yelling at him and was trying to find out when his film was going to open because I was worried he was going to steal my thunder.

"In my opinion, Matty's not going to be around long as a filmmaker unless he goes into the woodshed and learns his craft. I mean, he brags that he's never taken a class, that he's never been to film school: 'I ain't got no education in film; I ain't got this; I ain't got that.' His movie reflected that shit, too."[4]

When Matty Rich's second film, *The Inkwell*, was released in the spring of 1994, Allen Black, the associate producer of *Straight Out of Brooklyn,* told *Premiere* magazine, "People like Matty Rich become successful because they don't have a feel, or feelings, for people. Their goal, whatever the goal might be, comes first, and people are second. So they don't have a problem with stepping on people. I think that's what Matty is, basically."[5]

> **Terence Blanchard:** It was an experience. . . . Working with a guy like Matty as opposed to Spike was very different. Matty's young; he's new and has a lot of growing to do. Look, he's a talented guy, but I was not happy with that film at all for a number of reasons. First of all, Matty took some of the scenes from the script and cut them out and turned them upside down and spit them inside out. Secondly, I'm not happy with my score. It was a hard film to score because it wasn't a good film. I mean, the script was brilliant, just brilliant! And that's why I took the gig. Reading the script, I was like, "*Man*, these characters . . . ." It wasn't a *black* film in the sense of what a black film represents in Hollywood; that's why I loved it so much.

The creator of the script Terence admired so deeply was Trey Ellis. After Ellis sold his semiautobiographical tale to Touchstone Pictures, he was optimistic about getting the opportunity to direct. However, Touchstone had other ideas. In typical Hollywood fashion, the studio wanted to capitalize on the marketability of the hot young director of *Straight Out of Brooklyn*. Perhaps Touchstone figured they had the next Spike Lee in Matty Rich.

Admittedly, Ellis was disappointed over losing control of his project, but that had little to do with his contempt for the hired director. "In my first meeting with Matty," recalled Ellis in *Premiere* magazine, "he said, 'I want to make it "*blacker*."' I turned to the producer as if to say, 'If he has this essentialist view of blackness as poverty and wife beating and crack and AK-47s, he is clearly not the right person to do this.' But they didn't see it that way."[6]

In the end, Rich prevailed in actualizing his vision of Ellis's script by hiring Paris Qualles, a writer who, in Rich's words, "understands the black experience." When Ellis received word that his original screenplay underwent a rewrite, he was so offended that he opted to use the alias "Tom Ricostranza" for his screen credit.

Terence Blanchard: I have strong emotions about some of these movies being made about black life and Afro-American culture that are very one-dimensional. I'm worried that a lot of directors aren't respecting the Afro-American audience as they should. They think we only want to see one type of film. It's like the 1970s, the [Blaxploitation] period of *Superfly*. It's not the truth. I don't see myself in a lot of these movies.[7]

Branford Marsalis: One of the reasons I don't do too many scores is that the only time they call me is when they're doing a black movie. I ain't interested. I ain't interested in some white guy calling whenever they're doing one of those "Boyz N the Hood Part 10" movies. I'm like, fuck *that*. Those kind of movies are not something that I have an interest in doing.

Terence Blanchard: It was like that for me in the beginning, too, but I'm very grateful that I haven't fallen into that. I've been up for some very big films. I didn't get them [*laughing*], but I've been up for them. But I remember I turned down this one movie—it was so bad. I never saw it, but the script was so bad. It had these big ol' fat black women running around. It had every stereotype imaginable and not just pertaining to black people but just every stereotype. While I was reading the script, I thought it was a spoof because it just kept going and going. I couldn't believe it! It was at the beginning of my career, and I was really hungry to get work, but I said to myself, "I just can't do this one."

Of course, I think it's very disrespectful to make the same type of "in the 'hood" movie, but it's all about the numbers, man. Hollywood doesn't care about cultivating audiences; they're into making money! See, the thing that's interesting about Hollywood is that if they put out more diverse films—not only black films, any type—it would take a while for people to get used to that, especially in this country because people are so conditioned to seeing the same kinds of movies. I mean, you can basically tell if a movie's going to be a hit just by seeing the trailer. If it has a certain look, a certain sound, it will be a box-office success. And in order for audiences to break away from that, it's going to take time. But Hollywood isn't into taking time; they're only into overnight. Movies like *Independence Day*—it's just incredible how much money that movie made—that's what they look for. They're not looking for a guy who might bat .200 when they got a guy who can bat .390 all the time.

Branford Marsalis: The last film score I did was great. I had a good time. It was a movie called *Mr. and Mrs. Loving* about an interracial relationship in the mountains of Virginia. I wrote a bunch of hillbilly music, and it was great. It has to be something that's interesting to me. It was challenging to me to get a guy playing a guitar, a viola player, a bass player, and a piano player and write this music that they were sure I couldn't write because I'm a black guy—like *we* don't live in the country or something. I don't know. I mean, people who make movies come from society, and they spend their entire lives making movies for general people. And the reason they are successful is because they themselves are general.

Terence Blanchard: When I read the script for *The Inkwell,* I knew it was about black people, but I thought it was colorless, that it could've been about anybody. The whole notion of a Republican and a very militant brother-in-law from any ethnic group sitting down and having a conversation promises to create a lot of possibilities; the conversation can go in a lot of different directions, making intriguing points along the way. And that's what was in the script and why I was really excited about the project. There was no way I thought it would have turned out the way it did. Matty wanted it to be funny, and I don't think that worked. So when I saw the film, I sat back in my chair and said, "*Oh* . . . ." I was disappointed.

While we were working on that score, I had a couple of conversations with Matty and his whole thing was like, "Well, my audience . . . my audience." And I'm like, "Your audience? Man, this is your *second* film; you don't have an audience! You have to build an audience." We were talking about this jazz piece I had written for the opening credits that I thought was really interesting. I said to him that part of a director's responsibility is not only to entertain but also to educate when necessary. And I felt this was a great opportunity for people to hear a jazz piece in a very nonoffensive way. See, he was going to have these paintings of Jacob Lawrence's migration series, so I wrote this piece specifically for it. But he just didn't want to use it. Now directors do this all the time, so it wasn't such a big

> deal for me in the sense that he wasn't listening to me. But what really got me was that he wasn't particularly forthright with me all the time and didn't tell me the truth with what he was going to do with the music. In the opening credits, for example, he used this pop song I wrote for a party scene. And I remember there were a couple of scenes where guys from Disney [the conglomerate that owns Touchstone] asked me, "Why did you use a *clarinet* in this scene?"
>
> "I didn't use a clarinet."
>
> "Well, it's there."
>
> "Well, no, that's not what I had written for that scene."
>
> I found out that Matty had taken a piece of music from somewhere else and stuck it in to scenes where it didn't belong. So that's the kind of stuff that was going on.
>
> I'm not the kind of person to sit there and point fingers and say, "Man, you ain't shit." He was young, and I tried to encourage him. I was hired to do a job; I signed a contract and that's it. But it's funny because I didn't really know about all that stuff with Matty and Spike until Spike filled me in after I got the job. What did Spike say? You know, well . . . you know. You know what he said [*laughing*].

◆

The Inkwell tells the story of a sixteen-year-old boy whose family spends a couple of weeks on Martha's Vineyard in the summer of 1976. The movie, in Rich's hands, is an innocent comic fantasy, a coming-of-age tale that critics called an "amateurish mixture of *Summer of '42* and *House Party*."

When it opened in the spring of 1994 to soft business, internal finger pointing banded at Matty Rich. The young filmmaker felt the brunt of its failure and has consequently struggled to land another project.

Although his collaboration with Rich was mired in disappointment and ineffectiveness, Terence would benefit from the kind of working relationship most composers only dream of.

In early 1993, likely as her New Year's resolution, a young African American actress named Kasi Lemmons committed to a project that would finally utilize her prodigious creativity. Feeling unfulfilled as an actress and discouraged by the type of roles she had been offered, Lemmons informed her agent she would not be pursuing any acting jobs for the next short while.

Four months later, Lemmons emerged from a "very organic place" with a completed screenplay entitled *Eve's Bayou*. Set in the swamp lands of Louisiana during the early 1960s, the project eventually blossomed into her directorial debut. But the road to feature filmmaker (from an acting career that essentially pinnacled with a small role in *Silence of the Lambs*) had not been effortlessly paved. "Because I refused to negotiate the integrity of the script I had written," explains Lemmons, "it was a very difficult project to set up. I shopped the script around with Danny Glover, but we couldn't set it up. So then I was told that if I had Samuel L. Jackson attached, then people would be more interested, that they'd do it."

In the wake of his *Pulp Fiction* celebrity, Jackson had enough "juice" to get films green-lit in Hollywood. Luckily for Lemmons, she just happened to be old friends with the Oscar-nominated actor. "I knew Sam for a long time. In the eighties, the black show business community was so small that I literally knew everyone I cast in my movie. Sam, Branford, Roger [Smith], and I were all in *School Daze* together; Debbi Morgan is one of my oldest friends. But of course, having Samuel get involved in the project and supporting me as a director was absolutely *the* way."

With Jackson signed on to portray the dashing doctor, Louis Batiste, and to coproduce, Trimark Pictures launched *Eve's Bayou* in the fall of 1996 with a $4 million production budget.

A year later, the film celebrated its world premiere at the 1997 Toronto International Film Festival, where famed critic Roger Ebert proclaimed it the best film of the year and later elaborated in the *Chicago Sun-Times*, "If it is not nominated for Academy Awards, then the academy is not paying attention."

Many other critics applauded the realistic depiction of the film's all-black cast. In 1997, *Eve's Bayou* was certainly a needed respite from the gangster–drug movies that had been distributed ad nauseam by Hollywood studios.

> **Kasi Lemmons:** [The positive depiction] was important to me, but I wrote the script really without a political agenda. The Batistes were like ghosts to me. They were these characters that whispered in my ear, and I had to write them down just to get them out of my head. So because it came out in a very organic way, it was sort of pure art for me.
>
> When it came to scoring the film, I brought up Branford Marsalis. First of all, I cast Branford in the movie because I think he has great screen presence. His character is only on screen for a short amount of time, so I didn't want somebody you were going to miss. And so, I came up with Branford, because, to me, he's really charming and adorable. But I definitely mentioned Branford as a choice of mine to do the score even though he was on a huge tour. But there was a feeling that the studio really wanted somebody with more experience, who had composed a lot of movies. And around that same time, people started mentioning Terence to me. They were like, "Are you familiar with Terence Blanchard's work?

He's also from Louisiana, but he's done a lot of movie scores." So I sat with my editor and started listening to both Terence's scores and jazz albums, and I was won over. Actually, I wasn't entirely won over until I talked to him.

TERENCE BLANCHARD: Kasi had a lot of concerns, and because she didn't know that much about me and since this was her first film, she was understandably nervous.

KASI LEMMONS: He didn't say much to me when we first talked; he was kind of quiet. But one of the first things he said was, "I picture an elegant score and a timeless one, too." And he talked about how he wanted to use regional musicians, as well as a kind of classical orchestration.

At first, I was a little intimidated by Terence because here's this virtuoso jazz musician, and I didn't have a language to talk about music in. I'm not musical at all. So I'm trying to describe my movie and the kind of score that I want, and all I'm really coming up with is like "African-American-Southern-Gothic-melodrama." But somehow, he just *got* it. I really felt like he eavesdropped on my soul.

TERENCE BLANCHARD: You go through this whole process of casting and rehearsing, shooting, editing, and all that stuff, and then when you get your film down to its final touches, you have to hire this new person to come in and damn near screw up your movie. So I understood it, and we wound up becoming very good friends.

KASI LEMMONS: Yeah, we really get along. Terence is a great person. But after listening to his score, I felt like I loved Terence, his wife, his mother, and everybody related to him! I would have fantasies of baby-sitting for their kids—that's how much I love Terence. I'm so grateful.

TERENCE BLANCHARD: Kasi is a very passionate and sweet person. She's really great to work with, too. I was able to talk to her all the time about the film, which was very helpful to me because sometimes directors don't want to be bothered with a lot of questions. As a jazz musician, I can go in a number of directions, so I need to know which one they prefer.

When I first saw the film—it was an early cut—and it took me a while to understand what Kasi was doing. And that made me nervous because I didn't know if the film would turn out well. But when I got the revised cut, I really started to see the direction she was taking. Actually, she's similar to Spike in that she gives the viewer a lot of freedom of choice. She doesn't take you through it by the hand and say, "This is definitely the deal." So at that point, it really became apparent to me that this was really something special. And I think one of the reasons why I didn't see it at first was because everybody kept telling me it was something special. But when the story started to unfold to me—just to me personally—then I started to see how powerful it was and all that was in there.

KASI LEMMONS: I thought the score for *Eve's Bayou* was so extremely important; maybe more so than a lot of films because I really wanted to transport you to this place that's kind of a fairy tale but a part of Louisiana, too. And so, I wanted something special. I wanted the kind of score that as soon as you heard it, you knew that it was the music to *Eve's Bayou.* And that's what Terence gave me; it's very, very special music.

TERENCE BLANCHARD: This was my first score that I didn't really perform on—just on the last cue. For this score, I just didn't hear the trumpet. Also, sometimes when I hear my scores, to me, I sound like an egomaniac because the sound of the trumpet is everywhere. But I know that's what people hire me for. It's just weird, I guess, because you're writing all this music to feature me.

KASI LEMMONS: I assumed that was the choice that Terence made, and I supported it. I mean, as soon as I heard the orchestration, it was so incredibly gorgeous that I was just overwhelmed with joy. I cried the whole way through the [recording] session; I just burst into tears. We would get to a certain cue and I'd be like, "This is my favorite cue! No, this is my favorite cue!"

TERENCE BLANCHARD: That project was just great, and although we've only worked one time together, I love Kasi to death. She's the kind of person I'll do anything for.

KASI LEMMONS: There's this project that I'm up for now that's a composer's dream. It's about a homeless man who's also a classically trained pianist. And I already told everybody that if I do it, I have to do it with Terence. I'm going to work with him again and again and again.

◆

Terence's growing reluctance to perform on his own scores has not diminished the demand of his trumpet playing for other film composers' music. After working on the soundtracks for Miles Goodman's *Housesitter* and Don Was's *Backbeat*, Terence was a featured soloist on *Primal Fear* and *Random Hearts*, scores composed by Academy Award winners James Newton Howard and Dave Grusin, respectively.

TERENCE BLANCHARD: There's a slew of composers that I'd like to work for: John Williams, Thomas Newman, James Horner. I don't get a lot of offers since I started composing so much because people tend to think that I only want to compose. But I'm also a performer, and I have a strong interest in doing that, too.

I really love being involved in the process, whether I'm composing or performing but especially when I'm performing because I get a chance to watch people I admire at work. It's funny—I go in and try to do my part in one take so I can watch the rest of the score. I try my hardest not to screw up. I'm there looking at my part, listening very intently, trying to figure out what's going on, and then somebody else will blow a note and I'm like, "Damn, I gotta stand here for another take!" I want to be in the booth watching the composer with the orchestra!

I learned a lot from James and Dave. The thing that I learn most from these great composers is that there is no set way to do it. I mean, James Newton Howard's writing is very different from Dave Grusin's writing, and they're very different from mine. But the reason those guys have attained such success is simply because they have a great sense of drama and convey it in their own musical styles; it all basically boils down to developing a sense of drama.

Dave Grusin: Terence seemed to be terribly organized and intelligent about the function of what we were doing there. In other words, he knew we weren't just gonna go in there and play bebop. And that comes from the fact that he's had his own experience scoring and he understands that there's an exterior element hovering all the time, which are two questions: Do the people who are making the film like this? And, is it the right thing for the scene? Of course, Terence really understands that.

Terence Blanchard: Working with Dave was cool. First of all, he has a serious background in the music that I love, and secondly, he can write his behind off for an orchestra. So it was just great for me to watch and learn how he puts things together.

Dave Grusin: *Random Hearts* was a picture that required a lot of prerecorded music, so I started working on it six months before it was actually finished. The film has two settings, and we started in New York and then we were set to go to New Orleans. That's when I started thinking about Terence. I really like film music that has a geographic connection to the locale of the story. Even though there's a lot of great trumpet players around, especially from New Orleans, when I hear Terence, it triggers a unique emotional response. His sound has such an emotional quality, and I felt there was something deep in the story of the film that required that kind of thing. So the [main] theme itself was sort of constructed imagining Terence playing it. And then once I found out he was available and willing to do it, I was thrilled. The interesting thing in all of this of course was that the location was moved to Miami! It was the hurricane season in New Orleans at the time, so they decided to play it safe with Miami.

Terence Blanchard: Dave's music is very detailed in terms of what he's looking for creatively. But he still gives room for musicians to create and ad lib, especially for the guys he normally uses like Harvey Mason and John Patitucci. But the music is written with such detail that he gives you a very strong idea of what it is he's looking for in the score.

Dave Grusin: Terence was so perfect for that aspect of this thing because there are some details that you want, but you don't want to hamstring the guys. It's like a casting director calling this incredible ensemble and instructing them to do everything rather than letting them be creative. So there's always been this interesting dilemma of how much freedom you leave out there and how much you insist on being put down. And all of these guys turned out to be the perfect call for this thing. Harvey Mason and John Patitucci, who I've worked with a lot and have come to know what to indicate and what to leave to their discretion, have such great ears that, technically, you wouldn't have to write anything, you just go in and talk about it. And Terence fit into that mold perfectly.

Terence Blanchard: Working with Miles Goodman was also a great experience for me. When he first came onto the scene, he was dealing with a lot of the great film composers and passed a lot of that information on to me. Miles worked in a very different fashion from me and taught me a lot.

I first met him when he hired me to play on the soundtrack for his score to *Housesitter*, and we were friends ever since. Miles is my film mentor. He didn't like me to say that, but he is. I could call him up and ask him anything. As a matter of fact, we had just finished *Housesitter* when I was beginning *Malcolm X*, and I'll never forget this, he said, "If you don't call me up and ask me questions, I'm gonna be pissed at you!" He knew it was only my second film and that it was such a big project. He gave me so many suggestions that helped me a great deal. He hipped me to using muted strings because they don't get in the way of the actors' dialogue. And he was right. You can still hear what they're saying and also it gives the music this real icy kind of sound. But man, we became really great friends right off; we were just like really close right from the beginning.

◆

Miles Goodman, one of Hollywood's most notable composers, was born and raised in Los Angeles, but his passion for literature and theater prompted him to study abroad. He graduated with an English degree from Antioch College in Yellow Springs, Ohio (the institution has since implemented a scholarship fund in his name), and subsequently studied Shakespeare in London. But in the mid-1970s, after realizing his true calling, Goodman returned to Los Angeles and applied himself to the craft of film scoring. Before long, he landed his first film project as a composer for *Slumber Party '57*. Then in 1979, Goodman arranged orchestrations on the Peter Sellers comedy *Being There* for composer Johnny Mandel. Academy Award–winning Mandel was Goodman's mentor and older cousin. They would continue to collaborate with each other over the next few years, most notably to score Sidney Lumet's Oscar-nominated *The Verdict*.

Following his successful tutelage under Mandel, Goodman went on to establish his own name, scoring over fifty films, mostly comedies such as *Little Shop of Horrors*, *Dirty Rotten Scoundrels*, *Problem Child*, *What about Bob? Housesitter*, and *Sister Act 2*. Working so often in the genre manifested Goodman's reputation as the "King of Comedy."

Terence Blanchard: Yeah, he hated that [*laughing*]. It's funny because he wanted to do other stuff but got pigeon-holed into comedy because he was so successful at it. You know, Elmer Bernstein did a lot of comedies in the beginning of his career but eventually moved into other genres and Miles wanted to do the same. And I remember, Miles used to say, "Man, you know what? I must do them well because they just keep calling me for comedies."

Miles Goodman: There used to be an adage that if you didn't notice the score, it's a good one. The composer is a collaborator with the director in creating a motion picture experience and has to be satisfied that there's very little glamour associated with it, as much as our ego gets bent out of shape. We'll spend three months beating our brains out helping a film work, and everybody mentions the one Prince song he made in a weekend as the film's [only] music.

Michael Cristofer: I think that with contemporary films, one of the things that's happened is that the use of source music has become so important, which I'm not so sure is a good thing. It seems to be a marketing tactic, especially to younger audiences who have a relationship to that music. I've done previews for my films, and when you play a song in the background on the soundtrack, even just for eight bars, somebody in the audience would identify it, recognize it, and comment on its use in the scene. I don't know how bright they are or how fond they are of scores, but they're very attuned and smart about current groups and music.

Dave Grusin: A lot of film scores are not consciously being heard. And that doesn't make them a bad score. I think the score is supposed to support the film, and if the audience is listening to the music, that might not be the right thing. I mean, every composer loves a theater full of people tapping their foot because you know they're not tapping it to the dialogue. But if your attention is riveted over onto the music, you're obviously going to be missing something in the film. So there's a compromise. But I love film music that you're totally unaware of. I think the thing that we do better than any of the other crafts associated with the movie business is to manipulate an audience with subtlety.

Terence Blanchard: At its best, I think film music should work on the subconscious. It should help you relate to the characters, to the scenes, and the emotion that it's trying to convey subconsciously. If it becomes like its own character, then it's a separate thing that can detract you from

> the story. When scores are seamless but somehow make you well up with emotion, that's what I love. [Thomas Newman's] *Shawshank Redemption* is a great example of that. *Glory* is another. You know, you're caught up in all the battles and the drama and the acting in *Glory,* and then you're like, "Oh, yeah, there's music, too!"

◆

In January 1996, Terence and Miles Goodman successfully interviewed for Paramount Pictures' romantic comedy, *'Til There Was You.* Director Scott Winant (of television's *thirtysomething* fame) approved the duo, thinking the comical mastery of Goodman and the jazzy romance of Blanchard would make the perfect combination. Terence was so excited about collaborating with his friend and mentor that he rearranged his summer tour of *The Heart Speaks* around Goodman's ever-busy scoring schedule. Tragically, however, on the morning of August 16 that year, in the midst of preparing a musical concept for the film, Miles Goodman suffered a massive heart attack.

> **TERENCE BLANCHARD:** What happened was, we were working [at Miles's Brentwood house] on the music, and the director was supposed to come over that morning to hear what we had. So we were going to play the music for him, and then I was going to go back home to New Orleans.
>
> So the director was on his way over and that's when Miles had the seizure and everything and went to the hospital. When the director got to the house, he couldn't find us and didn't know what was going on.
>
> But the thing was, the night before everything was cool. We had been out on his deck with his daughter and his girlfriend having a nice time. And that day we had finally come up with a concept for the music and selected a lot of the melodic material for the movie, which Miles was excited about. So we were out on the deck that night, and then Miles said, "Man, I'm tired; I'm going to bed. I'll see you in the morning." And I'm like, "OK, cool," and went to bed, too.
>
> I was staying in the back area of his house—Miles had this area that was like a separate little suite for house guests—and the next morning I woke up feeling good and took a shower. But when I came out of the shower, I heard this noise outside my door. So I opened the door and Miles was leaning up against it: "Terence, dial 9-1-1!" And then he fell down on the floor. I had just come out of the shower, so I rushed just to put on a pair of pants and dialed 9-1-1. And as I did that, I could see he was just lying on his face. And I couldn't think of the address, but he told it to me: 13420 Chalon Road. So he started to come out of his seizure, but then he said, "Man, I think I'm having a heart attack." So I called back and I said, "This guy's having a heart attack! Get here, get here!" But as it

turned out, it was another seizure. He was having it right in the hallway with his foot against one wall and his back against the other wall. He was shaking real bad, and I couldn't turn him. Miles was a small man, but he was really strong. So finally I had to really wrestle with him to get him to lay down so he could relax—that's when he came out of his seizure. But when he came out of the seizure, his eyes went glassy. So I listened to his heart and I didn't hear anything, so I started pumping his heart. Then I called back 9-1-1 for the third time because I heard an ambulance pass by and go to the wrong address. So I called them again and I said, "You got to get here!" So when they finally got there, they started working on him and they put this thing in his windpipe and everything. They were trying to jump-start his heart with shock treatment, but you could see on the monitor that his heart never got into a rhythm. So they decided to take him to the hospital.

I got in his car and drove down to [St. John's Hospital and Medical Center in Santa Monica], called [musician] Oscar Castro-Neves and Robin, and they hurried over. So we were waiting in this sort of special privacy room for the doctor to come out, and I'm sitting there thinking how I'm gonna fuck with Miles once he got out. You know, thinking, "Boy, Miles, I'm gonna mess with your ass for putting us through all this shit."

Then the doctor came in the room, and he asked me what happened and what I did. So I told him and he said, "Well, you did everything you could do. You did the right thing, but we couldn't revive him."

I couldn't believe it, couldn't believe it. I was bent out of shape for a while, and I'm still in disbelief about it. But at that moment, I just lost it. Oscar lost it, too; they were like brothers. It was like a horrible thing to go through because you have this person that you really care about and you can't do anything—that shit is hard. It's really hard because there are a lot of situations in life where you can make a difference, so you start to feel like you can do anything, but then you realize, "I'm not God." And that's a hard situation to deal with because you're completely powerless.

I mean, it's weird how you're working with a cat, he seems cool, then a few days later, you're going to his fucking funeral. That shit was just, like, *out*. And you're like, "How the fuck did this happen?"

You know, I went to the place where you view his body, and you're sitting there looking at his body and you're going, "How the fuck did you get here?" Like, "Man, get the fuck up!" I mean, the reality of it still really hasn't hit you.

Three days later I was booked for a gig in Connecticut, and I lost it on the bandstand while we were playing "I Thought about You." Miles liked the way I played that tune, and it was hard because all I could do was think about him. Man, it was hard getting through that concert and then a whole week at the [Village] Vanguard right after the funeral.

But I guess that's just the way life is. I feel sorry for his daughter, and I feel sorry for him because he was just coming to terms with a lot of things in his life and his career. He was going to the gym, and he was eating right because he knew that his family had a history of heart problems. You know, it was a hell of a wake-up call for me, too. I've been going to the gym lately, trying to lose this weight and get my health together.

A lot of people said, "Well, it was a good thing that you were there because you were a good friend, and at least he had somebody there with him." He was like twelve years older than me but we were really close. He was a real generous man.

I remember this one film that I was working on with this producer who was a total asshole, so I ended up quitting the film even though he threatened to sue me. But the thing hasn't even come out yet. But the joke was, he went and called Miles Goodman (not knowing we were friends). So he called up Miles to do the film, and Miles turned it down. He said, "No, I think you should call Terence Blanchard; he would be perfect for this film." Naturally, they didn't like that too much [*laughing*].

Notes

1. *Larry King Live,* May 13, 1994.
2. Wayne K. Self, "Back from Frustration," *Down Beat* (August 1992): 30.
3. Michael Bourne, "In Tribute to Lady Day," *Down Beat* (May 1994): 19.
4. Spike Lee and Ralph Wiley, *By Any Means Necessary* (New York: Hyperion, 1992), 14.
5. Martha Southgate, "Isn't It Rich," *Premiere* (May 1994): 57.
6. Southgate, "Isn't It Rich," 58.
7. Bourne, "In Tribute to Lady Day," 19.

CHAPTER EIGHT
BACK ON THE BLOCK

> Those same people who said I was finished are now calling me for gigs, but I have a different attitude toward them now.
>
> —*Terence Blanchard*

As his new and exciting career was taking off in Hollywood, Terence Blanchard returned to the jazz scene in the spring of 1990. His rise and fall in the 1980s were dramatic, but his reemergence in the 1990s would demonstrate courage and resilience.

Since he was just a teenager, Terence labored through the intensive practice, exhaustive travel, and endless promotional obligations required to become among the first rank of young jazz musicians. For nearly a decade, he had wowed global audiences with his virtuosity. But when he dropped out of the glare of the performance scene for an entire year, concert promoters interpreted the sabbatical as his irrevocable collapse. After all, an embouchure change, according to critic Bruce Handy, is "the equivalent to Tiger Woods reworking his swing after winning his first Masters."[1]

It was only fitting that Terence's reemergence occurred in the spring, a season of growth and rebirth. With a new band featuring such young and talented musicians as tenor saxophonist Sam Newsome, pianist Bruce Barth, bassist Rodney Whitaker, and drummer Troy Davis, a new management deal with Robin Burgess, and a recording contract with Columbia, Terence gradually worked his way back from frustration.

> **Robin Burgess:** When I started working with Terence, *Mo' Better Blues* was on the table, and so was his deal with Columbia Records. Even though he was already on Columbia, we had to negotiate a new contract because he was signed as Harrison/Blanchard. Terence really wanted to stay with Columbia. He had some other offers, most notably from Blue

Note, but the money and prestige that Columbia offered determined that it would be them.

But then there was the embouchure thing, and after witnessing that whole experience, I think that it would have broken most people just because it was so intense. And I remember asking Terence if he would quit, but he always said, "Never."

◆

Terence's recorded debut as a leader is a self-titled piece composed of nine tunes, four of them original, including "Sing Soweto," a composition already immortalized in the movies. Terence featured his regular bandmates bassist Rodney Whitaker and pianist Bruce Barth throughout, while he alternated Sam Newsome and Troy Davis with Branford Marsalis and Jeff "Tain" Watts.

In 1991, upon its release, the album reached *Billboard*'s jazz Top 5 and spurred a North American tour. Terence was encouraged by the bookings, but when he hit the road, he had yet to master his new embouchure—there were good nights and bad.

RODNEY WHITAKER: When Terence started up his band, we did a couple of gigs, but because he was working on his embouchure, it prohibited him from doing a whole lot. But also there were a lot of promoters and critics who were just plain hard on him during that period.

ROBIN BURGESS: If I were to go back to that year and pull out all the reviews, you would not find a single one that did not speak about this grave embouchure change. And after a while, that grew really old because I think that Terence knew within himself that it was just a matter of time before he would have it all together.

RODNEY WHITAKER: I remember being with Terence, and sometimes he would talk about certain guys saying some nasty things about his playing. I tried to be supportive by telling him to hang in there and not to worry about the critics. My reference point was totally different from these critics. I was hearing improvement and a lot of growth on a daily basis. Terence, he's a person that I still love and that I was really close to at that particular time, so I wanted to encourage him to keep doing what he was doing. But I saw his playing diminish to its absolute worst.

ROBIN BURGESS: Oh, yeah, it was really dreadful because it *was* obvious that Terence was going through an embouchure change. I distinctly remember one of the first engagements that I went to. It was at the Top O' the Senator [in Toronto], and I was sitting at the edge of the bandstand. And watching Terence, I could see—just by looking at his face—what he wanted to play but couldn't because of his embouchure. He was struggling so hard to play out his musical thoughts, but his lips were not allowing him to do it. He would go through a riff but just couldn't hit the high notes and so, he would be cursing a lot. Like, after every other note was a curse word. And I told him, "Terence, I know it's difficult, but you're drawing more attention to yourself by cursing. If you didn't say anything, if you didn't go, 'Fuck!' maybe people wouldn't know that you were gonna go even farther and would just be satisfied with what you gave them." But it really was just painful for him.

Rodney Whitaker: He'd be playing the trumpet some nights, and air would be leaking out the side of his mouth or whatever. And sometimes, it didn't seem like he really enjoyed playing anymore. But on every gig I saw a courageous person get up on that stage and play night after night. I couldn't even imagine switching my whole concept—my instrument doesn't even have anything remotely close to like changing your embouchure! For me, it would be basically like switching to a totally different instrument and trying to play on the same level. So it was a courageous thing for Terence to take on. And now the results are incredible! But I think it was really unfortunate that some people were so hard on him.

Nicholas Payton: The whole thing Terence went through with the embouchure change was incredible. I remember when he couldn't play at all. And you know, to stick through all of that and still come out playing was remarkable. The amount of dedication! I really admire that. And now I think it's paying off. I see his name everywhere. So to me, that's a testament to his amazing dedication as a musician.

Rodney Whitaker: Terence was dedicated to getting to a certain level of musicality and excellence, and he wanted people in that band who wanted the same. And we strived to achieve that.

Troy Davis: I remember at that time Terence was hearing a lot of Miles Davis and Wayne Shorter-style music as far as trying to write songs that were not standard form. Terence was searching, trying to explore new ideas and was very adamant about not sounding like everyone else. When he first hired the guys in the band, he said he was looking for guys who were humble, who wanted to play, and weren't a headache [*laughing*]. You know, guys who are easy to get along with.

Terence Blanchard: I looked for guys who had similar goals as myself and were interested in improvement, not necessarily instant fame and fortune. Some cats spend so much time practicing for technical mastery that they seldom understand the importance of group development. I look for musicians who play with a certain kind of passion and emotion; the technical thing is not a big deal to me. But don't get me wrong—the guy has to have a certain level of proficiency on his instrument; he just doesn't have to be a technical whiz. If you can swing, if you can communicate your ideas, that's what I look for. If the guy is open to criticism, to trying new stuff, and if he's easy to get along with on the road, then he's got the gig.

But the hardest thing isn't hiring someone; it's letting them go. It's not an easy thing—at least for me. I think of the person's family, and maybe I shouldn't, but if you fire a guy, then there are other people who are affected. I mean, I know some people who can drop cats easily, "All right, bruh, see ya." I'm not a cold person, so I can't do that even though it would make life a lot easier for me. It's tough being a bandleader; there's a lot of different things you have to deal with.

TROY DAVIS: I didn't really think Terence wanted me to join his band because he never asked. I was there from the beginning doing gigs, but nobody said anything about being *in* the band. And I was doing other things like playing around with Marlon Jordan, Mark Whitfield, and Roy Hargrove, so I really wasn't clear. But all along, Terence was actually telling Sam and Bruce, "I got to find a way to get Troy in the band."

I actually auditioned for Terence and Donald's band a couple of years after I met Terence at the World Fair. I flew to New York to audition, and I stayed over at Terence's house. I did a pretty good job, but I didn't make the band. I wasn't quite ready in my development and in terms of the style that they needed and wanted at that time. So they hired Carl Allen, who was on the scene and had a lot more experience. I was still only like twenty, but at the time I was very disappointed because I had never been turned down musically before. I've been playing the drums since I was three years old and was a child prodigy here in town. And you know, being on TV here in Baton Rouge and throughout New Orleans, I had a big head, and you tend to lose sight of what's going on.

One of the great things about Terence is that he understood what I needed in order to become what you would call a "loyal band member." And that was just a commitment from him to keep the band working. As sidemen, if you don't work, you don't make money. We don't make any money on record sales, that's for sure. So he was committed to that, and when his film career blossomed, it added a foundation to help everything stay together.

RODNEY WHITAKER: Terence was always a great bandleader—really helpful and informative. He would make suggestions on what I should work on and who I should listen to. I was only eighteen when I joined his band with Donald, and I was so excited, but I was so green. So the guys would constantly make fun of me, but it was all good-spirited. I was extremely cheap, too. One time, Terence and I walked into McDonald's in Manhattan and I complained because the Quarter Pounder combo was fifty cents more than it was where I lived in Detroit. So Terence loved to tease me about that, but always in a humorous way. He and I became pretty good friends. I spent a lot of time with him, and I would stay with him and his family in New York. Terence is a talkative cat, but he always accused me of being talkative. We spent a lot of time communicating with each other; we had similar thoughts about a lot of different things. We had a lot of sympathy, in terms of the music, too. If I suggested something, he would always consider it; he is very considerate.

Unfortunately, when I was in Terence's band, we didn't work that much. For a band to really grow, you need to be playing all the time in order to achieve certain objectives. I mean, we *played*, but not as much as Terence is now. Some time after [*Mo' Better Blues*] came out, we started getting more gigs up until 1991. I left in the fall of that year. I was at a period in my development that I just needed to play; I was twenty-three. So I went with Roy Hargrove because I had an opportunity to play all the time in his band. He had an itinerary for like two years in a bunch of places that I had never been. So careerwise it was good for me. We were playing in so many different venues all over the world that it gave the opportunity for people to see who I was.

TROY DAVIS: Yeah, we weren't working very much at that time, and Roy was working a whole lot. He was hot, he was young, and his manager kept him working a lot. But Terence was disappointed Rodney left. He's always disappointed when a guy leaves, man. He almost takes it personal, but it's never been that way. No guy has left for personal reasons—and no guy has left for musical reasons! People love playing in his band. It's just sometimes things just don't work out the way you want them to.

ROBIN BURGESS: Well, you have the other side of the music industry—the business end—which really is the reality of it. When you're in the music industry, you're going to be involved in a very cutthroat atmosphere. You had people embellishing stories about how Terence would never be able to play again and how he really sucked. It was completely blown out of proportion. And there were some promoters who were very skeptical of booking Terence because of that. Promoters are not exactly known for believing in artists; they're just worried about their bottom line.

But I have to say *Mo' Better Blues* really started to change that. Denzel was really great about mentioning Terence a lot—they were really close at that time—and that did a lot for Terence. Also, even though Terence only scored one scene in that film, that was the beginning of his relationship with Spike. It was from that one cue that made Spike ask, "Terence, have you ever thought about writing for film?"

So because of the hype of *Mo' Better Blues*, that kind of dictated that Terence was now in demand, which pushed their hand a bit. I mean, promoters needed a hook—they always need a hook: "What's the latest album? What are you doing?" Blah-blah-blah. But we had this hook in *Mo' Better Blues,* and it really worked because it started to turn things around.

RODNEY WHITAKER: Terence is a person who really knows what it is that he's after, and there are not a lot of musicians who are like that. There are not a lot of musicians who know what it is that they're trying to say with the music. But Terence is a very conscientious human being and is very focused on his goals and objectives. And to him, this music is not just a means of support but a means of survival in terms of spirituality. Terence believes the music represents spirituality and love and all kinds of other aspects that are not necessarily addressed in these times.

◆

When the *Washington Post* hailed *Terence Blanchard* as "a solo debut revealing a 29-year-old trumpeter with a singular voice," the newspaper did not merely compliment him; it pointed out a remarkable fact: Terence Blanchard was still under thirty. For a musician who had experienced so much, he was very young. Now, with a new embouchure, Terence entered his thirties with unlimited potential, free to articulate his most profound ideas. As his climb back to prominence advanced, the critical sneering withered away. Though for all of his progress, Terence would not escape the shadow of Wynton Marsalis, an ugly distinction that had suppressed his reputation for a decade.

ELLIS MARSALIS: I don't know how anyone can really consider Terence in the shadow of Wynton, given what they do; they do too many diverse things. They're making their *own* statements. Besides, that stuff really only works in sports—what they used to do between Magic Johnson and Larry Bird. They both played basketball; they were both the best at it. It fills up the seats; it makes for great press. But Terence and Wynton both play *jazz*; there aren't any stats—you can't really compare. They don't really do the same things the same way.

RODNEY WHITAKER: Playing with both Wynton and Terence, I've realized that Wynton has a specific thing that he wants to hear, whereas Terence wants you to contribute a little more. I don't know whether it's because Wynton has an attitude of classical music, but there's just a certain thing that he wants to hear. But when I played with Terence, there wasn't so much of that. Whether it was sound or other ideas, Terence was more interested in the band's input. But those two people—Terence and Wynton—I don't think of them in the same breath. Wynton is an emotional player but in a different sort of way. Terence has this ability to speak to a person's spirit—not that Terence is greater or anything. Just that they're two totally different human beings to even think of as the same. They're always constantly being compared, but they're just too different.

NICHOLAS PAYTON: The fact that Terence is also from New Orleans and went to NOCCA and was in Blakey's band and on Columbia, people drew that comparison. It has nothing to do with music. The media will say, "Well, we already have one." And what can you do about that? You have to play through it. And that's exactly what Terence did. I mean, he could have said, "Forget it, I'll never be recognized for who I am." But he stuck through it.

TROY DAVIS: Well, in this society there's always a first. Wynton was the first guy coming up, and he did something that will forever keep him in the record books: the first guy to win a Grammy for both classical and jazz music in the same year. And that was unheard of. Wynton goes to perform for the queen of England and all these other prestigious gigs because of the classical music—it keeps him in that sort of elite genre. So I think the whole shadow thing was unfortunate because they're so different. To me, Wynton can play jazz, but Terence can *play* jazz. I mean, Wynton may have some technical things on Terence, but there's a fine line because Terence is a great technician himself.

CYRUS CHESTNUT: Those comparisons [between Terence and Wynton] should not be done. They're two different people. Terence is Terence. Wynton is Wynton. We need to look at these two gentlemen simply as who they are. Not try to say, "He does this, he does that." Uh-uh—don't put them against each other.

Terence is one of the masters. He has the ability of composition. And how he is able to communicate music throughout its language is really incredible. He will be one of the icons of jazz music, if he isn't already.

NICHOLAS PAYTON: I think Terence was in Wynton's shadow for a long time, but to no fault of his own. I've always loved his playing. Once a certain image is established, it's hard to break away from that. I think now that he's doing other things like film scores, he's definitely placed himself in his own category. And now people recognize him for being Terence Blanchard. When they want Terence Blanchard, they call him. They don't say we need another Wynton.

◆

Terence's growing status in the film industry illuminated him, especially among those who believed that he was in danger of eclipse by Wynton. With such a unique and successful career in film scoring (territory unexplored by Marsalis), the shadow was ultimately dislodged.

TROY DAVIS: For the longest time I couldn't understand why people weren't talking about Terence the way they were about Wynton. Wynton would be at the top of the *Down Beat* critics' and readers' polls, but Terence was never really a part of that stuff. And I used to say to Terence, "I wonder why?" Of course, Wynton and Terence were both on Columbia Records, and even Columbia was thinking about dropping Terence until they realized how well his film scoring career was going.

When Terence started getting involved in film, I remember there were more people starting to talk about him and more people were coming out to the shows, and they would say to me, "*Man*, where has this cat been? Now *this* is what I'm talking about!"

CARL ALLEN: There is something in jazz that is a sad commentary, but I'm glad of the end result for guys like Terence—it's that most jazz musicians of this generation that are really getting *serious* recognition is because of what they're doing *outside* of jazz. For instance, Wynton's popularity didn't really go over the top until he started making classical records. Branford, not until he did the Sting thing; and Terence, not until he started doing movie scores. And Terence and I used to talk about that.

TERENCE BLANCHARD: It's just the way the entertainment industry operates, but it's really pervasive in jazz because people feel alienated by the music. It's been the hardest thing trying to turn around the effect of that term *jazz*. When you say *jazz*, all of a sudden people's defenses go up. It's like, "Wait a minute, it's not a personal assault. This music has something to offer."

CARL ALLEN: It's almost as if being a great jazz musician alone isn't good enough. It's like you need a hook. And it's unfortunate because it doesn't make you any greater or any less of a musician, but I'm glad it's happening for Terence. Terence is worthy of all the accolades that he gets because he's a great musician.

MULGREW MILLER: They say you need a hook, but I think the hook syndrome is doing detriment to jazz, because some of the people who are being pushed and getting the most acclaim now are mostly all hooks and no substance. There was a time when if you could play, you could play. It's not about that anymore. If you can do something that's different from what everybody else is doing, then the record companies will take more of an interest in you. But I think Terence's [involvement in film scoring] is a wonderful opportunity, and I think he's very deserving of it. Terence is very talented: he's studied the piano, he knows keyboard harmony, and he's a studious kind of fellow. He's definitely done homework and research to be able to put himself into and maintain the position that he's in. But with all due respect to Terence—and I can say this without it being a put-down to him—I think there are many young musicians who are capable of that. But let's be realistic about it; Terence had a lucky break: his association with Spike Lee. And many of those who are capable did not have such an association. But I think it's to Terence's credit that he had the capacity to perform once that opportunity presented itself.

TERENCE BLANCHARD: When I got into the film industry, it set Wynton and me apart; there could be no comparisons. Up until that point, we were both on Columbia, and he had a quintet, and so did Donald and I. And I know Wynton didn't like the comparisons, either, because he wanted to be his own person. So frankly, I'm glad it's over with, because now I can go on and be who I am.

◆

Fresh on the heels of his debut recording, Terence would go on to record *Simply Stated*, his 1992 release dedicated to his newborn daughter. The composition "Little Miss Olivia Ray" is a beautiful solo piano ballad played by Terence, his only publicly issued performance on the instrument. Though dedicated to the precious new love in his life, *Simply Stated* paid tribute to Terence's mentor in the wake of his death. "Miles Davis always had the ability to play melodies in such a simply stated fashion," says Terence, "yet be very poignant and profound."

Simply Stated was another best-seller, reaching *Billboard*'s Top 10 in the spring of 1992. Terence was gratified with its commercial success but particularly pleased with the way his band was beginning to gel. He was dissatisfied with his debut effort because his obligations to *Jungle Fever* prevented the band from practicing the material before it was recorded.

Terence Blanchard: One of the things that you'll hear with this record is that the band itself sounds like a band. It really came together, and that's because after the first record, we went out on the road and tried to deal with the music all the time.[2]

On *Simply Stated*, as opposed to paying attention to South Africa with a composition like "Sing Soweto," I wanted to acknowledge a lot of the people who are suffering from this epidemic of crack and drugs that just seems to be rampant in our society. It's called "Glass J." And in the midst of that song, we play one of Ornette Coleman's songs, "Lonely Woman," because all too often, it's the people's loved ones who really feel the brunt of those kinds of situations. On a lighter note, I also wrote a song called "Lil' Fawdy" for Troy.

Troy Davis: Yeah, he named that one after me. Lil' Fawdy is an expression down south; it's a slang that everyone calls one another by. It comes from the tradition of Mardi Gras and New Orleans. It's just a friendly neighborhood thing that people say. You know, you say, "All right, Lil' Fawdy," instead of saying, "All right, man." We used to play that song all the time; it was kind of like the band's theme song. A lot of people told me they really like it—musicians, too. Nicholas Payton, Roy Hargrove, and Christian McBride, they all love that song.

Christian McBride: Terence means a whole lot to me, and that's why there's one part of our relationship that was a little heartbreaking and honestly still is. It was probably part of my wrongdoing for expecting this, but because Terence and I were so close, I was a little hurt that he didn't hire me after Rodney left his band. He hired Tarus Mateen. I remember thinking that I wasn't so hurt that he hired another bass player but that he didn't return my calls. I would call and call Terence, but, finally, I just gave up.

Carl Allen, who was really close to Terence at that time, actually turned out to be a really great friend to me. So I told Carl, "Man, me and Terence were tight when I was in high school, but I can't catch up with him now." And Carl was like, "Don't take it personal; Terence is extremely busy with the movies and other things." But I knew how busy the cat was and how he could spend a whole year doing a movie score. But I was like, "Dag, it wasn't like he was twiddling his thumbs when I was in high school; he was busy then, too." But then Carl told me about some of the personal problems that Terence was going through and that was why he wasn't getting back to me. And it was funny because I would meet cats in New York all the time and they'd say, "Hey, man, Terence talks about you all the time."

Troy Davis: When Rodney left the band, I recommended Tarus Mateen to Terence because I knew it would be an easy transition. I was familiar with Tarus's style because I had played with him in Betty Carter's band. He started with the *Simply Stated* tour and stayed about two and a half years until Chris Thomas came in.

Christian McBride: Around the time Tarus got the gig with Terence, it was when I first came to New York. I was going to Juilliard and Tarus and I were actually really close at that time. So I remember hanging out with him one day, and he said, "I got to go to Terence's house to pick up a few things. Why don't you come with me?" But I was thinking, "Oh, that might be a little awkward," but Tarus convinced me. So when we got there, Terence was real nonchalant, like everything was cool. And I guess everything *was* cool. It was just that I was disappointed that we weren't as tight as we used to be. I guess he saw it as something gradual, that we had just drifted apart and that there was no bad blood. So I don't think he realizes how significant an impact he had on me.

I didn't really see much of Terence after that until like three years later. In 1994, the jazz festival in Philadelphia was dedicated to me. They had like a Christian McBride day and wanted me to put together all of these musicians who meant a lot to me growing up. Terence played at the festival that year, but since he was headlining the night before, they said not to ask him. But I wasn't sure he would do it anyway. Ray Brown, Roy Hargrove, Wallace Roney, Joshua Redman, Jesse Davis, Benny Green, Billy Higgins, they all came out that day. It was one of the best days of my life! Freddie Hubbard was invited, too, and agreed to come, but then his lip blew out on him and he couldn't play anymore. So I guess festival productions got in touch with Terence to ask him if he'd come out. The next day when I saw him I was like, "Terence, this is a really significant day for me. I really thank you for hanging out the extra day." And he said, "All right, bro, solid," which is cool, but he just doesn't realize how big a part he played in my formative years. I really want to find the time to sit down and talk to Terence and let him know how I feel, but to this day I haven't had the chance to do it. But our relationship is still incomplete; the rest is still to come. Hopefully I'll be able to get with Terence again. I would love to do something with him.

◆

Although the *Simply Stated* tour took the Terence Blanchard Quintet around the globe, the departure was delayed until the summer. Terence was up to his ears listening to African and Arabian melodies while trying to find musicians who could play disparate music—all part of his preparation for his commission to compose and conduct the score for Spike Lee's new epic, *Malcolm X*.

When the tour finally did launch, Terence was able to resurface in New York just in time to celebrate the hugely anticipated release of the film. A couple of days before *Malcolm X* opened to the public in November 1992, its world premiere screened at Manhattan's Criterion Theater. For the glorious festivity, Terence wanted his mother to be by his side.

Terence Blanchard: I particularly remember the premiere of *Malcolm X* because when I got out of the limo with my mother, cameras were everywhere, just going off, and she was funny because she didn't know what to do. So I put my arm around her and guided her through. It was really great for her. She cried, and that kind of stuff makes me feel good. I was glad that I could do that for her. For *Mo' Better Blues*, she got the chance to meet Denzel Washington, and those kind of things are really great for me to see happen.

Mrs. Blanchard: I was at the premiere for *Mo' Better Blues* and *Malcolm X*. It was exciting! I remember the premiere for *Mo' Better Blues* because it was Terence's first movie. The mere fact of seeing Terence's name on the screen was fascinating to me. Actually, I don't think I saw anything else that night! It was mind-boggling, really. There were so many movie stars there that night that I almost tripped over Phylicia Rashad when I was getting into the limo. But I'll get used to it!

I didn't see Spike that night; I met him the night of *Malcolm X*, but only for a minute or two. There were so many people there that he had to see. But it's exciting. And what was more exciting to me was walking into

> the theater. I mean, you always see them on television—you know, the cameras, the red carpet—but to *actually* be there. . . . When we got inside, I met Denzel Washington and I was ecstatic. I shook his hand, and he gave me a big kiss. And as an old lady, that was wonderful. I fell in love with him when he was still on television, but I think everyone's in love with Denzel.

Clinging to her son, Mrs. Blanchard had entered a world unfamiliar to that of Odin Street. A woman of humility, she was unaccustomed to the vanity but awestruck by the glamour and celebrity. Although years have passed since those nights, a nostalgic smile reveals her pride to have witnessed a crowning achievement in her only child's career, an accomplishment that assured Terence Blanchard was indeed back on the block.

Notes

1. Bruce Handy, "Horn Again," *Vanity Fair* (June 2001): 78.
2. Wayne K. Self, "Back from Frustration," *Down Beat* (August 1992): 33.

CHAPTER NINE

NICE WORK IF YOU CAN GET IT

> Terence is out there writing those movie scores for Spike Lee and others, and I think it's great—and I think he's great at it!
>
> —J. J. Johnson

In launching a lucrative second career as a film composer, Terence Blanchard has fallen victim to startling backlash in his primary career. For whatever reason, the jazz industry has not responded favorably to Terence's success in Hollywood, which disturbs him deeply.

Among all genres of music, jazz has always most prized individuality, emphasizing its artists to write and perform the music in innovative ways to achieve an original voice. With over thirty film scores to his credit, Terence has initiated a rebirth of jazz in the orchestral world, stretching the reach of the music to wider audiences. "I always try to bring the elements of jazz into every score I do," he says, "no matter what style it is."

Lately, the jazz industry has begun to violate its tradition, inducing the music into a monolingual voice. If its musicians embrace an aesthetic that is considered "out of the box," their artistry is nullified as a legitimate contribution to the jazz idiom.

TERENCE BLANCHARD: It's amazing how the whole notion of being a jazz musician is to be experimental, but in this certain climate of the business, when you do that you're viewed as being unfaithful to the music. It seems to me as though there's a tendency for people to not want you to be as adventurous. It's like they want you to stay within a certain niche because they think that's what jazz is. It's interesting to see how certain journalists who call themselves experts are twisting around the meaning of jazz.

BRANFORD MARSALIS: I don't think that there is a movement for the perpetuation of ignorance in jazz because that makes it sound like there are intelligent people who sit around and decide to make ignorance the rule of the day of jazz. Actually, what it is is that there are these people who are musically ignorant and have very powerful positions in terms of being writers and editors. They make arbitrary decisions on music based on their own lack of knowledge, and once they are confronted with what could conceivably be the truth—since it is not their view—they decide to make the truth the enemy, or distort it to the point where it is actually a farce more than anything else. That is the basis of this big war going on with the writers. Why should I listen to a writer when I know more about what I am talking about than he does? There is no real reason to respect what they do or listen to what they say. Their reviews are not going to break me as an artist. What affects me is the misinformation, the irresponsibility, and that pisses me off. The only person that can fuck my head up is Sonny Rollins; if he tells me to hang it up, then I will have to consider it.[1]

Herbie Hancock: I'm not happy about the idea of limiting jazz and discouraging jazz musicians from the freedom to [experiment] with other music or instruments. I think when you limit jazz, you destroy jazz at the same time. Because jazz is not limited. I think jazz expresses the heart and human emotion. That's why people all over the world from different cultures can relate to jazz. When you start limiting it, you're getting away from its true meaning.[2]

Edward Simon: I think film is another avenue for jazz to be heard. So I think the jazz industry should welcome and cultivate that because we need more people to listen to jazz. Terence is becoming very popular, and they can try to invalidate him, but that's wrong. Terence is writing some beautiful music. I have been very impressed by his film scores, and for me, it's a great experience to be involved in those projects [as his pianist].

I just think there's probably some jealousy there. I don't know why, but there's so many purists in the industry who close themselves to any other musical possibilities.

Robin Burgess: Yeah, I just think it's based on envy. There's a lot of envy out there, and it's a shame. I mean, there are those who may say Terence is a film composer and no longer a jazz musician, but what's interesting is I see so many jazz musicians wanting to get into film music. A lot of guys who call me seeking representation ask me, "I want to get into film scoring—can you help me get into that?" But for Terence, he's never said it any other way: jazz is his love. He's always said that. And he's missed out on a lot of film opportunities because he decides to tour with his jazz band.

Terence Blanchard: Over the last few years, my sincerity as a jazz musician has been put into question, which is ludicrous. I've been touring with my band on the road. I've put out a record every year with the exception of one year, and that's more than some of the young rising stars have done. I love playing jazz, and it will never be my choice to give that up.

ROBIN BURGESS: When you become successful, the overall attitude in the jazz community is that they no longer view you as a jazz musician. You know, you're supposed to remain downtrodden, poor, and strung out on drugs. It's like they watch too many bad foreign films on jazz musicians. But that mentality still exists.

◆

In spite of the apparent stranglehold the jazz industry has on the career paths of many of its artists, Terence continually moves in a new direction—*his* direction. And while his extraordinary exposure in the film industry provides added accessibility for wider audiences, Terence has resisted the temptation of trumpeting his talents for commercial gain. By remaining true to his cultural roots, Terence's successful merging of the two media into a unique, diverse body of work recognizes him as the most prolific jazz musician to ever compose for the motion picture industry.

ROGER DICKERSON: I think a lot of musicians get to a point—once they get involved within the industry—that an ego takes over and begins to damage their talent. But Terence remains serious with a high sense of integrity in his work, which counts for everything. And he's continually developing his talents not only as a performer but as a writer—and a writer of notated music. There's a difference between that kind of writer and one who gets a bunch of guys together in a studio and says, "OK, let's take this chord here, and then we'll play something around this, and then we'll make something out of that," and then comes out of the studio and says, "Yeah, I wrote that." A lot of that goes on!

The whole idea of developing oneself as an improviser and coming up with tunes in your head is one kind of thing, but when you start to deal with writing in the full content of the piece, you learn to broaden your personal expression. When you become a writer in the notated tradition, you are faced with another situation entirely. And Terence is on that road, and he has the opportunity to do it, especially in film.

TERENCE BLANCHARD: One of the things that I'm trying to do [in my writing] is bring the music I love to film. Duke Ellington was probably the only composer who got to score film using [jazz] with some degree of integrity. I get tired of seeing downtrodden figures, and all of a sudden you hear saxophones swinging. Jazz can be funny, can be sad, can be serious. People score movies using European traditional techniques, but to me it's all about interpretation. It's how musicians look at an eighth note with a triplet feeling. They phrase like jazz musicians. I want to take that language and use the orchestration techniques for composing film with a jazz band. You don't have to hear drums all the time or hear a bass walking all the time. There's a lot of room for this music to be used in very creative ways. It can bring something very fresh to this industry.[3]

Ellis Marsalis: I didn't know that Terence was studying piano and composition with Dickie until Terence came to NOCCA. But once Terence was at NOCCA, the school was able to nurture their personalities and talents so they could choose the directions that they wanted to go in. Now, I had no idea that Terence would lean more toward composition, especially the things he's doing with Spike Lee. That's great! When I was in college, that was something that I really wanted to get into.

Not too long ago, Terence gave a great workshop here [at the University of New Orleans], and people wanted to know about his film compositions. Terence basically credited Roger with a lot of that. And I've been trying to funnel people to Dickie, but he can't take *everybody*!

Terence Blanchard: Here's a guy, who I consider to be a really great composer, who took the time out to teach me. I mean, that's the way I look at it. People say, "Well, he *is* a teacher." But Roger Dickerson is more than that—he's an artist. He's like an Art Blakey. He made me feel comfortable with who I am. He used to ask me what I wanted out of music. He'd say, "Tell me, what do you want to do?" This is a piano lesson; you know, I'm like, "Can we get to some music?" But he made me think about all of that stuff; he planted the seed for me to really deal with being an artist. He's just an amazing cat.

Willie Metcalf: Terence, Wynton, Branford—they're *doing* what they're supposed to be doing. They're taking care of business, serious business. Monk, Bird, Diz, Art Blakey, all of those cats would be proud of them because they're carrying on the tradition at a very high level. Look at Terence and what he's doing with his movie compositions. That's innovative. How many jazz guys are able to do that? But you know, that's Roger Dickerson coming out. Roger is a genius. He has such great insight into composition. And it opens up whole new areas of thought depending on your imagination and intellect. There's no end to the possibilities of the mind. That's what I used to *tell* my students, but Roger can *bring* that out of his students.

Roger Dickerson: Terence comes back once in a while to speak with my students. One time during the jazz festival in New Orleans, he did a workshop at Southern University. I stopped in just to say hello, and then I left. Later that day, I saw some professors, and they said, "Your ears must be burning."

"Why's that?"

"Oh, Terence was really singing your praise."

During a question-and-answer period, students were asking Terence,

"How do you start writing? How do you do this?" And he said, "Well, I went to Roger Dickerson." And he does this a lot because he's that kind of person, which is really nice to hear.

CHRISTIAN MCBRIDE: I'll tell you another reason why Terence is very important to me: I admire him for those movie scores he does. In the 1960s, it was the norm for jazz musicians to be an integral part in writing the music for movies. I mean, there was Duke Ellington, Oliver Nelson, Benny Carter, Quincy Jones. And I can't think of any true jazz musicians that have continually done that type of work in the last thirty years other than Terence. Terence was the first to bring that tradition back. I really look up to him for that because I see it as a way where other jazz musicians today can get into that kind of work. I'm not making a conscious effort to break in, but if it happened, I'd definitely welcome it.

JOE HENDERSON: The first time I heard Terence play was out here in San Francisco at the Keystone Korner, but I never met him that day. I was actually sitting in my car in front of the club with a lady friend of mine. But with no traffic, you could hear the music as clearly as if you were sitting inside. He was with Art Blakey at the time, and I remember having a good impression of Terence. He sounded really good.

It's been really great to see Terence get involved in the movie industry. I mean, I've thought about doing film scores—as a matter of fact, I still do—so it's great to have those possibilities dealt out to you. I'm sure Terence is a person who's exercising a considerable amount of influence over some of the youngsters because he's dealing a lot of cards out there. What I mean by that is, he's showing that there are great possibilities out there for jazz musicians, particularly in film scoring. Just seeing Terence deal out those cards for people to pick up will influence the scene because it will get jazzers to think much broader in terms of their career goals. I mean, that's a pretty fair amount of power there, so I hope Terence is aware of that, but I'm sure he is.

NICHOLAS PAYTON: I think to a certain degree, film scoring goes beyond jazz. You have to be open to a lot of different things, and I think that is part of Terence's appeal. I mean, Terence *is* a jazz musician, but he doesn't bogart jazz on everything because that's not realistic for a film. You have to be open musically and flexible enough creatively to do other things when scoring a film. And to me, that goes beyond being a *jazz* musician. That's about being a *great* musician. Developing to that point. And that's what Terence has done.

◆

Through Terence's scores, more people are being exposed to jazz; it is his hope that these creations will trigger interest in youngsters, specifically black youths, to seek out its historical legacy. Even though jazz is recognized around the world as an original African American art form, few blacks are seen in its audiences nowadays. Art Blakey used to say, "Black people know less about jazz than anybody else in the world." This is a disturbing fact to many of its artists, one that was adeptly articulated in a scene from *Mo' Better Blues* between characters played by Denzel Washington and Wesley Snipes.

SPIKE LEE: If you go to see jazz musicians anywhere in the country, we're not going to be in the numbers there. We're there for Luther [Vandross] or [rapper] Snoop Dogg. But, you know, that's all right. You want to get support wherever you can get it from.

But I always felt that it must be something jazz musicians think about; that's the reason why I brought it up in the film. They must think, at least initially, "I'm playing my ass off out here. Where are all the black people?" Then after a while, they probably get used to it. One of the funny things about that scene, though, is that we've got "Mercy, Mercy, Mercy" by Cannonball Adderley playing on the soundtrack.

TERENCE BLANCHARD: One of the most frustrating things for me is to play a gig and the majority of people there are not black. It's disappointing, but at the same time I understand it. A lot of these kids grow up with no respect for themselves *and* others. The things that they deal with every day do not have anything to do with jazz.[4]

NICHOLAS PAYTON: It's an abstract concept to think that a fifteen-year-old is going to sit down and listen to jazz just for the pure enjoyment of it. I mean, it's just not "hip" to a teenager. And certainly, none of their friends are into it.

For so long, jazz has been outside of the community that it came from, and now it's almost lost. And there's so many arguments for that. For one, jazz, sad to say, probably has no social significance to most black people's lives.

If jazz is brought into the schools, the kids will gain an awareness of who Duke Ellington was or who Ornette Coleman is—or even some of the musicians who are closer to their age that are out here playing this music. I'm not saying that they have to become musicians—I'm not worried about a lack of musicians, because there are a lot young guys coming up—but I don't see any people in that age group coming out interested in the music unless they're musicians themselves. You look at the crowds coming out in the States—they're all middle-aged and above. Ten, twenty, thirty years from now, when those people have passed, who are we going to be playing to if people don't even know what jazz is?

As far as the race thing—well, I know a lot of black people say, "Well, this is expensive. I'm not paying $17 plus a $10 drink minimum to see, you know, Terence at the Vanguard." OK, that's expensive, but if Snoop Dogg is at Madison Square Garden, they'll pay fifty-five bucks to see him. The whole concept of just listening to music is gone. It's got to be a show. And jazz has this stigma that it's just for older people to come to a club and sit in a seat and just listen. But I don't want people to come and see me play and just sit in their seats—even if I'm at Carnegie Hall. If I play something you like, shout out or whatever. If you feel like jumping up or tapping your feet, do it. That's what this music is all about.

I know younger people have a very short attention span, and if somebody's playing the same song for fifteen, twenty minutes, well, that's boring to them. No one wants to listen to a cat play a solo for five minutes. And I don't blame them because, to a certain degree, I don't want to hear that, either. So, it's sad to say, but jazz will never be accepted by the masses because of what it represents.

CHRISTIAN MCBRIDE: As long as I'm a musician, my all-time goal is to try to draw more black people to the music, especially young black people. When Terence and I are in our sixties and fifties, it's going to have to be the younger generation to support it. I mean, I appreciate all the people who come to see us perform. There have always been whites supporting the music, but at one point, blacks were the main supporter because they realized jazz was their music, and it was cool to like it. Then all of a sudden, after the 1950s, we know less about it than anyone else in the world.

You go to Canada, Asia, Europe; you go to South America; they have all these jazz festivals dedicated to these wonderful jazz musicians. They pay them good money, they're appreciated, and they treat them like kings. That's fantastic. But you go to where you're from, and they don't know who you are. That has to be changed, but obviously we can't do it ourselves. We need the help from black press and black radio.

TERENCE BLANCHARD: Black radio ain't doing nothing. That's what it is. There's no education going on. If we had some education going on, it would be happening. There used to be a period when Dinah Washington, Nancy Wilson, and Diana Ross would all play on the same station. It doesn't even come close to that happening now. But that's just the tip of the iceberg; I don't want to put all the responsibility on that. I feel that the other part of it is schools have to get more involved in helping these kids feel proud about its great legacy.

DONALD HARRISON: Well, I think that we lost something when we said that this music is not dance music. Africans relate to music in a different way than Europeans. We have taken the African experience out of our music and tried to make it something that Europeans relate to, which is to sit in a concert hall and listen to Mozart. But if you go to Africa, you'll see they don't do it like that. So I think jazz has just deviated away from the African American experience. Of course, there are some African Americans who can relate to it that way, but a lot of people also say jazz got too intellectual. But the fact is, their minds have not been keeping pace with what's happening today.

Branford Marsalis: Yeah, you have musics that start out, then they deviate from their folk-form roots. Classical music did. The majority of white people don't support classical music. When classical music was baroque music and it was all like a nicer version of traditional folk music, everybody loved it. Then when Beethoven came along, he took the shit out. I guess Mozart actually started to take it out, and then it just started going out. And people liked it less and less because it was just too heavy for them. That's what happened to jazz; it deviated from the folk form. Charlie Parker changed the music forever; it no longer was dance music. As long as it was dance music, everybody was fine with it. But when you do what Charlie Parker did, you leave the people behind. That's the way it goes. I mean, so it ain't got nothing to do with the color of your skin. It has to do with your ability to intellectually process the information that your brain has received. When we're dealing with shit on that level, God does not dole out intellectual ability based on race. And if people have the intellectual ability to ascertain the information that John Coltrane and Ornette Coleman are putting down, then they will also dig Stravinsky and Puccini and all this other shit. You know what I mean? And they will be able to read from the magazines. And they won't watch Oprah and they won't watch . . . you know? But I mean, jazz is completely antithetical to what the average person likes and feels comfortable with. Jazz is completely antithetical to the Hamptons, and being seen, and hanging out with the beautiful—that ain't got nothing to do with jazz. You know, going to a nightclub and wearing suits; all that dumb shit that people do—relaxing in a suit. I work in suits. I don't think the idea of relaxing is putting on a suit. Just look at what the average person does with their time, and jazz is like the opposite of that; classical music, at its highest level, is the opposite of that.

I mean, when jazz is played at its best level, very few people know what's going on. You get blank looks—from black people, from white people—but you'll have like five people in the back going, "*Yeah*!" And they can be any color because they can *hear* it. So it ain't got nothing to do with being mad when there are no black people there. I'm just happy when I see five people who know what we're doing. You know, *if* I can find five, I'm happy.

Like, just last week we were playing at the Vanguard—me, Tain, and Veal—and we were tearing the shit up, and we got a good review in the *New York Times*, so we got a big weekend crowd. You know, all the wannabe hip people, "Hey, let's go to the Vanguard and see that Marsalis guy; he got a good review in the *Times*." I don't think people come to my shows for the music. They come because of the hype.

So we were playing "Citizen Tain," which is a tricky form, and it went totally over their heads. But in the corner of my right eye, I see this little nineteen-year-old white kid—if he's that old—and he's just nailing the shit, just right on it! And I started laughing, man! I'm playing; I'm looking at this kid going, "*Oh, man!* This kid is right there!" And that makes us happy, man. I don't go, "Too bad it wasn't a black kid." I was just like, "Damn, man, out of all these corny motherfuckers in here, this one little kid hears what we're doing." But then we changed the subdivision of the song from four to five—lost him! So when the song was over I said, "Did you get what that was?"

"No, man . . . ."

"It was five."

"Oh, five fives?"

"Yeah, one time it was five, and one time it was three sevens and a four."

"What?!"

"Twenty-five beats, man." I'm talking to this kid in the audience, and the people were like, "Oh, it's so cute that he's talking to the little boy." You know, they see *that*. But I'm like, "Yeah, that's *charming*. I'm giving this kid information!" He was diggin' the music, and I felt good about that so I wanted to help him get the music because I know I'm going to be seeing him one day playing and he'll say, "You remember me, I was sitting in the audience . . . ." And I'll say, "Yeah, I remember you—you're from North Carolina." That's going to happen because he's going to be one of them cats.

Terence Blanchard: People talk about Charlie Parker and bebop. They say that it had an effect on it, and it did. But, while that may be a point that people can debate over, I don't necessarily think that it holds water in the long run because it's been my experience that when you have people exposed to the music, they like it. So that's cause for me to believe that it just takes more people to get exposed to it. And I think there's a lot of potential for that. That's what I tried to do when I was at Columbia, but they didn't get it.

Robin Burgess: I started out working for the senior vice president of black music at Columbia Records, Ruben Rodriguez. At that time—this is like 1987—jazz at Columbia fell under the black music department; it didn't have its own division. Dr. George Butler was reporting to the black music VP, which is very interesting. And on the jazz roster at that time was Sonja Robinson, Branford, Terence, and Donald, Wynton, and Kent Jordan—those were the "it" players. Even though jazz was a part of the black music department; it was just automatically assumed that you worked constantly with R&B. No one was paying attention to jazz, but I had like a serious love for it so I used to go to the label meetings and take notes about what was being said about it. Then I would come back and share my thoughts with Dr. Butler—George has always been a social kind of character. He wasn't really into the daily running of this jazz department. So I would talk to him and to my boss about doing some promotion for jazz. I mean, there was no one servicing radio, no one was paying attention to the roster, but my boss didn't really want to hear about it: "*Please*, jazz is not on my agenda."

At that time the black music department had like fourteen number one songs in one year. They were dealing with George Michael, Michael Jackson, New Kids on the Block, Lisa Lisa and the Cult Jam, Regina Belle, and Jeffrey Osbourne; it was all blockbuster sensations. They were not thinking about Terence and Donald's *Crystal Stair*, Branford's *Royal Garden Blues*—that was not a priority.

Terence Blanchard: I have some friends in the black music department at Columbia, and I told them, "Look, whatever you all need me to do, let me do it." I said, "I'll be your guinea pig." I want to go out there and reconnect jazz with all of these folks. We don't need to sit here and act like they don't exist because they do. I didn't grow up in a totally white environment; I grew up in a mixed environment. So I just want to let them know that I'm cool and that they have nothing to fear. They can come to this music; nobody's going to intimidate them. We're not stuck-up musicians. I hate that whole notion.

◆

Terence is eager to dispel many of the myths associated to those in his profession and the music that he plays. Such a lofty undertaking is not only admirable but, to a degree, reminiscent of preceding generations of African Americans. Blacks in the United States have long been forced by a society saturated with stereotypes to challenge misrepresentation of who they are. At no time has this been more apparent than during the civil rights movement.

Notes

1. Dave Helland, "The Marsalis Tapes," *Down Beat* (November 1989): 17.
2. Unknown Internet source (1997).
3. Michael Bourne, "In Tribute to Lady Day," *Down Beat* (May 1994): 19.
4. Wayne K. Self, "Back from Frustration," *Down Beat* (August 1992): 33.

CHAPTER TEN

MALCOLM AND MARTIN: A COMMON DREAM

They might have had different means, but they were after the same end: dignity and rights for black people, and all oppressed people.

—*Spike Lee*

For Terence and especially more recent generations of African Americans, the horrors of the segregated South are a distant nightmare. But for those who were victimized by it, the vivid memories of injustice and maltreatment remain.

MRS. BLANCHARD: Segregation was the biggest thing in New Orleans when I was young. There were certain things we weren't supposed to have. You know, we were all supposed to live in shacks. It was hard at times, but we managed mainly because of the strong values and pride that our mother instilled in us. She taught us that we were no different from anyone else, and I believed her. But I can't say that I wasn't affected by it.

When we moved [to Odin Street] in 1969, although it was predominantly black, we had whites coming over from Gentilly Woods, and they'd throw eggs and tomatoes at the house, even bottles and bricks—anything they had in their hand. The whole experience demoralized me to a certain degree. Knowing that another race looked at me as being inferior was awful. Not being able to go to certain places, shop in certain stores. But there was this one store where I had a special saleslady. She knew what I liked and was always nice to me. So it was a pleasure to shop there because they didn't look down on you. But for the most part, the whole experience was horrible.

◆

When the U.S. Civil War abolished slavery, America was heading to legitimize its own declaration, "All men are created equal." Congress had passed the Civil Rights Act of 1875, giving equal rights to blacks in public accommodations and jury duty. However, eight years later, the Supreme Court invalidated the new bill, dismissing it as "unconstitutional." It sanctioned the principle "separate but equal" and imposed the notorious Jim Crow laws that legally segregated blacks in southern states. And so, the Land of the Free continued to suppress the advancement of its people of African ancestry.

Over the next seventy years, such prominent black civil rights leaders as W. E. B. Du Bois, Marcus Garvey, Medger Evers, Malcolm X, among many others, devoted their lives to fighting against these discriminatory barriers. However, no leader captured the hearts and hope of Afro-Americans like Dr. Martin Luther King Jr. An emotionally stirring speaker, millions of blacks and whites alike were attracted to King's high moral stature. King fervently believed in the wisdom of Mahatma Gandhi's nonviolent disobedience and set out to apply the credo in the hostile South.

Born in Atlanta, Georgia, on January 15, 1929, King has had his birthday celebrated in the United States since 1983 as a national holiday. After graduating with a doctorate in philosophy from Boston University in 1955, King moved back south to Montgomery, Alabama. In December of that year, a fellow Montgomery resident, Rosa Parks, defied the mandate pertaining to segregated seating on city buses. She refused to grant her seat to a white passenger. The courage and heroism exhibited by Parks inspired King to lead a boycott against the city's bus lines. Eventually, the city relented to King's demands of desegregation and allowed black passengers the freedom to sit wherever they chose. King's successful organization of the boycott and his humane policy of passive resistance to segregation garnered national attention and elevated him in the public eye as the prominent leader of the civil rights movement.

In the aftermath of Montgomery, King traveled throughout the South with intentions of ending the segregation of buses, lunch counters, hotels, washrooms, and other public facilities everywhere. He delivered inspiration and optimism while emphasizing the importance for African Americans to register to vote.

In 1963, one hundred years after the Emancipation Proclamation, the symbolic high point of the American civil rights movement occurred in the nation's capital. There, over two hundred thousand people gathered for the King-organized March on Washington. On the steps of the Lincoln Memorial, King addressed the world with his eminent speech entitled "I Have a Dream." (The speech and the march were the first-ever televised events to be carried internationally via satellite.)

This historical event is accredited as a major factor in the crumbling of the remains of legal segregation. King's essential function was not to lead black people but to educate white people. His articulate, idealistic vision for the United States had a profound effect on the conscience of white America.

In 1964, King became the youngest recipient ever to be awarded the Nobel Peace Prize. Yet just four years later, this young life was snuffed out prematurely by an assassin's bullet. On April 4, 1968, King was in Memphis, Tennessee, to lead a nonviolent march in support of striking sanitation workers. There, this man of peace suffered a malicious death.

Although James Earl Ray was convicted for the murder, many believe, including the King family, that Ray may have been innocent; who committed the cowardly act is unclear. One thing is for certain: America lost a towering figure of moral righteousness and social progress. Dr. Martin Luther King Jr. was thirty-nine.

MRS. BLANCHARD: Dr. King was something of a little Moses to me. He had made a difference with all of us. He gave us a sense of hope, inspiration and courage. Rosa Parks, too. I've had many experiences riding the streetcar and the bus where they'd ask you to move to the back, or to stand for someone else to have the seat. So naturally, I felt bad. It took Rosa Parks a lot of courage, and should I say *guts*, which meant a great deal to me. It was an inspiration. But most of the time we would just walk instead of taking the streetcar to avoid the humiliation. There would be times where we'd have bags full of groceries, but we'd still walk home.

MRS. DOUGLAS: Although segregation was difficult, it was a part of life for us, so we just tried to go about. Obviously, it was difficult going in stores, riding buses, all that; everything separated by "white" and "colored." You really felt like a second-class citizen. "What is so bad about me that we need to have these two separate water fountains here?" It's not a good feeling.

Martin Luther King Jr. meant freedom. He gave us a chance to be and do some of the things we wanted to. And Rosa Parks—here's a woman who's giving me a chance to feel like a human being. You know, but then you ask yourself, "Why couldn't I have been that kind of person?" We could have said no, but we feared going to jail. So you do have warm feelings for someone strong enough to do what she did. She inspired all of us to be strong and to start standing up for ourselves. "I'm not going into the stores that say I can't try on a hat anymore; I'll shop somewhere else." So Dr. King and Rosa Parks helped us a great deal to come up with the strength to make those decisions.

MRS. BLANCHARD: Terence had experienced some of it but not as much as we did. I don't think it really bothered him; I think he understood it. But Terence is the type of person that doesn't talk very much. I don't think he was affected by it because he has always been *music* from a little fella. And nothing else seemed to bother him.

TERENCE BLANCHARD: I grew up at the tail end of segregation, so I didn't really experience it the way my mother and father did. But people always talk about how integration may have been the *worst* thing that ever happened to the black community. While things were segregated, the black community had their own role models, their own establishments, their own places to do things; the black community was thriving. Not to say they were as financially secure as the white community, but emotionally, there were a lot of positive things happening because they were functioning *as* a community. With integration, a lot of those things were lost, especially in the educational system. A lot of the teachers couldn't understand African American culture or the neighborhoods in which we came from. Consequently, they didn't know how to deal with the social issues of the African American students.

DENZEL WASHINGTON: The fact is, not a whole hell of a lot has changed. When we took one direction instead of another, people said Martin Luther King was safer. That seemed to be the doctrine, and they got a lot of good things done and changed a lot of laws, but what you come to find out is, you can't change the way people think.

In the 1950s and 1960s, somewhere in there, we got mixed up with integration and assimilation. We lost part of our own culture and strength, and I think that Malcolm X was telling us, know who you are, learn who you are, learn what your true history is—so that when you walk out the door, you'll feel good about yourself because that's what the Italian American does. That's what the Jewish American does. That's what every nationality does; they're solid about who they are, and the African American was the one who said, well, we just want to be able to fit in.

Now people are realizing that the things Malcolm said then make a heck of a lot of sense. To know who you are, to be economically strong as a community. He called it nationalism. They called it separatism, but all he was saying was, "Hey, if you live in that community, why not spend your own money in that community? Why not own the business in that community? Everybody else does that."[1]

◆

Malcolm X was a man of complexity, a fascinating leader whose evolution as a human being never ceased. In his stirring eulogy, actor Ossie Davis summarized the slain leader's profound influence on an entire race in four short words: "Malcolm was our manhood."

Born Malcolm Little in Omaha, Nebraska, on May 19, 1925, he was a victim of a turbulent childhood. His father was a Baptist minister who dedicated his life to the "back to Africa" preachings of Marcus Garvey. This doctrine antagonized the local Ku Klux Klan, for they believed it was "spreading trouble" among the "good Negroes" of Omaha. After initial resistance, the Littles ultimately submitted to the violent coercing of the terrorist group and fled Nebraska for Lansing, Michigan—a town that would not prove to be their safe haven.

Late one night, six-year-old Malcolm awoke to the shrill cry of his mother. He scrambled out of his bed to the living room where police officers just informed Mrs. Little that her husband was dead—his skull crushed and body cut almost in half. Reverend Little was thought to be attacked by the Klan and then placed across streetcar tracks to suffer a violent death. Mrs. Little was so devastated, both emotionally and financially, that the state Welfare Department eventually deemed her unfit to care for her children. Malcolm was removed from his family and placed in a foster home. Although he lost contact with his mother, he remained close with his four siblings. In fact, many of them would play pivotal roles in his adulthood.

While in the seventh grade, an incident involving Malcolm's English teacher, Mr. Ostrowski, proved to be a major turning point in his life. One day after class, the white teacher sat alone in a classroom with Malcolm, discussing his aspiration to become a lawyer. Malcolm was among Ostrowski's elite students, but the teacher told the youngster that it was an unrealistic goal for a "nigger." Although, in retrospect, Malcolm believed the teacher meant no harm, that his advice was just in his nature as an American white man, Ostrowski's remarks made him feel uneasy at the time. No longer did he feel immune to the derogatory remarks that were thrown his way. Malcolm began to feel withdrawn from his white peers, for Ostrowski had planted a seed of contempt inside the boy, one that would later blossom into deep-rooted aversion.

WILLIE METCALF: During the recesses at the academy, I played the records of Malcolm X's teachings over the PA system. Anyone could tell that Malcolm was an angry guy, but by playing his records, I was hoping the kids would take that anger and channel it into something positive, whether it's self-awareness, whatever. I didn't know at the time, but I later found out that it scared the shit out of Terence. But it prepared him for the movie *Malcolm X*. After the movie came out, I ran into Terence and he said, "Hey man, thanks for introducing me to Malcolm X."

TERENCE BLANCHARD: I'll never forget the first time I heard Malcolm X speak. We were all in this park on Jackson Avenue. We played a lot of concerts there with Willie Metcalf. And on breaks, Willie played Malcolm's speeches. Malcolm was talking about how this one's tongue needs to be cut out and blue-eyed devils and it scared me to death. I had never heard anything like it in my life. But I remember everybody else being into it. And it was weird because not only was I ignorant to Malcolm X, but you're around all these people who are your friends, and all of a sudden something shifts and you discover something you never knew or suspected about them. It was like finding yourself in the middle of a cult or something. I thought they were just normal people [*laughing*]. It caught me off guard, but I was just naive.

◆

Malcolm X was a much maligned figure, his message often misconstrued, but understandably so—the focus of his leadership kept evolving throughout his life. In his final year, even he conceded his uncertainty with which philosophy to adopt. But the fact that most associated him to his twelve years with the extremist Nation of Islam, when he verbally assaulted whites and preached separatism, irrevocably damaged his image.

Unlike Dr. King, Malcolm X did not believe in turning the other cheek. Advocating violence was not his theme either, but because whites were threatened by Malcolm X, the mainstream press and some Negro leaders strived to discredit him as a "raging hate-monger."

By promoting this image, it more than muddled Malcolm X's tireless efforts in the civil rights movement. It demonstrated an ugly ignorance. The militant years of Malcolm X were an instinctive, defensive counteraction to America's treatment of blacks. His hate could be attributed to the effect persecution has on an ancestral line that dates back several hundred years.

TERENCE BLANCHARD: I didn't read Malcolm's autobiography until I got to college. See, I kind of moved away from that for a while, but then when I got to college—the militant part of your life—you discover new things and really a new world. So I started to understand more at that point. While I was reading it, I actually felt embarrassed. I felt embarrassed that history has taken his life so far out of context. But I think that's what happens in general in America with Malcolm X. I've always believed that people only choose to take bits and pieces from his life. They dwell on the militant aspect of his life without fully understanding how he got there and, more important, where he went afterward.

SPIKE LEE: Malcolm was a very complex person. There were three or four different Malcolms. He was constantly evolving, his outlook and his ideology, and always trying to seek the truth. If he found it, he was not scared of being called a hypocrite. If he found a higher truth, he would say, "I was wrong. All that stuff I said before is wrong, and this is what I believe." That's something that very few people do.[2]

◆

As a teenager in the mid-1940s, Malcolm Little was lured into the underworld of crime. He hustled, pimped, ran numbers, and pushed drugs on the streets of Harlem and Boston before eventually getting convicted on fourteen counts of burglary in February 1946. Three months short of his twenty-first birthday, Malcolm was sentenced to ten years in jail at the Charlestown State Prison in Massachusetts. In the joint, he rediscovered education, diligently studying English and Latin. But it was a letter from his older brother Philbert that focused Malcolm's new passion: religion. Philbert's letter joyously announced that he had found the "natural religion for the black man" and that he had joined the "Nation of Islam." After initial befuddlement and reluctance, Malcolm embraced the Islamic faith as well.

For more than forty years, the leader of the Nation of Islam was an African American from Georgia named Elijah Muhammad. Referred to as "The Messenger of Allah," Muhammad's fundamental message was that the "blue-eyed devil white man" had kidnapped the "so-called Negro" from his homeland and stripped him of his language, culture, family name, and familial structure. He believed that through his teachings, the Negro would rise up and return to where he had begun—at the top of civilization.

A message this outspoken was unprecedented in America. Never before had a Negro spoken so contemptuously of whites on such an area. His teachings reached and inspired African Americans across the country from churches to prisons. To inmate Malcolm Little, Muhammad was a guru, and he worshipped him unconditionally.

In 1952, after serving six and a half years, Malcolm was released from prison. He immediately joined the Nation of Islam and began spreading the message of Elijah Muhammad. In addition, he no longer replied to the name Malcolm Little.

During slavery time, most blacks had their African family name stripped and replaced by their slavemaster's surname. The Nation of Islam believed the letter *X* (representing the unknown in mathematics) should supplement the slave name. Thus, "Little" was erased, and Malcolm X was born.

For the next twelve years, until his disagreeable split from the Nation in 1964, Malcolm X, who often described himself as "the angriest black man in America," articulated black rage with highly controversial rhetoric.

But in March 1964, Malcolm announced that the Nation of Islam and Elijah Muhammad himself did not meet the standards they had set for others and divorced himself from the hypocrisy. A considerable rift developed between the Nation and their most celebrated apostle to the point where Muhammad allegedly issued an order for Malcolm's assassination.

With the financial assistance from his sister, Ella, Malcolm escaped the hostility and ventured to Mecca to make a *hajj* (a religious pilgrimage that all orthodox Muslims—if able—are obligated to do). There, he encountered a spiritual awakening and underwent a complete philosophical reconstruction.

Upon his return to the United States, he held press conferences, where for some, the unthinkable materialized. Malcolm X stood before the world and admitted a critical error in judgment regarding his cultivation of the teachings of Elijah Muhammad. He announced that he had become an orthodox Muslim and that if America desired an end to racism, it should embrace the ideals of the Islamic faith. His travels throughout Africa and the Middle East had produced a more optimistic view for the potential of peace and brotherhood. In fact, Malcolm ceased all talk of racial separation and embraced the idea of the "oneness" of man. Such newfound enlightenment spawned a sharp contrast to the "hate" that had gained so much momentum throughout his twelve years with the extremist Nation of Islam.

Mere months after his return from Mecca, Malcolm X's fascinating life and career came to an abrupt end when he was shot in New York City on February 21, 1965. The assassins, although never charged, were thought to be connected with the Nation of Islam. Like Martin Luther King Jr., Malcolm X was gunned down at the young age of thirty-nine.

> **Donald Harrison:** I think Malcolm—after he left Mecca—is the person that I really relate with. It wasn't about color; it was about *human beings*. Everybody hasn't learned that lesson, but if you don't think of the world in those terms, then you're really creating problems. After you get past race, we're all humans. I do understand that this country was built upon a certain segment—my segment—being subservient. And I think when we play this music [jazz], we're saying that we are people of great intellect, we are distinguished people, and we're people who can achieve anything and will achieve anything. But when Malcolm came back, he was really spreading something that would have taken the whole country—not just black people—to another level, and it would have come at an opportune time. So it's unfortunate that the message he was spreading before he was assassinated wasn't fully blossomed.
>
> **Terence Blanchard:** Yeah, you really felt that he was about to make a significant difference. I think he was on the brink of something in terms of the areas where black people really needed the help. It's hard to say, but the possibilities were endless.
>
> **Branford Marsalis:** Malcolm was a bad brother, man. He stood on his moral convictions, right or wrong. And he was a real man because he woke up one day and realized that some of the philosophies that he was preaching were incorrect and he was man enough to say, "I was wrong." That's a special cat.

SPIKE LEE: I was a convert when I read the book in junior high school. It's the most important book I'll ever read. The book gave me courage to do what I need to do to make the types of films I want to make. It takes commitment, and it takes backbone not to go along with the status quo. You could easily be sucked into smiling and grinning and going for the money. That's not the route I've chosen to go.[3]

[When] I read it, I thought, "This is a great black man, a strong black man, a courageous black man who did not back down from anybody, even toward his death." And then I woke up to other things that were going on around me that had nothing to do with the arts. People had pushed Dr. King's philosophy and his legacy to the forefront—they were both dead by this time, around 1970. . . . And Dr. King was chosen for a national holiday. And there are times when Dr. King is a vehicle for my true feelings about the racial situation. But from what I read of Malcolm X, I immediately knew that what he said was much more in line with the way I felt. I have a deep respect for Dr. King, but I've always been drawn more to Malcolm. I think that I've really grown to love Malcolm more. What he stood for and what he died for. I just cannot get with Dr. King's complete nonviolence philosophy.[4]

People should try to learn from both men. They were different, they might have had different means, but they were after the same end. Simply dignity and rights for black people, and all oppressed people. It's something we could apply to ourselves today, to make it work for today, for the world we live in now.[5]

TERENCE BLANCHARD: Considering my introduction to Malcolm, it was very, very ironic for me to be doing the music for the film some fifteen years later; I think about that all the time. But I believe my experience is probably similar to a lot of people hearing Malcolm speak for the first time. But now I understand what happened over the course of his *entire* life and identify with it all because it was all a part of the process.

To me, Malcolm X was a person in search of something. His quest to unravel the truth about human injustice and to acquire human rights in the U.S. and abroad never wavered. Malcolm was a very sincere person who put everything out front for everybody to see, which leads me to believe that he had a large sense of humility. See, that's what I love about his story because if the humility wasn't there, then you don't leave yourself open to change. I consider Malcolm one of my heroes because of how he evolved. He accepted the fact that everything he was taught by Elijah Muhammad wasn't all it was cracked up to be. So I'm really amazed when people get offended by the mere mention of Malcolm X. I mean, here's a guy who admitted his mistakes to the world! He understood racial segregation wasn't the key and tried to make amends with the community. He realized the teachings that he was delivering were wrong, and he owned up to it, unlike anybody else in that arena. I think a lot of people don't have the courage and the integrity to do that. I mean, we saw what happened with Nixon and Watergate, and with Clinton and all his scandals. I'm a Clinton supporter, so it's not like I'm trying to bash him, but none of those cats ever sat down and really tried to make amends for any of that stuff. But Malcolm did. So for me, my level of respect for Malcolm at that point goes sky high. That's what life is supposed to be about. Those are the principles and values that we're taught as kids but forget as grownups. So it was really inspiring to see a person who maintained those kind of values throughout his life.

Notes

1. Roger Ebert, *Roger Ebert's Video Companion 1994 Edition* (Kansas City, Mo.: Andrews & McNeel, 1994), 806.
2. Elvis Mitchell, "Playboy Interview," *Playboy* 38, no. 7 (July 1991): 68.
3. Ebert, *Roger Ebert's Video Companion 1994 Edition*, 794.
4. Spike Lee and Ralph Wiley, *By Any Means Necessary* (New York: Hyperion, 1992), 3.
5. Lee and Wiley, *By Any Means Necessary*, 6.

CHAPTER ELEVEN

BY ANY MEANS NECESSARY: THE MAKING OF *MALCOLM X*

I thought it was really important that the film was made because so many kids focus on a very small portion of Malcolm's life—the militant part.

Terence Blanchard

In 1990, twenty-five years after he was murdered at a podium in Harlem, Malcolm X's legacy galvanized many to realize their highest potential. Still, for most Americans, he was remembered as a symbol of violence and white hate. Others didn't remember him at all.

Hollywood studios, of course, were not in the habit of making big-budget movies about black leaders who were either feared or forgotten. But film producer Marvin Worth remained undaunted. Since acquiring the movie rights to *The Autobiography of Malcolm X* in 1967, Worth made several attempts to produce the picture. More than a marketing issue, adapting the sprawling and sincere autobiography into a screenplay was a demanding assignment. Such accomplished writers as James Baldwin, David Bradley, Calder Willingham, and David Mamet had each authored scripts that did not satisfy expectations. Even award-winning directors like Sidney Lumet and Bob Fosse failed to create a vision for the material.

Then in the summer of 1989, following a two-decade search, Worth thought he found his man. After seeing *Do the Right Thing*, the producer sent a letter to Spike Lee offering him the director's chair. Somehow, Lee never received the letter, and since he heard no reply, Worth figured he was not interested.

Finally, in early 1990, it was announced that Denzel Washington had signed on to portray Malcolm X, and Norman Jewison would direct playwright Charles Fuller's screenplay. Jewison and Fuller had successfully collaborated in the past on 1984's *A Soldier's Story*. Adapted from Fuller's

Pulitzer Prize–winning play, Jewison's film won rave reviews for its vivid depiction of racism at a Louisiana Army base during World War II. Coincidentally, in a small but pivotal role, the film featured an up-and-coming young actor named Denzel Washington.

Jewison, a white filmmaker from Canada who was also at the helm of the famous and groundbreaking *In the Heat of the Night* with Sidney Poitier, showed he was capable of directing African American subject matter with both sensitivity and discernment. However, when the news of Jewison's involvement reached Spike Lee, he publicly vented his disapproval. "I have a big problem with Norman Jewison directing *The Autobiography of Malcolm X*," he told the *New York Times*. "That disturbs me deeply. Blacks have to control these films. Malcolm X is one of our most treasured heroes. To let a non-African-American do it is a travesty."[1]

Lee, who has a tendency for creating enemies by saying exactly what he thinks, shook up the industry with this outburst. Although some, like esteemed playwright August Wilson, stood in his corner, others, including Sidney Lumet and David Bradley, the black novelist who was once involved in the project, took Lee to task: "[This] is the story of a man who learns to transcend race. It's a stupid notion that there's a black aesthetic, a black experience. Malcolm was never a Christian—does that mean you have to have a black Muslim director?" Added Lumet: "Where do you stop? Only an Irishman can direct Eugene O'Neill?"[2]

"With some films, not every film," retorted Lee, "the director needs to come from the background. Francis Ford Coppola, being Italian-American, enhanced the *Godfather* movies. Martin Scorsese, being Italian-American, enhanced *Mean Streets*, *Raging Bull*, and *GoodFellas*. And me, being African-American . . . well . . . ."[3]

In the end, Jewison announced that he and Fuller were not able to come up with an effective script, and they bowed out. Jewison explained that Malcolm was an enigma to him but encouraged Lee to follow through because it was important the film was made. Spike Lee couldn't have agreed more.

"I can't think of anyone more qualified or more prepared to do this movie than Spike Lee," said Denzel Washington, who would remain to portray Malcolm. "He lived that man's life over again. He retraced his steps. He loved—*loves*—that man. And, you know, it could be argued that he *is* that man, in his own way."[4]

When America's movie-conscious public caught wind of the upcoming motion picture, Malcolm X's fading and distorted legacy got an unexpected marketing boost. Dozens of companies took to producing and selling products that bared his name or image.

Millions of inner-city kids who knew nothing of Malcolm's message started to sport T-shirts, jackets, and embroidered "X" caps. While it created something of a rediscovery of Malcolm, many black leaders were repulsed by its superficiality. "People running around with X hats on who don't know anything about Malcolm, who embrace him as a figure of rage, [have] emptied him of his complexity,"[5] said Harvard professor Henry Louis Gates Jr. Spike Lee echoed Gates's criticism but saw the hype from his film as a potential springboard for kids to do more research and learn what Malcolm X actually represented.

As early as the fall of 1990, during the postproduction of *Jungle Fever*, Lee began his own research as he reworked the *Malcolm X* screenplay. While he liked David Mamet's, he decided to work from a James Baldwin version cowritten by Arnold Perl in 1969. The legendary Baldwin, who had the benefit of Malcolm's friendship, was first commissioned by Marvin Worth to adapt the book but experienced difficulties dramatizing Malcolm's assassination and his split from Elijah Muhammad. This, coupled with his alleged alcoholism, forced Worth to hire another writer named Arnold Perl to complete the project.

Spike would revise the Baldwin–Perl version with new information from interviews he conducted and finish with a 190-page script—well, beyond the 110-page Hollywood standard. The screenplay spanned over thirty years, called for thousands of extras, and included several locations from Nebraska to South Africa, all translating to three and a half hours of screen time. From the very beginning, Lee only envisioned a sweeping historical epic, one that would fully and earnestly tribute his hero.

Now he had to convince Warner Brothers, the studio that would produce the picture, to finance such a vision. Lee and his longtime coproducers Monty Ross and Jon Kilik submitted a $38 million production budget only to have it rejected. Spike would admit that his initial proposal had a small cushion, but he knew the film could not be made for less than $33 million. Warner Brothers made a final counteroffer of $18 million, which offended Lee and his partners. They vehemently argued that the importance of *Malcolm X* was comparable to that of *JFK* (the Oliver Stone epic the same studio just put into production with a much larger budget). Warner dismissed the comparison and would not relent on their Scrooge-like negotiating tactics.

Lee managed to pick up $8 million more by selling the foreign distribution rights to Largo Entertainment, and he began shooting that September hoping Warner Brothers would eventually make up the shortfall. Consistent with their game plan, the studio refused, and when the project went over budget in November, the bond company that insured the film's completion took control of production.

> **Spike Lee:** We never had the money to shoot the film we wanted to do from the beginning. And that is what made it tense. But this was *always* a $33 million film, and when I make a $33 million film, it's actually a $50 million film, because you *know* we have to know how to cut corners and do all kinds of stuff on the cheap or the quick without compromising the work. Black people have to do this all the time, making do with what you have. You always have to stretch everything double. Everything! What kills me is, all it's going to do is make money for Warner Brothers in the end. You got to spend money to make money.[6]

Meanwhile, the Completion Bond Company (CBC) was in a state of panic. Liable for all costs that exceed the studio budget until the film is in theaters, they were desperately trying to keep their loss to a minimum and began advising thriftier shooting locations to cut down on the escalating budget. Instead of going to Egypt to shoot Malcolm's pilgrimage in the Holy City of Mecca, they thought the Arizona desert and the New Jersey shore would suffice, which only infuriated the director: "Now, how are you going to shoot fucking Cairo or the Sahara desert and Mecca in fucking January at the fucking New Jersey shore? How can you have 160 minutes of Malcolm saying white people are blue-eyed devils and then not spend the time or money to shoot the pivotal moments that caused him to turn around on that line of thinking, which occurred in Africa and in Saudi Arabia?"[7]

Ironically, when the CBC ultimately relented on this matter, it contributed to filmmaking history. Shooting in Mecca was a monumental feat, as the *Malcolm X* crew became the first ever allowed inside the holy city during the *hajj*. But Lee had no intention of stopping there. He wanted to carry the momentum into South Africa to shoot the ending with Nelson Mandela. "Since Malcolm always talked about Pan-Africanism, I wanted to end the film in Africa, to make the connection between Soweto and Harlem."[8]

Already troubled about financing location costs in Egypt, the CBC balked at paying the crew's travel expenses to South Africa and ordered them to "come home!"—a demand to which Spike Lee quipped: "Kiss my ass. We're going anyway."[9]

Lee had now reached a point, not unlike Francis Coppola on *Apocalypse Now*, where he was overcome by his passion for the project and was spending money he did not have.

SPIKE LEE: When we flew back to the United States [in February 1992], the bond company immediately wanted a rough cut of the film in five weeks, which is a crazy, stupid request. And they were appealing to Warner Brothers and Largo to help defray this overage. Usually when a film goes over budget, the studio will kick in, but Warner said you're stuck. So in actuality we were stuck in a war between the bond company and Warner Bros. The bond company said, "If we don't see a rough cut in five weeks, then we're going to cut; off funding." Five weeks came and we were not ready to show them a rough cut; we were not going to rush this film. So therefore, they sent a telegram to all the editing staff that their services are no longer needed until further notice. They fired our editing staff and tried to shut us down.[10]

At this desperate point, Spike tossed $2 million of his own back into the film and entertained ideas of attracting outside investors. However, he realized there was no incentive for them because Warner had the profit lines drawn and had no intention of relenting to ensure the completed quality of the picture. Quality notwithstanding, the completion itself was in serious jeopardy. With nowhere to turn, Spike did the one thing that made sense: he put Malcolm's dictum "By any means necessary" into action. He secretly contacted a few fellow industry heavyweights to put the TKO on the CBC and Warner Brothers.

SPIKE LEE: I called up Bill Cosby. I told him that we really needed some help, and he asked me, "How much do you need?" Now, I didn't want to be greedy, so I gave him a little figure—my mistake—but regardless, he said, "Spike, tomorrow the check will be there." Tomorrow came and there was a check from Bill Cosby, Federal Express. So I said to myself, "Maybe we have something here." I called up Oprah Winfrey and said, "In my days of ignorance, I might have said some ignorant statements about you wearing blue contact lenses, but now I'm much wiser; before I was blind but now I can see! So she said, "What do you want, Spike?" And I told her the deal and oh, by the way, Bill Cosby sent me a check yesterday. So she sent me a check. So then I called up Magic Johnson: "Bill and Oprah kicked in." Magic said, "All right, fine," and sent his check. Then I called up my main man Michael Jordan. I said, "Mike, you got the money and plus, you can't let Magic outdo you." So Michael sent a check. Then it was Prince, Tracy Chapman, Janet Jackson, and all these people gave me money so we could finish *Malcolm X* the way we wanted to. These were not loans; they were not investments in the film; they just gave out of the hearts so we could finish the film the way we wanted. Their only request was that I not divulge how much money they gave.

> It took two months before we started to need funding again, which, by coincidence, happened [on May 19, the sixty-seventh anniversary of Malcolm's birth]. We held a press conference that day on how we were able to survive over the last two months. This made national news, and I guess Warner Brothers did not like the fact that I had to go to prominent black Americans to get the film finished—you know, they don't look so hot. So two days later, they started to send money. And this is how the film was made, and to me, this was one of the most important things about the film because here was a specific, concrete case where prominent African Americans in the entertainment and sports world came together, put aside their differences, and gave big checks out of love and respect so we could finish this film. And next time, who's to say that these people can't get together and finance a film and just forego Hollywood altogether.[11]

◆

At the heart and soul of *Malcolm X* is Denzel Washington's portrayal of the martyr. Two years prior, Spike's production team marveled at the method actor's transformation into a jazz musician—a mere introduction to Washington's remarkable acting talents.

In the late 1970s, Denzel studied journalism at Fordham University in the Bronx before gravitating toward acting. Upon graduation, he landed small roles in theater and television before winning the role of Malcolm X in a small, off-Broadway production called *When the Chickens Come Home to Roost*. At the time, in 1981, Denzel had little interest and even less knowledge of the man he would immerse himself into a decade later.

In Hollywood, Washington is known as a meticulous performer, a method actor who researches and prepares for each role by entering the world of his character before each shoot. For *Malcolm X*, Denzel left his family and home behind in Los Angeles for New York, the city Malcolm made his home for several years up until his assassination. There, Washington absorbed the setting, hired a Muslim tutor, and devoted up to twelve hours a day to study: reading speeches, reviewing videotape, and examining FBI reports. Additionally, he sought instruction from the Nation of Islam on the fiery delivery of Malcolm's speeches.

> **DENZEL WASHINGTON:** I didn't sit at home with a pedestal. We had a few guys come in from the Nation of Islam, and we had a training course. I would rehearse all day long, and at six [o'clock] I would start the classes with the Nation of Islam. We would march and recite and they would discipline us. Finally they made me get up and speak and that helped a lot. That sorta got me going, getting in front of people and not feeling afraid. And a lot of prayers.[12]

TERENCE BLANCHARD: I saw firsthand how talented and brilliant an actor Denzel is on *Mo' Better*. He really got into the role of Bleek but not like Malcolm X. Noooo. Denzel *became* Malcolm.

A couple of friends and I have talked about how when we play sometimes that we have to put our egos aside and let the Creator enter. That is true creativity, when you are nothing but a vessel. You've got to let it speak through you. Sometimes when I play, I feel it's not me; somehow, and invariably, those are my best performances. Denzel once told me he felt the same way when he was portraying Steven Biko in *Cry Freedom* during the courtroom scene. He said it wasn't him anymore. And when they said cut, nobody called him Denzel for awhile. They just looked at him. Somebody called him Steve.[13]

For *Malcolm X*, you could see that he was all over him, and it was absorbing for me to watch. Actually, it was kind of eerie sometimes. I had a conversation with him over the phone just after we finished *Mo' Better Blues*, and man, he was talking about Malcolm X, how he was getting into the role, and then he started talking like him, "Revolution is bloody . . . ." He went into this whole Malcolm X speech, and a chill went up my spine. He was ready to go! I would imagine that he probably grew up with Malcolm being ingrained in his thoughts for a long period of time.

DENZEL WASHINGTON: Believe it or not, I was in my twenties before I'd heard of Malcolm X. But I had done a play about the man ten years [before the movie]. When I took that job, it was strictly $125 a week, and I needed the money. And one guy's name was Malcolm, and the other's Elijah—bet. Let's get busy. Which one am I?[14]

SPIKE LEE: I think that that's typical with a lot of African-Americans. Denzel was raised in the Church, his father was a Pentecostal Minister. But a year before we began to shoot this film, Denzel said to his agent, I don't want to do anymore work, or accept any scripts. He began to prepare for this film in the same way you might say a fighter prepares for a heavyweight championship fight. Denzel dedicated himself totally toward the film. He changed his diet. He completely cut out alcohol, cut down very low on red meat, cut swine completely out. (There's no way you can play Malcolm X and eat pork chops and barbecued pork grinds.) He started to read the Qur'an, he started to fast, he did all these things in preparation for the part. Denzel knew he could not be Malcolm X. He knew he could not impersonate Malcolm X. At best, all he could do is capture the essence of the man. And the only way he could accomplish this, he had to be in the correct place spiritually. Possibly then, the same God that passed through Malcolm would pass through Denzel. And I was a witness to that. It was *scary*. Many times watching Denzel throughout this role, he actually *became* Malcolm X. And although you may think I'm talking this hocus-pocus voodoo stuff, I'm on the up-and-up. When he did those speech scenes, and once we came to the end of the take,

> I would keep the cameras rolling, and until he heard cut, he kept on going. He would go on for five minutes after the actual scripted speech ran out. And everything that came out of his mouth was Malcolm. I would say, "Cut," and he would stagger over to me and say, "I have no idea what I just said for the last five minutes." And that's how much he was a part of that man.[15]

> **Denzel Washington:** This is the first film where I did not want to stop shooting. Especially the speeches. Once I got used to it, I just kept going and going. The hardest scene for me to shoot was probably the assassination. There was a dark feeling on the set and I felt shackled in it. Throughout the film I lived Malcolm's life whether the cameras were on or off. The guys that were my bodyguards in the film went with me everywhere in the course of the day. Now here was the one scene where I wasn't in control, and I felt like I had abandoned my friends, especially the guys who had to shoot me. The first take that we did, we had to stop and some people were crying and upset. It was an emotional couple of days.[16]

◆

In the filmmaking process, there are three major phases: preproduction (scouting for shooting locations, rehearsals, etc.), principal photography (the actual filming of the movie), and postproduction. During the last step, the raw material is molded and sculpted into the final product. Picture editing, sound mixing, and music are integral parts of that process. Spike Lee commissioned Terence Blanchard to place his musical voice on *Malcolm X*.

> **Terence Blanchard:** When we were doing the score for *Jungle Fever*, we all knew *Malcolm X* was next for Spike—he was already signed on. So I was working really hard to get the job to do *Malcolm X*. At that point I really wasn't sure if Spike had any confidence in me as a film composer because I was a real novice at it.

> **Alex Steyermark:** Spike is generally a very loyal guy, and when a director finds a composer they can work with, you'll find that they'll continue to work with that same composer. The music is like the last emotional imprint that's put on the film, and since most directors can't write music, they have to rely on the right person to make that last statement for them, which is a really critical thing. And I think that if Spike's going to have someone write a score for him, he just sees Terence as that person.

> **Terence Blanchard:** I knew Spike was loyal to his crew, but I don't like to count my chickens before they hatch. You set yourself up for disappointment that way. But I wanted *Malcolm X* real bad. I wanted to be a part of this, man—not just to see my name up there on the screen, but to be a part of something that I felt was a monumental project, something that would go down in history as a great film.

Roger Dickerson: One of the most exciting moments for Terence was when Spike contacted him to score *Malcolm X*. I remember he stopped by my classroom while I was teaching. He tapped on the glass, so I told him to come in. It was great for me because here he was coming back years later and touching base with someone who had been a center in his life.

Afterward, we went into my office and he told me Spike asked him to do the movie. He asked me for some advice, but mostly, he was just very enthusiastic about tackling the project.

Terence Blanchard: For me, *Malcolm X* was an intense project. So when Spike called and gave me a shooting script, I started working immediately. Ideas just started popping into my head. Let me put it to you this way: a lot of people say my writing is very dark in the first place, and when I think of Malcolm X, I think of a solitary person in search of a truth all alone. So I was constantly hearing singular instruments portraying that kind of emotion.

This film could've been overwhelming to me for any number of reasons [because] the character himself, Malcolm, is overwhelming. But I am one who has always trusted my instincts.

When it came to writing the theme for Malcolm, I went back to all the fears, frustrations, and anger that I felt as a kid and combined that with what I felt when I read the autobiography. And from that, I was able to create the musical identity for Malcolm.

That was one of the hardest parts because I had to see the film before I could commit to an idea. So I kept pressing Spike, saying I had to have a copy of the film. I had gone to the very first screening that he had, but I needed a tape. I'd also seen the dailies, but that isn't the same. But Spike didn't want to give me a tape at all. He said, "Can't you just write from the script?" But I didn't want to do that, especially the theme, because I needed a vision of what was going up on the screen. See, Spike was having problems with the studio and the bond company and was worried about losing control of the film to them. So he didn't want any tapes out there at all, even with his friends and coworkers. He played it close. But what I would really have liked to have done was to be able to sit down alone and watch the entire film over and over again, so that the film could speak to me. [I like to] get a feel for the flow of dialogue and where the empty spaces are because all that has to be incorporated into the music because dialogue is musical. When you see great Shakespearean actors orate, that is very musical. I saw Denzel in [Central Park] as Richard III, and I called him later and talked to him for like three hours because it just blew my mind. I'd read Shakespeare before, but it can be hard to read. But to hear it read right—you have to have someone who really knows how to draw on the potency and the rhythm of those lines. Film is the same way. And music is the exact same way.[17]

Alex Steyermark: It was a major moment when we were doing the score for *Malcolm X* because it was such a *big* score. There were like seventy musicians in the orchestra, and Terence conducted and had [his saxophonist] Sam Newsome as the copyist. But it was a massive amount of work because the orchestra was so big and there were a lot of parts for Sam to write out. He was doing everything he could to just keep up.

The first day of the session, a journalist and TV crew came to the studio to do a piece on the recording of the *Malcolm X* score. So we were all sitting there, but there was no music on the stands—Sam overslept. At this point, Spike was pouring his own money into the film, and we're sitting there for an hour and a half with seventy union musicians who are getting paid [regardless]. And Spike is just like boiling over in a way I had never seen. Suddenly, he picked up a chair and said, "Where's the music?! This is my fuckin' money! My motherfuckin' film!" and throws the chair across the control room. The casters go flying and almost take out this journalist's kneecap. We didn't let him forget that, and we used to tease him that we were going to start using Nerf chairs.

But that was such an intense, anxiety-ridden time for Spike. We got a new copyist, but Sam did continue to play on the session. For the most part, though, everyone who worked on *Malcolm X* was so focused. It was just one of those films that when you were working on it, you just felt like you were doing something *really* special. I mean, I worked on that film for over a year. It was a major endeavor, and Terence's score is phenomenal.

Joe Henderson: The writing and orchestrating of the score were very impressive to me. As a composer, Terence created another spark to the film that's like another character. His music tied scenes together [and captured a real sense of emotion]. I recall a particular scene when a crowd of people were standing across from the police station and Denzel as Malcolm led a march toward the hospital and you hear this drum . . . the way it was put together was just creative imagination. Terence's ability to capture the mood of that particular moment with music was incredible. And, of course, I didn't know Terence in that way. I just knew him, like most of us did, as a jazz musician. So I really stood back and took note. I really admire that diversification in Terence.

Terence Blanchard: To me, all the time and effort that went into the making of this score will have been for naught if the viewer and listener don't come away with an emotional attachment to Malcolm X and his struggles. I feel that we captured a certain kind of solitary side of Malcolm throughout the score. I've gotten comments from people who heard the score before seeing the film and really got a sense of what the film was going to be like before they had seen it. And that makes me feel good because that's what I was trying to capture in writing the score.

Spike Lee: I put the same emphasis on the music in my films that I do for the cinematography, production design, costumes, casting, et cetera. Terence himself, his voice and his music have enhanced this film tremendously! I've seen it with and without his music, and the difference is significant. Terence has successfully captured the four decades we span in the film. With his score we hear the joy, sorrow and the celebration of the African American experience, which is really also the story of Malcolm's life.[18]

◆

At last, the financial bickering and artistic disputes were put to rest, and the Thanksgiving release of *Malcolm X* charged closer. The hype was mounting, the world was waiting, and "it was clear," declared Roger Ebert, "after all the years of publicity and months of controversy, that *Malcolm X* had better be a good movie or Spike Lee would go down with it. He had talked the talk, and now it was time to walk the walk."[19]

Indeed, Ebert's observation was true, but it seemed inconceivable that Lee would permit a single film, albeit his most ambitious, to destroy a career he had worked so hard to achieve. Putting himself on the line for *Malcolm X* was more than just an admission of reverence for the subject; it was a remarkable display of self-confidence. By championing the resistance from Warner Brothers, the CBC, and the media, Spike benefited from a huge growth experience.

Alex Steyermark: *Malcolm X* was the film where Spike really grew up as a filmmaker. He was under a lot of pressure not only from the studio but from the black community, and, you know, he changed. It was like he really went through the fire and came out on the other side. That was a major, major endeavor.

Spike Lee: All human beings are periodically tested by the power of the universe. Whether you're an athlete, entertainer, businessperson, et cetera, how one performs under extreme pressure is the true measure of one's spirit, heart, and desire. Sometimes, I think that may be more important than talent.[20]

Everyone got in some swings. But you know what? This is the only way the film could have been made. We had to fight tooth and nail, fight like hell to get what we wanted on the screen.

When you do something this big and you have so many obstacles, either it can kill you or it makes you stronger. And after going through the fire with this one, I feel I can do anything. [*Malcolm X*] was the hardest thing I've ever had to do in my life, and Denzel and the other filmmakers and the cast knew that we had to make a great film.[21]

◆

On November 20, 1992, *Malcolm X* was released to sell-out crowds around the nation. Over three hundred thousand people attended the film's opening day. And after a lengthy theatrical run, it collected over $50 million in box office receipts, a heap of critical acclaim, and numerous awards.

In fully realizing the extraordinary course of an American life into a movie (the literature of this generation), Lee has made an important contribution to history. *Malcolm X* will forever introduce people to the great leader as well as dispel many misconceptions about him. His film reveals a sincere man who, with self-education, uplifted himself from a life of crime onto an uncharted journey to seek and expose the truth about human injustice. He had been misled by his emotions and by those he trusted until he found redemption in embracing the ideals of interracial brotherhood. It is a story that transcends color to provide inspiration for all peoples who seek the courage to change their lives because it renders the wisdom that circumstance does not have to determine outcome.

Notes

1. James Earl Hardy, *Spike Lee* (New York: Chelsea House, 1996), 14.
2. Hardy, *Spike Lee,* 14.
3. Roger Ebert, *Roger Ebert's Video Companion 1994 Edition* (Kansas City, Mo.: Andrews & McNeel, 1994), 794.
4. Spike Lee and Ralph Wiley, *By Any Means Necessary* (New York: Hyperion, 1992), 114.
5. Harry F. Waters and Vern E. Smith, "Malcolm X," *Newsweek* (November 16, 1992): 70.
6. Lee and Wiley, *By Any Means Necessary*, 32.
7. Lee and Wiley, *By Any Means Necessary*, 102.
8. Harry F. Waters and Vern E. Smith, "Spike's Mo' Better Moviemaking Blues," *Newsweek* (November 16, 1992): 71.
9. Waters and Smith, "Spike's Mo' Better Moviemaking Blues," 71.
10. Spike Lee, "Speaking Engagement at the University of Toronto," March 1, 1993.
11. Lee, "Speaking Engagement at the University of Toronto."
12. Ebert, *Roger Ebert's Video Companion 1994 Edition*, 805.
13. Lee and Wiley, *By Any Means Necessary*, 150.
14. Joe Wood, "Denzel Washington," *Rolling Stone* (November 26, 1992): 40.
15. Lee, "Speaking Engagement at the University of Toronto."

16. Ebert, *Roger Ebert's Video Companion 1994 Edition*, 806.
17. Lee and Wiley, *By Any Means Necessary*, 146–47.
18. Spike Lee, *Malcolm X Score*, liner notes.
19. Ebert, *Roger Ebert's Video Companion 1994 Edition*, 793.
20. Lee and Wiley, *By Any Means Necessary*, xiii.
21. Hardy, *Spike Lee*, 103.

CHAPTER TWELVE

ABSOLUT-LEE SPIKE

> Spike Lee has done things as a director that nobody else has even thought about.
>
> —*Terence Blanchard*

For Spike Lee, and for black cinema itself, *Malcolm X* is a triumph. By successfully challenging the status quo and becoming the first black director ever to film a big-budget epic about African Americans, Lee took another giant step in overthrowing the color barrier in Hollywood.

Today, Spike continues to produce quality films on a range of African American subject matter. He has demonstrated, through a body of work, the diversification of his race, destroying the stereotype that African Americans are a monolithic group. And his success has blazed a trail for many other black filmmakers to surface in Hollywood and tell their own stories. Unfortunately, his barrier-breaking efforts have also cast a burden of representing all African Americans with every image he films.

"It's a responsibility," says Terence, "that no other director has to deal with. Black people expect him to be the end-all, which is impossible. I mean, he made movies like *School Daze* and *Crooklyn*, which are obviously based on his own experiences growing up, but a lot of people had many bad things to say about them."

Some African Americans have charged the filmmaker with furthering stereotypes and endorsing myths about their culture. Nola Darling, the title character in *She's Gotta Have It*, was cited as an example of Lee supporting the cliché that black women are promiscuous.

Television's Bryant Gumbel condemned *School Daze*, Spike's second film that lampooned the racism blacks have for one another based on the complexion of their skin. Gumbel chastised Lee to his face on the *Today*

Show for airing the black community's "dirty laundry" in public. African American women also expressed their disdain for *School Daze* and its creator, claiming the female characters were weak and pushed into the background of their men.

Prominent writers and social critics Stanley Crouch and Amiri Baraka have each engaged Lee in well-publicized verbal slugfests. Crouch ignited a stir when he used the word *fascism* to characterize *Do the Right Thing*, while Baraka staged a rally to protest Spike's involvement with *Malcolm X*. There, he termed Lee "petit bourgeois" and suggested that he would sanitize and distort Malcolm's legacy "so middle-class Negroes could sleep easier."[1]

"What did James Baldwin say?" Lee asks rhetorically. "He said, 'When white people criticize me unjustly, it makes me stronger. When black people do, it makes me want to cry.' What really hurt me is that you never heard one peep out of Baraka when Norman Jewison was going to direct this film."

Spike has also been bothered by the white journalists who have depicted him as an angry racist. Most infamously was a 1992 *Esquire* cover story entitled "Spike Lee Hates Your Cracker Ass." Two years earlier, Jewish American critics branded him an "anti-Semite" for his portrayal of club owners in *Mo' Better Blues*. And before that, critics from *Time* and *Newsweek* steered potential viewers away from *Do the Right Thing* with irresponsible predictions. "A lot of white moviegoers were scared to see it because they read it was going to cause riots. The media just plays on white hysteria. Every day white people say to me, '*Do the Right Thing* was one of my favorite movies.' But 75 percent of them never saw it in the theater."[2]

> **TERENCE BLANCHARD:** Some people may not agree, but Spike is a great filmmaker. A lot of journalists, white and black, may have a lot of bad things to say about him, which is fine because they're entitled to their opinion. But it doesn't matter because the bottom line is that Spike Lee has done things as a director that nobody else has even thought about. And, in the end, his work will speak for itself.
>
> **ALEX STEYERMARK:** I think Spike Lee is one of the great American filmmakers. He's truly original, he takes big chances, and he's really prolific. And I think the fact that he is so prolific puts him in a certain category of filmmakers where no film is flawless. But since he already has another film going, he's going to solve that problem on the next project, and he just keeps going like that. I think he's probably even among the great international filmmakers. He's a real universal filmmaker, and I think his popularity around the world attests to that. His work should not be limited to this idea that he's an African American filmmaker.

Terence Blanchard: White or black, Spike is one of the best filmmakers today. But I think it's unfortunate that he's considered a "black director." I mean, even though Woody Allen, more or less, deals with the same type of movie (upper-middle-class, neurotic, intellectual white people in Manhattan), he's not considered a "white director." He doesn't have that race classification. But that's just how this country is, and it's a shame.

◆

In February of each year, the nominations for the Academy Awards are announced in Hollywood. Since 1927, Oscars have boosted careers and certified films as classics. When *Malcolm X* opened to exceptional critical acclaim, delivering on its hype with brilliant performances, sweeping cinematography, emotional music, and a knowing direction, Lee's epic was expected to garner several nominations. Instead, it was accredited in only two categories.

Terence Blanchard: On *Malcolm X*, everybody gave 110 percent. There was a real special vibe working on that project; everybody was excited and they all wanted to do their best. And the finished result reflects that attitude. Sure, it's a shame it didn't get a lot of the nominations it deserved. [Actor] Delroy Lindo was ignored, as was Al Freeman for his portrayal of Elijah Muhammad. [Production designer] Wynn Thomas and [cinematographer] Ernest Dickerson should have been nominated, but when you see how Hollywood works, you begin to understand why. Spike and I have talked about this, but he still gets upset that I don't get nominated.

Spike Lee: We were glad that Denzel got his nomination, and we were elated that Ruth Carter, an African American woman, got nominated for costume design. But of all the things we felt that we should have shown in, we only got two.

It frustrates me that Terence doesn't get the recognition he deserves. For some reason, people don't want to acknowledge the great music that he's written. I read these film composer magazines, you see the nominations, and it's always the usual suspects: John Williams, James Horner, Jerry Goldsmith.

Racism permeates the whole fabric and structure of America, so why should the entertainment industry be unscarred by that? We could go to the Hollywood studios and go right down the line and see how many black executives there are, number one. Number two, we could see how many black executives there are who can green light a picture. Well, if you did that, and then asked them point-blank, is it racism? They will say no, it's not because of racism, it's really because Hollywood is built on a network, an old boy's system.

Terence Blanchard: An argument could be made that *Malcolm X* was ignored because it's a so-called black film. *Malcolm X* is not a black film; it's an American film about American history. Unfortunately, a lot of people don't agree; they don't feel it's a part of their history even though it is. I mean, why is it that people classify John F. Kennedy's story as *my* history? Because it is; American history is *my* history.

But I think it all comes down to one basic fact: you're either a part of Hollywood or you're not. Spike Lee is not. He's not a part of that club, so [all the snubbing] doesn't really surprise me. It's just the way it is.

So I don't think it has so much to do with race or, for that matter, your intelligence, artistry, or qualifications. It's just a tight-knit community, one with a social rapport that doesn't really welcome outsiders. It's all about whether or not they know you and feel comfortable working with you—that's how you get hired.

Spike Lee: It's like a fraternal order—you know, a clique. And if you're not accepted, then, you know, just forget about it. There's a community in Hollywood, and I'm not really part of it. I don't live there; I live in New York. I don't hobnob; I don't go to the parties and other stuff. And really, I came from the world of independent filmmaking, so I'm navigating the high wire where I have one foot in Hollywood and the other foot in independent filmmaking. So the only reason I come [to Hollywood] is to get my financing. "Give me the money and put the film in the theaters."

◆

After the grueling production of *Malcolm X*, Spike Lee made an announcement: after six movies in seven years, he needed a vacation. Meanwhile, with Terence's star on the rise, the phones at Burgess Management were ringing off the hook. Despite Oscar's omission, Hollywood wanted to know more about this new composer.

Robin Burgess: I remember between *Mo' Better Blues* and *Jungle Fever*, I had called some of the top film agents in Hollywood [to get Terence representation], and they wouldn't even return my calls. Then *Malcolm X* comes along and they were calling *me*. And I was like uh-huh! Now, whose phone calls should I return?

Jungle Fever was really great, but the only thing with that was Stevie Wonder also did music for it. And you would have a lot of folks saying, "*Jungle Fever*? Oh, yeah, Stevie Wonder wrote that score." And Terence was like, "Ah, man." But if there was anyone to be in great company with, it was definitely Stevie Wonder. Actually, a couple of years later, Stevie asked Terence to perform on his album *Conversation Peace*.

But then with *Malcolm X*, because it had so much hype and hysteria and controversy behind it, Terence got five film offers and all kinds of demo requests outside of Spike all in a matter of months. Terence did a great demo for *Get Shorty* and had a wonderful conversation with [director] Barry Sonnenfeld, but he had already hired John Lurie. Barry said, "If I had gotten your demo before I had hired him, it would have been a totally different thing."

◆

The five films that Terence was commissioned to score included a true story based on the life of Johnson Whittaker called *Assault at West Point.*

During the late nineteenth century, Whittaker became the first-ever African American cadet to attend the United States Military Academy in West Point, New York. Just mere months before his scheduled graduation, Whittaker, while he slept, was brutally attacked by fellow cadets. With his ears slashed, body bound and beaten, Whittaker was discovered in a pool of his own blood the next morning. This was a racially motivated assault that led to his *dishonorable* discharge from the military and a year-long sentence of hard labor in a military prison. The court falsely claimed that Whittaker inflicted the monstrous beating upon himself in an attempt to discredit the institution.

Assault at West Point was adapted from the John Marszalek book and directed by Harry Moses. The film concentrated mainly on the efforts of two lawyers (played by Samuel L. Jackson and Sam Waterston) appealing the case in a military court. Despite presenting their case with compelling evidence on the implausibility of Whittaker's so-called scheme, the court upheld its original ruling and sent him to military prison.

Terence's score is a thoughtful and somber one that evokes a great deal of emotional attachment to Whittaker's fight for justice. Needless to say, Terence was proud to contribute to such a noble project. *Assault at West Point* debuted on Showtime, a U.S. cable network, in February 1994.

Upon completing the *Assault* score, Terence buried himself in his home studio to create the music for *Sugar Hill*, Leon Ichaso's urban drama starring Wesley Snipes; *Trial by Jury*, the Heywood Gould thriller featuring William Hurt; Matty Rich's comedy *The Inkwell;* and an epic documentary for the Discovery Channel entitled *The Promised Land.* The latter, an acclaimed three-part series about the great migration of African Americans from the impoverished South to the North, was narrated by actor Morgan Freeman and garnered Terence an Emmy nomination for Best Original Score for a Documentary in 1995.

Carl Allen: I marvel at the fact that Terence has been able to do quite well for himself in film scoring and to see that he's been able to develop that from literally nothing is quite exciting. And not only with Spike's films, but in a number of other movies as well. And that's great because he won't get pigeon-holed into a certain thing.

TERENCE BLANCHARD: Oh, that's very important to me because although me and Spike have worked together several times, I've never felt like an employee. We're friends, and he's always just hired me to do a service. So I hate the whole notion that just because we work together we think the same. People do that all the time, and that's a very prejudiced thing.

You know, it's crazy, but I've lost a bunch of films because I work with him. The number of them is outrageous. After *Malcolm X*, a producer offered me a job, but then the director said he didn't want anyone working on his film that works with Spike Lee. So Hollywood hasn't really embraced me because they don't like Spike. But because I work with him, more people definitely know who I am. I guess it's kind of like a catch-22.

SPIKE LEE: I think it's kind of humorous that people have held it against Terence for scoring my films, but it's also very unfortunate. Frankly, it's just plain stupidity because filmmakers should want what's best for their film, and getting Terence to score their film is what's best. The fact that we have a relationship should have nothing to do with anything.

TERENCE BLANCHARD: There was this one producer who was very interested in hiring me for a major movie but then backed out. He told a friend of mine, who's also a film composer, "I love Terence's music but I hate Spike Lee." And I said, "OK, fine. What does that have to do with me?"

I don't know how someone can assume that anyone who works with Spike Lee is a puppet. Naturally, I take that as an insult. It's like saying that I'm going to come on their movie wearing Spike Lee paraphernalia telling everybody they should work like Spike. It's ridiculous!

Me and Spike probably don't agree on everything, but I respect his opinions and have always admired his ability to stand for something. I mean, this is a cat who sticks his neck out every time for something he believes in, and I think you have to admire that. Look, he made a movie about Malcolm X when no other black director even thought about doing it. He fought for the job, then had to fight for its completion. And now he's going through the same battle to make the Jackie Robinson story.

◆

In the summer of 1993, Spike Lee ended his brief respite and started preparing to film his next movie, *Crooklyn*. In an amusing coincidence, the film's release in May 1994 coincided with Matty Rich's *The Inkwell*. What's more, other than featuring Terence's original music, both films are semiautobiographical, coming-of-age tales about Afro-American youths during the 1970s. This time, however, there was no controversy between Lee and Rich at all. In fact, *Crooklyn*, Spike's seventh film, was his first that did not cause an uproar of conflict, debate, and other controversy among his critics. With the warm and sentimental family drama, Lee revealed another layer of his multidimensional artistry and delivered an interesting contrast to the sweeping *Malcolm X*.

SPIKE LEE: Denzel and I talked about this a lot; he said, "Spike, what role can I play? I just had the role of a lifetime. What can I do after Malcolm X?" It wasn't so extreme for me, but I just felt that I did not want to box myself into "Spike the filmmaker that only does films about racial issues in this country." [Those films] are very important, but I have many different interests. I want to do musicals, sports films, science fiction. But it was very important after *Malcolm X*, the biggest one, not to duplicate that right away.

I felt that after *Malcolm X* it was good to do something about a family, a strong African American family, where you have both the mother and the father running the household. The father's not on heroin, the mother's not walking the corner, the girl's not getting pregnant at six years old, and the sons aren't out mugging or shooting people; I just wanted to get back to that with this film.[3]

TERENCE BLANCHARD: *Malcolm X* was so dramatic that the music kind of wrote itself. *Crooklyn* is a lighter thing, so in a way, it was harder to score than *Malcolm X* because you can't be heavy-handed. The instruments have to have the right timbre to hit the different moods you want. It was definitely more of a challenge for me scoring this film because of its humorous elements. It's a nostalgic slice-of-life dramedy about a family growing up, a real nice family film.

SPIKE LEE: Crooklyn is what they call Brooklyn now. It's sort of like a nickname, a prey upon [its] reputation for being crime- and drug-ridden now. So the title of the film is really referring to how it is now in comparison to when I was growing up.

When I was growing up, I think that I really had a relatively happy childhood. The difference between then and now was that there was no such thing as crack. I mean, the worst thing that we were scared of were the glue sniffers. And, also, the only guns we had were pop guns and water guns. You know, any kid can get a gun nowadays. So that's the difference between the two eras.

The film takes place in the early 1970s and is told through the eyes of the young girl [played by] Zelda Harris. And it's sort of a coming-of-age picture. It was my sister Joie's original idea. She got together with my brother Cinque and they came to me with the script not knowing I wanted to do it, just, "Can you help us get this film made?" I read it and

I loved it and said I would like to work on the script also. So we got together and we shot it.

It's loosely autobiographical, but people, you know, want to make it seem like every single incident that happened in the film happened to us growing up. But there are a lot of similarities: the family growing up in Brooklyn, four brothers, one sister, with a jazz musician father and a mother [who's] a teacher. But no dog ever popped out of a convertible stiff and dead. That never happened.[4]

◆

Clockers is the baby of the eminent American writer Richard Price. After extensive research in a New Jersey housing project, Price wrote an authentic yet fictional account on the underworld of drug dealing and murder investigation in the inner city. Published in 1992, the harrowing, best-selling novel was embraced by critics around the country as a dazzling odyssey of cops, drugs, survival, and power. *People* magazine echoed what most of its readers felt: "Price displays a near perfect ear for street language. . . . He gets so deep under the skin of both the cops and the clockers that it's hard to believe he himself has never been either."

RICHARD PRICE: Well, there's no substitute for osmosis. Jimmy Breslin said about Damon Runyon: "He did what all good journalists do: he hung out."

I started out with the police in Jersey City, and then at some point I wanted to leave the police and start hanging with the reverse angle, the policed. So I started running with the drug dealers. But not just the bad guys; I was hanging out with the people in the projects—you know, the mother with four kids that was trying to get her children to the age of eighteen without stepping on a land mine. I hung out with legal aid lawyers, at methadone clinics, social workers, basically anybody who would have me.

I grew up in a housing project in the Bronx in a different time and place. It was the 1950s and the 1960s, so it's not like I'm coming from Scandinavia or something. But what surprised me most [in the research] was the give and take in the street between the police and the policed. It's a world where everybody goes to work on the same street: the cops, the dealers, the hustlers, the guys who have the craps games, the numbers runners. Everybody has to show up for work, and you're going to see each other everyday. Now, you're on the job twenty years and this guy's been hustling twenty years, you might as well say hello, you see him all the time. So when he buys a pack of cigarettes and you're in there [too], say hello. But if there's a warrant out on him, you'll grab him. But that might not be until next week. Meanwhile, we all have to get along. What has to happen, too, is that they need each other. What I realized is that the cops, in order to get the information they need to become effective cops, have to have sources. And the only way somebody's going to talk to you is if you do them a favor. Well, a guy's in a jam, he didn't show up in court when he was supposed to, and now there's a warrant out on him. You go tell this guy, "You didn't show up yesterday in court."

"Well, I was in jail yesterday on something else."

"Well, OK, I'll go down and tell them that. But you better show up tomorrow."

"Yeah, I won't forget that."

Two days later, there's a murder. This cop's out on the street trying to figure out who did it. There's that guy you just did a favor for and he's going, "OK, talk to me later."[5]

◆

Sensing potential for a box-office boom, Universal Studios purchased the film rights for Martin Scorsese and Robert De Niro, who, respectively, had directed and starred in several films from Price's pen, including *The Color of Money* and *Mad Dog & Glory*. But when the opportunity arose to actualize a film adaptation of Nicholas Pileggi's *Casino*, a real-life account of the Italian mafia in Las Vegas, they withdrew from the project. Scorsese did stay on as a producer and recommended fellow NYU alumnus Spike Lee to replace him in the director's chair.

In accepting the position, Spike was very adamant about ensuring *Clockers* would not exploit the inner city. "I didn't want to do a film that could be lumped into that Black hip-hop–shoot 'em up–gangster–drug movie. All these guys making films use the excuse 'It's real. That's the way it is on the streets.' Even if it's real, it's not news. Sometimes art should be about elevation, not just wallowing in the same shit."[6]

And so, Spike Lee's *Clockers* neglects gratuitous violence for a collection of poignant images that conjure up thought-provoking commentary. "I can't speak for other films," said an approving Richard Price, "but I've never seen violence used as a weapon against violence as it is in *Clockers*." Price went on to speak particularly about the opening sequence where an abrasive pictorial of young black murder victims exposes the reality of violence and sets a lucid tone for what lies ahead.

Spike Lee: In the research for the film, I spent a lot of time with the Crime Scene Unit here in New York City. They're the guys that show up at homicide scenes, and they take the pictures. And they have this album—they call it the "family album"—which has the most gruesome homicide photographs ever seen. So we re-created those for the opening credits sequence of the film. What we wanted to do was just to grab the audience's attention right from the beginning. You know, put down the popcorn and your watery Diet Coke that you're sipping through the straw and just pay attention to what's on the screen. What we tried to do in this film was have no heroes or villains. Most human beings, cops or clockers, are made up of good and bad parts, and I think that makes more interesting moviemaking when all the heroes don't have the white hats, and the villains wear the black hats.[7]

Richard Price: Everybody knows that by the time the drugs are on the street, the war is over. The only war is who gets the best spots. And most of the police that have been out there long enough know that if but for the grace of God, if I was living in this turmoil, and I had this kid's life, and I was nineteen years old and seen what this kid has seen, there's a good chance that I would succumb also. I mean, the main character of the book and the movie is this kid Strike, this nineteen-year-old crack dealer. And people would often ask me, "What do you want people to get out of the book or the movie?" And I'd say, "Well, it's not a public service announcement, but if there is something, before you demonize this individual, try to imagine yourself having been born in, say, the Jersey City Medical Center in 1971, living in this particular housing project under these circumstances, and now it's 1991, and you're twenty—what are you gonna do? Are you gonna be a novelist? I don't think so." You know, if you're lucky, there's always the baseball player that gets out, the basketball player, the actor; you know, the real heroes just make it to eighteen.[8]

Terence Blanchard: That was the component that I tried to implement in the score. I didn't want *Clockers* to be a gangster score. I didn't want to show the evil side of these guys. I wanted a little more majesty in these characters but with a slight edge. Plus, I knew the soundtrack music would take care of the hard stuff because I know how Spike is, that he would have all of that hip-hop stuff in there. So I knew that in my area of the film I could soften things up a bit. In showing a personal side of these guys, I wanted audiences to really relate to them as people and not as just these gangsters with no names; that's the main thing about the story. This guy, Strike, is really upset about what he's doing with his life and wants to make a change. So in order for that to be effective, people have to feel something for him.

◆

In the fall of 1995, *Clockers* attracted a charge of endorsement from America's leading film reviewers. Yet, like *Crooklyn*, the critical support did not spread to the box office. Both films had disappointing showings (the first two of Lee's career). In spite of this, Spike proceeded to make films that did not adhere to a mass *Jurassic Park*–type audience. By remaining true to his independent roots, he resisted the temptation of making the mundane Hollywood blockbuster.

Such integrity would have its pitfalls. For years, Spike had planned to film a biography of baseball legend and civil rights activist Jackie Robinson. In 1997, on the fiftieth anniversary of Robinson's remarkable feat of breaking the color barrier in baseball, Lee had high hopes of having such a film in theaters. Movie studios like Fox Searchlight and Miramax showed interest but eventually backed out. Spike's difficulties in raising money for the film can be attributed to his less than alluring box office responses to *Crooklyn*, *Clockers,* and his subsequent effort, *Girl 6*. Furthermore, in light of the controversial cost overruns on *Malcolm X*, Hollywood studios were not anxious to revive their relations with the filmmaker on an epic biography of an African American figure.

Instead of wallowing in self pity or harboring a grudge against the system, Spike Lee reinvented himself with two earnest joints, each chronicling separate eras in American history. This successive rendering produced inspirational, educational material and marked Lee's return to more personal filmmaking.

First was *Get on the Bus*, a fictional account of a diverse group of black men on their cross-country journey to the Million Man March. Then came *4 Little Girls*, a full-length documentary on the Birmingham church bombing that claimed the young lives of Addie Mae Collins, Denise McNair, Carol Robertson, and Cynthia Wesley.

Get on the Bus was distributed in theaters by Columbia Pictures on October 16, 1996, to commemorate the one-year anniversary of the march but was produced independently of the Hollywood system.

> **SPIKE LEE:** *Get on the Bus* is a low-budget film, but our aspirations weren't necessarily low-budget. In trying to keep true with the spirit of the march, which is about self-reliance and self-dependence, fifteen African American men financed this film, and it was later picked up by Columbia Pictures. Some of the men being Wesley Snipes, Will Smith, Johnnie Cochran, Danny Glover, and myself.[9]
>
> **WESLEY SNIPES:** I didn't get a chance to actually go [to the march], but I could sympathize with the interest and the concern that the brothers had with being there. So I wanted to do something, you know, that showed that I was down for the cause even though I couldn't be there. A lot of people who are not economically inclined believe that those of us who come into Hollywood lose touch; you know, we become kind of disassociated to the issues that affect your average brother or sister in the street.

Quote, unquote, "We sell out." That's not really the case. A lot of us still live in the 'hood and are affected by the same issues that affect brothers and sisters who don't have the economic means. And this is an example of those of us who have a little bit of something, that we haven't lost our connection to the neighborhood, to the grass roots.[10]

DANNY GLOVER: I think one of the things that people often talk about when they mention the Million Man March is the apprehension behind it. I happened to be touring about ten colleges [the following] January and February, and at every one of those colleges, invariably, men got up and talked about their experience—the emotional experience they had at the Million Man March. And I was so moved. Men talked about what they received. Some had taken their sons. And it was a profound experience. So people who had apprehensions about what this march was about, whether it was about [Louis] Farrakhan's march or whoever's march, it was about these men's march, their journey to become better men.[11]

SPIKE LEE: A million people came together; there were no incidents at all. No alcohol, no drugs, nobody got shot, nobody got stabbed, and people made a commitment that day that if things were going to change, then we have to do it ourselves. I think it was great. I think there might be some cynical people who think that this thing happened, people just atoned for one day and then went home and started doing the other crazy stuff, but I don't think so. I think it really struck a chord.[12]

◆

Birmingham, 1963. A single explosion rocked a community and awakened a sleeping nation. When a bomb tore through the basement of a black Baptist church, as Reverend Jesse Jackson reflects in the film, "The bad news is four innocent babies were killed. The good news is we were able to transform a crucifixion into a resurrection—new life, new energy, and more determination." The massacre, the Oklahoma City bombing of its day, became a focal point in the civil rights movement, confronting the atrocity of racial hatred in America head-on.

Twenty years later, writer Howell Raines revisited the bombing with a *New York Times Magazine* cover story. Spike Lee, inspired by the article, wrote a letter to Chris McNair, father of Denise, asking permission to film the girls' story. When McNair did not reply, Lee decided he would wait a decade before pursuing the issue.

SPIKE LEE: I was not a filmmaker when I read that story. I was still at NYU, and my skills as a filmmaker were nonexistent. It took ten years of myself making movies for this to come together.

With *4 Little Girls*, the original idea was to tell the story dramatically, but I changed my mind over the course of ten years. It had to be a documentary; no way can I write dialogue in the words of a parent who has lost a child. We could have reached a larger audience having made a movie, but I don't think that was necessarily the best form, the best way to tell the story. A lot of people had to dredge up a lot of painful memories, and the subject was not to be played with—lives were lost behind this incident. All we had to do was just tell the truth and stay close to the four girls.

Terence Blanchard: I knew of the four little girls and everything as innocent victims, but Spike's documentary gave them a real identity, which I guess makes it even more tragic.

Another thing that was interesting to me was that I didn't realize how much bombing was going on at that time—at least to that degree. I think we have a tendency to fall into that "out of sight, out of mind" thing where if you're not talking about it, then it's some unimportant stuff that happened way back when. But when you sit down and watch these mothers—one woman still had the brick that was launched in her daughter's head—it really strikes a chord emotionally.

Working on this film score was just one of those things where the music wrote itself. It's not like writing for a [fictional] film because you don't really pinpoint a lot of stuff. In a documentary you just put in some background to the dialogue. And there's a lot of heavy dialogue, interesting dialogue, and there's some funny stuff in there,too. That stuff with [former Alabama governor] George Wallace and his assistant is hilarious!

Spike Lee: That was some major footage we got with George Wallace. We never thought he'd give an interview. It's funny, when you know you're about to die, you try to fix things. That's the only reason why he even agreed to [participate]. And he definitely was trying to change his legacy. The more he said that he befriended Negro people, the more he hung himself.

Terence Blanchard: Spike came over to my house in New Orleans, man, and we were sitting up just watching that scene: "Run it back, run it back!" But in the end, the film had me in tears. It was really touching and the music just sort of came to me immediately. Actually, when a project is this good, it's always very easy and such a joy to do.

◆

Spike Lee's first foray into documentary filmmaking was a highly acclaimed endeavor, as *4 Little Girls* won him an Oscar nomination for Best Documentary Feature in 1997. "I think doing documentaries is a serious talent of his," enthused Terence. "When you look at Spike's films, there's a lot of information and heavy statements in them, so it makes sense that he'd do a documentary well."

After his basketball drama *He Got Game* (scored with Aaron Copland's classic compositions), Spike Lee's next film, *Summer of Sam,* would also document the past. In the summer of 1977, David Berkowitz, who called himself the Son of Sam, rained terror on New York City. His demoniac killings gripped the metropolis and caused the biggest police manhunt the city had ever known. The tabloids ran sensational headlines like "No One Is Safe from Son of Sam" and printed the threatening letters they received from Berkowitz himself, compounding concern into citywide panic and paranoia.

"The summer of '77 was one of the hottest summers ever," remembers Lee. "New York City gets crazy sometimes because of the heat. It's stuff I've demonstrated before in *Do the Right Thing*. Everybody had their air conditioners on, and that's why they had the [citywide] blackout. Everything was just wide open: the whole disco thing; drugs were still happening; the wild pre-AIDS days were at their height. It was a pivotal summer. Combine that with the Son of Sam hysteria that was being fueled by the *New York Post* and the *Daily News*, and you have complete madness."[13]

The film follows a fictitious group of Bronx youths who become so obsessed with finding the killer that they form a vigilante group to hunt him down. Their inept undertaking merely produces outlandish suspicions of their own neighbors founded on prejudice and hysteria.

"The vigilante group we show in the movie used Son of Sam as an excuse," explains Spike. "He gave them license to just fuck up the people they didn't like. They had a very narrow vision of what is normal. If you're gay or a punk rocker or you've got long hair, you're potentially Son of Sam material. So the film is about intolerance."[14]

For the soundtrack, Lee and Steyermark chose music that evoked the period, such as Abba's "Dancing Queen" and the Who's "Baba O'Reilly." Terence's original score was another orchestral effort featuring more than seventy musicians that suavely elevates the tension.

Terence Blanchard: When we talked about *Summer of Sam*, Spike said he wanted it very melodic but very low, which I could understand because there's a lot of haunting stuff in this film. So the thing that I tried to do was embellish that feel and tone for the movie. This score took me a little longer to write because there was a lot of interesting detail in the scenes. There's a lot going on in the plot and I thought an orchestral score was necessary.

With [his next film] *Bamboozled*, I suggested to Spike that we should go for a small ensemble. He wanted to do it with an orchestra, but we've done that a number of times and since the subject matter is so strong on that particular film, I thought we should try something different. Spike agreed, but he was adamant about having strings for the final montage of the film. I thought it would be melodramatic if you're listening to the score with a small ensemble and then all of a sudden, at the end, sixty strings come in. So I thought we could start small then have it slowly build to an orchestra. Halfway through the film, strings come in and it just kind of builds from there.

◆

Bamboozled, released in October 2000, is among Spike Lee's most controversial and least commercial projects. It's a scathing satire of television's pitfalls and prejudices that was hailed by the *New York Times* as "an important Hollywood movie," even though they refused to print an early version of its advertisement on the grounds that readers would deem it racist.

The film stars Damon Wayans as a beleaguered TV writer whose more meaningful ideas are dismissed by his racist boss, so he cynically sets out to make a point. He drafts a black-faced minstrel show starring "two real coons" named Mantan and Sleep 'N Eat that is so flagrantly racist that he expects to be fired for insubordination. Instead, the network produces the concept into a hit sitcom called *Mantan: The New Millennium Minstrel Show* featuring tap dancing, grinning, and watermelon eating.

Not unlike *Do the Right Thing*, *Bamboozled* mixes comedy with intrepid social commentary to bludgeon viewers out of their complacency. "It is the work of a master provocateur," said the *Los Angeles Times*.

SPIKE LEE: In the twenty-first century, you don't have to put on blackface to be a minstrel act. There are shows on American TV today that are minstrel shows. A lot of these gangsta rap videos, I think they've evolved into minstrel shows. So I hope people are more astute in knowing that you just don't need the blackface.[15]

TERENCE BLANCHARD: It was really interesting to see Spike pull off something so outlandish as this one. The subject matter is real strong, and I think he handled it really well. I think it's one of his best and most important projects to date.

The score is a serious departure from anything that I've ever written before. Melodically and harmonically, it's more pop oriented. The harmonic motion really comes from the pop culture, not like a jazz thing and definitely not like a classical thing at all. Spike wanted that kind of theme. He played some things for me, stuff that he was looking for. He played a Bruce Hornsby song that he actually used in the film. We talked about concepts; he wanted the stuff to be very melodic as usual but very kind of light. It's different.

Spike Lee: In addition to Bruce Hornsby, I kept telling Terence that I wanted this Cannonball Adderley feel; that's the vibe I wanted. I didn't use a temp score, though. In the beginning, I used to temp my films, but I think it really contaminates a composer's mind and a director's, [which happened on a film I produced called *Love & Basketball*]. And the reason it happened was because that was [director] Gina [Prince-Blythewood's] first film. She was inexperienced, and it created some problems with Terence. You know, I tried to talk to her, but a lot of these things people just have to learn on their own.

Terence Blanchard: I've had mixed emotions about temp scores in films. With certain directors, it doesn't bother me because they understand that it's just that: a temporary score. But I've worked with other directors where it has become a problem. They fall in love with a piece of music that they've stuck in just temporarily and think that the score should be based on that—it's what we call "temp love." That's very limiting in terms of giving a composer freedom to create something original for a film. So in those instances it can be something that is very troubling for a composer to overcome.

Basically, what's happening with temp love is that [directors] develop a habit of hearing this particular piece of music—not necessarily that they love it—just that it's become an integral part of the scene and they become accustomed to it.

Spike Lee: Yes, exactly. You know, they keep hearing that shit again, again, and again. And that just creates problems on both sides. Number one, the composer tries to write something just like it, and number two, the director will never be satisfied because they're expecting something else. So, for me, I prefer to just leave it to dialogue, describing what I'm looking for, rather than having a temp score play.

Gina Prince-Blythewood: [My editor] put together such an amazing temp score that it was so hard for me to separate myself and give Terence's score a shot. In the beginning, everything I heard just didn't sound right. It took me [a while] to separate myself from the original score. And now, when I watch the film, I so appreciate how great it is, which I wasn't able to do initially.

Terence Blanchard: You have to work through those things. What I try to do is try to show some alternatives. I'll do exactly what they wanted me to do [based on the temp score] and then do an alternative that I think would probably serve the film a little better. And then I let them hear both so they can make a final judgment.

Spike Lee: When we're working on the main theme, right away I know it's the one when I hear it. Just by the melody I can tell whether it's going to be strong enough to support the entire film. So I want to hear something I can *hear* throughout. I mean, you have different variations, different arrangements of it, but it has to hold up. Sometimes I hear it right away, sometimes I don't and you gotta keep working on it.

For *Bamboozled*, we had to go back three or four times. It took a while for the right theme to be revealed to me. It was one of the more difficult films to score.

Ultimately, I liked what Terence did with the score, where the first half is just his jazz ensemble and then as the film gets progressively darker, it moves into a full orchestra. It was Terence's idea to try something different like that, which was interesting. He really understands how to make music fit the film, that it's not the other way around. *Summer of Sam* is a perfect example of that—his music worked so well with that picture.

I love all of Terence's scores: *Malcolm X* was huge; *4 Little Girls* was wonderful but on a much smaller scale; *Jungle Fever* had a beautiful melody—it's a strong theme. But I would say *Summer of Sam* and *Malcolm X* are my two favorites.

Terence Blanchard: Basically, Spike wants a strong melody that will transcend the story and give people something to walk away with. That's what Spike has always drummed into my head. There have been times when I've tried to write very subordinate themes for Spike, very sparse melodies, something that won't get in the way of dialogue. Whenever I've submitted those, he rejects them every time. If I come back with something that's a little more melodic and has more notes, he'll say, "That's what I'm looking for."

One of the things that people always ask me about Spike is what he's like to work for. A lot of them envision this guy standing over me with a whip beating me in the back telling me what he wants. But he's totally the opposite.

Alex Steyermark: Spike is a very honorable and very loyal person. It's a very respectful environment to work in. I mean, I see more of the private, the more "in the trenches" side of him that may be different from the public persona, at least the early one. But I think he's certainly changed a lot. Spike has really strong principles, and he's a really decent human being. I remember the first time I worked with him—he's a little too busy for this now—but he used to be the first person in the studio and the last person to leave. I would show up at nine o'clock, and you knew he had been there since 8:15 because his breakfast was almost done and he was halfway through the *New York Times*. Nowadays he has other commitments and his time is much more structured, but he lives for this.

I feel privileged to have had such [a long-standing relationship with him]. It's a very special relationship in my mind. Spike is somebody who has allowed me to grow professionally and given me a lot of opportunities to push and move out of what was sort of narrow confines of being a music editor into a bigger thing of producing and supervising. You know, he's *the* guy. He's really allowed people to grow, and I think he's done the same thing with Terence.

Terence Blanchard: Spike's quick to tell me that he doesn't have a [musically] trained ear, and we joke about that all the time because I think he does. As soon as someone's out of tune, Spike's practically the first to notice. He'll come over and say, "Man, that cello is out of tune." And I'm like, "Oh, the untrained ear, huh?"

Alex Steyermark: Spike's got a great ear. But he's just one of these guys who's like a walking database of pop culture. He remembers who did what song and when, what color the label was on the forty-five, who wrote it, everything. Spike's one of these guys that really impresses, and he keeps you on your toes. Music is a really big part of our society, but Spike has made it a point of just knowing it. He claims not to [play an instrument], I've never seen him play anything, but I think the fact that he's grown up with music—you know, his father being a jazz musician—it's just essential in his life.

Spike Lee: Well, yeah, I grew up in a musical household. I gained an appreciation of music from my father. He had very defined views, like, anything that wasn't jazz or acoustic was bad music: "Turn that bad music down!" It didn't matter whether it was the Beatles or the Supremes, if it wasn't acoustic, he'd say, "I don't want to hear any of that bad music!"

From an early age, I saw my father perform at the Newport Jazz Festivals and all around various clubs in New York City—not just jazz venues, but with [folk artists] like Judy Collins, Bob Dylan, and Peter, Paul, and Mary. So even though I'm not a musician and I can't read a note, I think my appreciation of music helps me understand how it can be used effectively in films. Also, I think I have a gift of looking at something visual and knowing, through intuition, what style of music would work well with it.

Terence Blanchard: When we were recording the score for *Mo' Better Blues,* there was this trombone player who was begging for a solo all week long. So finally, at the end, Spike agreed to let him play one. So the guy steps up to the microphone but just before we're about to start recording, he leaves the stage to get something out of his trombone case. Of course, everybody's freaking on him. And then on his way back [to the stage], he stepped on the tuba player's headphone wire and got his foot caught in it, but since he didn't realize it, he kept walking back to the stage. Then all of a sudden, the tuba player tumbles out of his chair, falls to the ground, makes all kinds of noise, and Spike's so funny—he comes over and yells, "That's a wrap! It's over! No solo for you!"

But Spike is at his funniest when he's at a New York Knicks game. I'll never forget this one time he took me to the game. We're sitting courtside—you know, first row on the floor—and he argues with the refs on every call that goes against the Knicks. And I had this box of Crackerjack sitting on the floor. And all of a sudden Spike jumps out of his chair to argue a call and kicks the box, spilling all the Crackerjack out onto the court. But he was so busy arguing the call on the other side of the court that he didn't even notice what he did. So there I was standing on the court trying to sweep them back under my chair with my feet before anyone noticed!

Spike Lee: Terence and I both love sports, so that's always been a bond. I have a lot of fun going down to games with him, but since he moved [back to New Orleans], we haven't been as much. We just have so many good memories though, and I'm very honored that I've been able to work with Terence and have a true collaboration. I think we work well together and that we complement each other, too. He's composed eight scores for me, and I'm looking forward to the next eight. I'm looking forward to him doing the music for this [documentary that I'll be directing on football legend Jim Brown for HBO], which will probably be a small ensemble thing like *4 Little Girls.* And then hopefully we'll get [a studio to greenlight] a script that I'm writing about [boxer] Joe Louis. That film is going to be an epic on a bigger scale than *Malcolm X.*

Terence and I have been able to build a relationship and a body of work, which has been great. A collaboration between a director and a cinematographer or an editor is just as important to me as the one with a composer. We've always given as much respect to the music as we've done to the [other departments]. They're all essential tools that help tell a story. So my relationship with Terence is very important to my filmmaking. He brings the stuff that's missing; Terence's music fills in the holes. I'm telling you, when I see the film without his music, it's a lot different than with it. A lot! Terence lifts it up to another level. It's uplifting. But it's not just a score in general. There have been many bad scores that have dragged down films. Terence's music has never been detrimental to any of my films. If something didn't work, it wasn't the music—it was the scene.

Terence is a great composer, and we both want to continue building on our relationship. We have a lot more great films and great scores to do.

Terence Blanchard: My relationship with Spike has been great. I'm very thankful to him for a number of reasons, but mainly because he gave me such a rare opportunity to do something that I love to do.

People have a misconception about me. People think that I do so much film work that I don't want to go on the road—but that's what I really want to do. Writing for film is fun, but nothing can beat being a jazz musician, playing a club, playing a concert. When I stood next to Sonny Rollins at Carnegie Hall [on a gig in 1993] and listened to him play, that was *it* for me. I didn't give a damn if I ever wrote another film in my life.[16]

Notes

1. James Earl Hardy, *Spike Lee* (New York: Chelsea House, 1996), 92.
2. Karen Brailsford, "Spike Lee," *Interview* (November 1992): 105.
3. *The Arsenio Hall Show,* May 11, 1994.
4. *Larry King Live,* May 13, 1994.
5. *The Late Late Show with Tom Snyder,* September 8, 1995.
6. Lisa Kennedy, "Spike Lee," *US* (October 1995): 51.
7. *Late Night with Conan O'Brien,* September 15, 1995.
8. *The Late Late Show with Tom Snyder,* September 8, 1995.
9. *The Late Show with David Letterman,* October 15, 1996.
10. *The Oprah Winfrey Show,* "Get on the Bus," October 16, 1996.
11. *The Oprah Winfrey Show*, October 16, 1996.
12. *The Late Show with David Letterman*, October 15, 1996.
13. Oren Moverman, "Son of Sam Spiked," www.findarticles.com (accessed July 1999).
14. Moverman, "Son of Sam Spiked."
15. Tom Lyons, "Look Black in Anger," *Eye Weekly* (October 19, 2000): 22.
16. Michael Bourne, "In Tribute to Lady Day," *Down Beat* (May 1994): 21.

CHAPTER THIRTEEN
CENTRAL FOCUS

I'm at a point in my life where I know what I want—which is to focus on becoming the best jazz musician I can be.

—*Terence Blanchard*

In early 1993, music pundits were raving about Terence's new album, *The Malcolm X Jazz Suite*, an inspired and fiery jazz rearrangement of his orchestral score. Noted critic Peter Watrous described the suite as "hugely ambitious; a meditation on a historical event using the language of the period, amplified without cliché, made intelligent and useful by the present." Geoffrey Himes of the *Washington Post* declared the album an "extraordinary landmark" and distinguished Terence as "Wynton Marsalis' only real rival as a modern composer of jazz suites in the Ellington mode." K. Leander Williams also fashioned comparisons to the legendary Duke Ellington in his *New York Times* review, where he wrote, "Both [Blanchard and Ellington] brought heightened force and energy to the extended suite form and like the extended compositions of Ellington's later years, Mr. Blanchard's suite has succeeded in creating music that, while illuminated by his players, is indelibly shaped by its composer."

Coinciding with its release, the Terence Blanchard Quintet launched another world tour from New York City's world-famous basement club, the Village Vanguard. Later that spring, around the time his modified embouchure turned four years old, Terence reached a new level of stability and confidence in his playing. He began contemplating a switch from his standard five-piece band to a quartet, which was encouraged by his longtime drummer and close friend, Troy Davis.

Troy Davis: I thought if Terence went quartet, it would help him get even stronger because he would have to play most of the solos.

So he did go quartet, and throughout that year I saw an amazing development.

There was one incident at the Vanguard where we went to sit in with Roy Hargrove's band. Terence didn't bring his horn, so Roy gave him his. And, man, let me tell you a little story about that: it sounded as though Roy's horn was literally about to explode! That's how much wind and power and strength Terence put into that horn. And Roy was stunned, just looking at him like, "Wow!" And Rodney Whitaker, who was there that night playing with Roy, was like, "Man, Terence, you really sound good."

But I specifically remember when Terence was back to back with Wynton Marsalis at the Lincoln Center for an Art Blakey tribute. Of course, Wynton's technique is practically flawless, and he sounded very good on his solo. But on that night, Terence just literally wiped him out! When Terence stepped to the mike, oh, my goodness, he had the crowd screaming and hollering—it was amazing! Mark Whitfield was sitting right side of me and he couldn't believe it. He was like, "Man!" And Wynton—I know him—he's very competitive. I could see the look on his face; he wanted to solo again but didn't because of time purposes. But he still wanted revenge!

Terence's embouchure was just coming on, and I had told him before the concert, "Man, you go out there and play your butt off." And, boy, did he ever. The next day I went up to him and hugged him. But he just laughed and said, "Oh, man, get out of here." He has a lot of confidence in himself, but you'd never know it because he carries himself in such a humble and modest way.

Branford Marsalis: I think that Terence's decision to change his embouchure changed him as a person and changed his musicianship. There was a mild competition between he and Wynton, which is only natural—they play the same instrument, and both want to excel. Terence was willing to undergo two years of absolute misery for long-term gain. For a professional working musician to decide to take a hit like that shows an enormous level of personal honesty that is rare even among musicians who make our living by trying to be relatively honest.[1]

◆

During the final week of October 1993, Terence Blanchard led his quartet and a string orchestra through material for his fourth album for Columbia Records. Like *The Malcolm X Jazz Suite*, Terence was drawn into a project that would celebrate another one of his heroes. The finished product is a jazz orchestral homage of twelve songs to the revered Billie Holiday. "I've always had a strong attraction to singers, and I've always loved Billie Holiday. She was so distinctive and had such a strong influence on everybody."

Although mainly instrumental, Jeanie Bryson sings on five tunes including Holiday's composition "Fine and Mellow." Bryson, the daughter of another jazz giant, Dizzy Gillespie, is a fine addition, bringing a Lady-like spirit to the piece. Miles Goodman also contributed his talents as both arranger and conductor to a terrific string orchestra.

Upon its early 1994 release, *The Billie Holiday Songbook* soared to the top of jazz charts, became Terence's biggest-selling record to date, and catapulted him onto the May 1994 cover of *Down Beat* magazine—the first such distinction of his fourteen-year career.

TERENCE BLANCHARD: I tried to show my appreciation for Billie rather than just re-create her style. I didn't want to try to sound like her on trumpet or even imitate one of her trumpeters, like Charlie Shavers. I just wanted to play her songs as they affected me—and do justice to the music, so I had Miles do the arrangements. The funny thing was, I was hoping he'd give me some orchestration lessons, but he wouldn't because he didn't want to influence my musical style in any way. He believed your weaknesses are your strengths. But it was a great thing for me to just be the performer for a change because it enabled me to really work on these tunes and on my instrument.

JEANIE BRYSON: Terence's trumpet sound is a really beautiful one to sing with. I loved the interaction that we had. But the actual sound that he has, especially on a ballad, was really nice to bounce off of.

I was really excited when Terence called me to do this project. We had known each other for a long time (we both went to Rutgers), but after that, I think I had only seen him twice over a ten-year period. But right before that album was to be recorded, I was singing at a little club in New York, and Terence ended up there one night. Then the next day I got a phone call from him, and I was just totally thrilled.

I had never sung any of the tunes before that I was expected to sing, and we only had about ten days before we were going into the studio. But that was good in a way because I didn't really have too much time to get daunted by the idea of doing a Billie Holiday record. I mean, I just loved her singing so much.

TERENCE BLANCHARD: When I listen to Billie Holiday sing [the lyric] "My man don't love me" [on "Fine and Mellow"], it doesn't matter what mood I'm in, I feel her pain. To me, that's what music should do. And that's what I want to do with my music.

I've always had fantasies of what it would be like just to stand next to Billie as she sang a song. If it were possible, I would love to go back in time just to be there for one day. I don't even need a day; just give me a half an hour and I'm cool.

I was really excited about going on the road and playing this music because it was different every night. Playing with Jeanie, Troy, Bruce Barth, and [bassist] Chris Thomas was great; it was a really special combination. We really matured as musicians and had a lot of fun learning new things. Bruce would play something one night that would change the whole sound of the band. Or sometimes Troy would change the groove unexpectedly and the next thing I knew, we were playing "Lady Sings the Blues" in a totally different way. I couldn't wait to hear the music a month after being out on the road. It was a real exciting time for me.

Jeanie Bryson: My experience with Terence on the road from March '94 to about September '94 was such a wonderful experience in every way. I learned so much about being on the road and just what that entails. We went to about ten different countries, and seeing the world the way I did was great because I had never really been on tour to that extent before. We started in Sweden, went to Italy, France, Canada, Ronnie Scott's in London, and even *The Tonight Show.*

They're probably gonna kill me for saying this, but I used to tease them because there they were, four nice-looking young men who'd be looking at girls, but nevertheless, we would all end up in somebody's hotel room every night watching Jenny Jones with our jammies on. And I had to laugh. I'd say, "Yeah, you guys are real big jazz stars sitting here watching Jenny Jones at three o'clock in the morning." The life of a jazz musician just sounds so glamorous, but there we were watching some silly talk show almost every night. But we had so much fun—we really did. And musically, I loved playing with the guys; every night was a joy. It was just so fulfilling in every way.

Terence Blanchard: The thing about that whole project was that it helped me focus on the things that really matter musically for me. I'm always working on my technique, I'm always working on learning more about music theoretically in terms of composition, how to structure things, and how to manipulate ideas. But when it boils down to it, none of that matters. The only thing that matters to me after it's all said and done is that people really get something out of what I do.

You know, I'm not trying to prove anything anymore. And I think I'm relaxed with that now. I'm having fun playing, and learning more about this music is really a joy for me now. I don't feel obligated to uphold this tradition of being a jazz musician. I just love being a jazz musician.

◆

With two successive tribute recordings, Terence's next album, *Romantic Defiance*, would utilize his compositional skills to articulate the pain he felt from his failed marriage to his high school sweetheart, Jackie DeMagnus. After seven years, the relationship, which had produced two children, ended in divorce and left Terence pondering what went wrong. "The thing that I was really thinking about was that nobody ever talks to us about relationships. We can learn how to go to the moon if we need to, but nobody really teaches us about marriage. I was very young—I was twenty-three when we married—and any type of relationship requires a large amount of compromise and understanding that only comes through age and experience. I tend to think I was like a lot of people who get married too young; you don't get a chance to discover who you are and don't really become comfortable with yourself."

Following his divorce, Terence wrote "The Premise," "Romantic Defiance," and "Morning after Celebration" on commission from Jazz at Lincoln Center and premiered them in quintet at Alice Tully Hall in 1993. However, the band was on the road covering material from *The Malcolm X Jazz Suite* and then *The Billie Holiday Songbook*. It wasn't until the end of 1994, after writing five film scores that year, that Terence would find the time to return to this music.

His commissioned material would provide the framework for four new compositions, and a rearrangement of "Central Focus" from his album *Simply Stated* would round out the eight-piece recording.

For *Romantic Defiance*, Terence applied his experience in film scoring, a medium that heightens drama and fleshes out character, to shape the recording into a quasi-soundtrack for his own personal tale. "I try to write music that is personal rather than just difficult." Terence believes, "Music right from life—that's how it has to be."

The recording, his fifth as a leader, featured notable firsts and changes. Special guest Kenny Garrett, the proficient alto saxophonist who played in Miles Davis's last band, made his recorded tenor sax debut on three tunes. Edward Simon replaced Terence's longtime pianist Bruce Barth, and although Chris Thomas recorded on bass, David Pulphus made the tour and became the band's bassist for the next four years.

The personnel revisions to the ensemble would lead to high praise from critic Jim Macnie in *Down Beat* magazine, who identified Terence as "leading one of the era's most fascinating bands."[2]

> **TROY DAVIS:** Musically, the band has changed over the years. When Rodney, Bruce, and Sam were in the band, we had a different message. Back then we were trying to develop by being a little different and creative. Then over the years, we started thinking about all the people who were left out in the dark. We wanted to broaden our audience. Terence and I discussed all those greats like Louis Armstrong and realized what

made them great: the entertainment they provided. So we started to talk a little more to the audience and to make them feel like a part of the show. Terence tells a few jokes here and there.

David Pulphus: The [*Romantic Defiance*] tour was amazing because first of all, it was a government-funded tour, so everything was top-notch. The U.S. government was funding certain artists to expose certain smaller countries to our music.

For five weeks we toured South America and went to places like El Salvador, Panama, Ecuador, Paraguay, Uruguay—all over. It was unbelievable and just incredible for me. And Terence, who had been playing for fifteen years prior to that, said it was one of the best of his entire career. Everywhere we went, the audiences were *so* into it!

The American embassy in each country we went to discounted certain ticket prices, so people who normally wouldn't be able to afford it came to check us out. And at each country, the embassy would greet us at customs, which was cool. We stayed at the best hotels, got paid top dollar, went to really great museums, and we didn't even play that much! We only played like two or three times a week. The first day we got there we went horseback riding! It was beautiful.

Edward Simon: I was born in 1969 in Cardon, Venezuela, a small town where everybody knew each other. The access to jazz music there was very limited, but someone in our town managed to get a video of Dizzy Gillespie, Stan Getz, and Chick Corea playing at the White House for Nancy Reagan's birthday. Chick made a big impression on me, but hearing improvisation over changes and intricate jazz harmonies blew me away. Up until that point I had only been playing Latin American music, which is intricate rhythmically but somewhat limited harmonically. I immediately fell in love with the sound that I would later become a musician of.

When I moved to Philadelphia I began playing in the local jazz scene there, doing a steady gig every weekend with [bassist] Charles Fambrough. Through Charles I met people like [saxophonists] Bobby Watson and Greg Osby. In talking with Greg, he really expanded my concept of the music. He talked about breaking patterns and going beyond the norm. Greg was actually the first musician to record me on an album. He also introduced me to [guitarist] Kevin Eubanks, who was living in Philly at the time. Kevin came to check out our gig, and I guess he really liked my playing because two months later, he called and asked me to join his group. I was with Kevin for about three years until I joined Bobby Watson.

Terence Blanchard: When Bruce Barth announced he was leaving, I bought a bunch of CDs of a lot of guys. One of them was Carl Allen's *The Pursuer* that featured Edward on piano. He had this short solo on a tune, and when I heard it, I kept running it back wanting to hear more. So I talked to Carl about him, and he was really impressed with Ed. But the funny thing was, nobody had his current number, so I couldn't get a hold of him. He was moving back and forth from Jersey to Philly, and I was like, "Damn, how does this cat make a living?" Then I finally got a number, and when he answered the phone, I was like, "Gotcha!"

EDWARD SIMON: There were several things that helped me make the decision of joining Terence's band. One was that Terence does not use any monitors on stage. The sound of his band on stage depends completely on the acoustical sound of the instruments. I think that is very important. Also, musically speaking, having the opportunity to play with some young musicians, guys who are interested in expanding their horizons and breaking the limits is something I've always welcomed. There's just that whole edge of young musicians that I really like. They have a certain hunger that really attracted me to the band because I needed some of that.

The reason I moved to this country was to learn more about music, particularly jazz. And Terence, being from New Orleans, couldn't be a better connection to the roots of that music. He's right here with the history of jazz. So to me, that is very important because he is a source that I can really draw from. When I listen to Terence play, I can hear the history of the music; I can hear everyone from Pops to Miles. I think that just by the nature of where he comes from, Terence is more in touch with the music from the guys that I've played with.

TERENCE BLANCHARD: There has to be a certain kind of sensitivity that one needs to be a pianist in my band. I don't care if you have great technique; I like somebody with a touch, especially on ballads. The piano is a very beautiful instrument with wonderful colors and wonderful tones, and if that's missing, then there's nothing there for me. I mean, when you listen to Herbie Hancock, Oscar Peterson, and some of those older guys play ballads, there's a certain way they approach their instrument, and that's what I look for. And there's very few younger guys who have that. But Edward Simon is one who definitely has it.

EDWARD SIMON: The first gig I did with the band was in Monterey, California. I was a bit nervous because it was a new situation for me, and I didn't know the music that well. In fact, it took me quite some time—at least a couple of months—to get adjusted to playing not only with Terence but with Troy as well. They had been playing together for a long time and had a really strong *thing* together—it's very intricate. And I had to figure it out before I could even think about what I was supposed to add to it. So for the first two months, I was just trying to find my place. But I always felt very welcomed, and I was given a lot of freedom musically. You know, it's still a constant learning thing, and the more I learn what Terence expects from me, the more I can fill his piano chair.

◆

Out of Terence's desire to expand as an artist and embrace other musical forms came *The Heart Speaks*, his interpretation of the music of Brazilian singer/songwriter Ivan Lins. "Upon learning more about Ivan and his music," says Terence, "I realized that I wanted to do something with his compositions. I had known about Ivan's music for awhile, but admittedly, I only knew his voice—I didn't even know his name. I didn't have any of his recordings or anything like that. But whenever I heard that *voice* singing on the radio, I'd say to myself, 'I really like this music!'"

Luckily, it just so happened that his friend Miles Goodman had worked with Lins, producing a project for him and Toots Thielesmans. "I had really wanted to do a Brazilian album, so Miles suggested that we get in contact with him because we knew that working with Ivan would be ideal."

> **Ivan Lins:** As a Brazilian, it was a real surprise to me to know that a mainstream jazz trumpeter as excellent as Terence Blanchard was interested in recording only my songs. I was also very excited that Miles Goodman was backing the project and that Terence was from New Orleans. I had the opportunity to meet an amazing trumpet player, an exceptionally gifted musician, creator, and incredible human being.

For the recording, Terence rearranged a dozen of Lins's sensual compositions, including "Just for Nana," a ballad dedicated to the soulful singer Nana Caymmi. Caymmi is often compared to Sarah Vaughn, who, along with Ella Fitzgerald, is among those to record Lins's music. Miles Davis had also hoped to work with the Brazilian songster. Lins composed a tune for him called "Congada Blues," but unfortunately, he passed away before he was able to record it. Then Lins presented the song to Terence, who was so intrigued by the unique rhythm that he wanted to add it to his album. *Congada* is Portuguese for "African root," a rhythm that derives from northern Brazil. On the recording, the rhythm kicks in at the song's conclusion, showcasing Terence's fiery horn playing.

The Heart Speaks may be complete with congada, galope, and samba rhythms, but the album still embraces Terence's jazz roots, particularly on the exquisite ballads. "I wanted to take the aspects of Brazilian music that I love and personalize it. I didn't want to make a 'strictly Brazilian' album because no one needs me to come along and try to imitate what they do."

One of the highlights of *The Heart Speaks* is "Menino," a composition that borrows its name from a Vitor Martins poem. Lins, who wrote it in 1992, was so thrilled by Terence's New Orleans rendering of the "galope" rhythm that he implemented a new lyric, "O Menino da Tijuca meets the kid from New Orleans." Tijuca was Ivan's childhood neighborhood, so the lyric translates to "the kid from Tijuca meets the kid from New Orleans."

IVAN LINS: Terence captured all the different moods of the Brazilian soul and rhythms and achieved the precise connections with his personal roots from New Orleans. He created a very unusual, innovative jazz album, and I'm very proud and honored to be a part of that.

TERENCE BLANCHARD: Working with Ivan was a great experience because he is a true genius. One of the first things that Ivan did was open my eyes to composition. Most musicians compose through the instruments they play, but the writing will be heavily dictated by the limitations of being able to play that instrument. Ivan composes by actually singing. And by doing that, I've learned that you can stretch your music to new heights.

Playing a melody behind Ivan's singing was one of the most challenging things for me because the human voice is so complex and vast in its tonal colors and its flexibility. There were so many variables that I had to deal with on my instrument to be able to play behind him and stay on that high level of musicality because, you know, there are no lyrics for a trumpet player.

I've always wanted to do different types of projects like *The Heart Speaks,* but it was definitely a departure for me. People may think that it's my most innovative album, but it wasn't about trying to have the most innovative rhythms and harmonic structures. For me, each song had its own personality. There was a personal feeling that I went through during the process of recording each tune. But really, all the music that I've done has always been personal to me. I think of it all as a documentation of where I've been and what was going on in my life at the time. On *Simply Stated* I was dealing with going back to the basics. *Romantic Defiance* was obviously about personal things that have happened in my life. *The Heart Speaks* is something I wanted to do, something where I can relax a bit and not have to be on the cutting edge all the time.

EDWARD SIMON: *The Heart Speaks* was a special project for me; it was like a dream come true. I've been listening to and studying the music of Ivan Lins for quite some time now—he's one of my all-time favorite singer/songwriters. I have always dreamed of being able to play with him, so I was very excited when this actually happened. I was like a little kid.

I've always thought that you get great results when you have jazz musicians play that style of music. We have our own approach to music and when we apply that approach to such beautiful [Latin] music, the result is *The Heart Speaks.*

The result of *The Heart Speaks* was Terence's first Grammy nomination as a leader and an accompaniment of flattering acclaim. *Billboard* magazine applauded the recording as "one of the most exceptional cross-cultural meetings (Rio meets New Orleans) to come along in a while," and *The New Yorker* hailed Blanchard as "a thrilling virtuoso with a romantic streak." Although he did not win the Grammy for Best Latin Jazz Performance (Paquito D'Rivera did for his *Portraits of Cuba*), Terence regarded the nomination as a great honor, especially considering he was the only American up for the award.

> **DAVID PULPHUS:** I remember in August of '95, right when school was supposed to start for me [at the University of New Orleans], I went to my first day to tell my teachers that [I would be away for a week]. I told them I was leaving the next morning for Los Angeles to record *The Heart Speaks* with Terence Blanchard. It was my first ever recording on a CD, and it got nominated for a Grammy!
>
> **EDWARD SIMON:** I really feel like I'm growing musically and would like to stay with Terence for a good while. I'm getting a lot of experience in different areas—not only with the film stuff and not only musically. I mean, Terence is a great mentor to me as far as an artist and bandleader. Seeing how he leads the band, how he acts in front of an audience, and how he develops his whole artistic personality has been great for me. And Terence is great, a really warm guy. He likes to hang out with us guys in the band. He's a very nice person to be around. He's strict about the music, though. If something's not there, he'll demand it out of us—and I like that, too.
>
> **TROY DAVIS:** Man, I just hope it continues, because so far it has been a wonderful experience. But you never know—if you're not cutting the muscle, if you're not making the music that Terence needs, if you can't do the job, then you have to move on. And I've always respected that in Terence. And I've told him, "If we're not pleasing you, man, it's your band; do what you gotta do."

◆

Terence Blanchard's career, now in its third decade, is distinguished as much for its diversity as its longevity. But it is his prolific pace that is truly astounding. And with each new project, whether it be jazz oriented, film related, or a hybrid of both mediums, Terence keeps going, his sights set on satisfying his passion for making music—a jazz musician is an ever-progressing artist, one who develops and nourishes a voice that communicates his artistic sensibilities.

Terence's loyalty to his artistry forced him into making some difficult decisions recently. In the fall of 1998, after eight enriching years together,

Terence replaced his friend Troy Davis with the young, driving drummer Eric Harland. That move was followed by a change on bass—Derek Nievergelt for David Pulphus—and then an addition to the front line with tenor saxophonist Brice Winston.

Terence Blanchard: We're doing our best to keep this edition of the band together because we've been playing a lot together, and I'd like to document our development. The longer these guys play with each other, the more I feel like they can really have a great impact on jazz. And I don't say that because it's my band; if these guys were in anybody else's band, I still think the same thing. The thing that excites me most about this particular group of guys is that their heads are in the right place. Derek Nievergelt is a very smart guy and a very musical guy. He has a broad background in music and is very open to trying different things. He kind of puts me in the mind of a younger Dave Holland.

Brice Winston lives here in New Orleans, and once in a while I'd call him for gigs. I remember this one time in L.A., Ed, Eric, and myself fell out laughing because Brice was playing like, "Oh, you gonna remember me!" He was playing his behind off!

He's an extremely analytical and inquisitive guy—so much so, that sometimes it puts him in a bind. But I love that about him. I love the fact that he questions everything and that he's always working on different aspects of his playing.

Eric Harland has a lot of technical ability, which you can see from the first time you hear him, but he plays straight from his heart with a large amount of emotion. Having him in the band brings a different flavor. He's a guy with an endless amount of creative ability when it comes to molding and shaping tunes. And he's only going to get better at that because he's still a little young. But he has a natural gift that's immense, and as he works at understanding orchestration and how to develop a tune, he'll become an amazing force in this business.

You know, it was a very difficult decision with Troy, *very* difficult. I felt Troy really helped shape the sound of the group. His background of coming from Louisiana, understanding that whole culture musically, brought a certain flavor to everything we did, which I thought was unique from what everybody else was doing.

Troy is still a close friend, and I love him as a person. I miss him on the road. I mean, we had the kind of relationship, both being from the same area, where we could sit down and talk about stuff that nobody else could really grasp, and we always had a lot of fun together.

So it was hard, but it was one of those things where I knew it was time for a change. It was just a need to do something different because the time came for me to take that next leap.

◆

Although Terence took many important forward leaps in 1997, two regressive leaps that year proved just as memorable. In mid-February, during Valentine's week, he reunited on the bandstand with an old friend for an extraordinary musical engagement at New York's Iridium Room. It had been eight years since that lethargic Sunday afternoon under the scorching Arizona sun, the last time Terence and Donald shared center stage under the Blanchard/Harrison billing.

Since parting their ways in 1989, Harrison traveled an adventurous and bumpy road. He recorded a couple of assured straight-ahead albums and did some enterprising work that included a pop/fusion record and another with New Orleans Indians, but he struggled to receive his just due from the jazz industry. Unable to re-sign with Columbia, Duck was forced to distribute his eclectic music on significantly smaller labels such as Candid and Sweet Basil, consequently diminishing his exposure. "I used to worry about whether the industry was just going to try to overlook him," remarked Terence about his longtime friend before the GRP/Impulse label nabbed him to a lucrative record deal. "I think Donald's definitely one of *the* guys, but since he doesn't fit into a certain kind of mold, the industry has practically said, 'See you later, Donald.' That's one of the things I hate about the jazz industry. If you don't fit into what it considers how jazz is supposed to sound like, then screw you! But now that he has his deal with Impulse, hopefully things will turn around and his talent won't go to waste."

For six nights, Blanchard and Harrison retraced the steps from all those glory years as they shared the MC duties and led Terence's rhythm section through tunes from each of their songbooks. "I'm really glad they've become friends again and have now reconciled whatever differences they had," remarked Rodney Whitaker, the duo's last bassist. Whitaker was out on the road with Wynton Marsalis and unable to visit, but New Yorker Carl Allen managed to attend, sitting in on drums for a couple of tunes. "It was a lot of fun," said Allen. "I had a blast!"

"Playing with Donald is like riding a bicycle," discovered Terence. "There are certain things that he'll do, and you'll go, 'Oh, yeah, right. I remember that.'" Conversely, Donald was surprised that an eight-year layoff had no ill effect on their chemistry. "I don't know how it happened," he quipped, "but if I did, I would put it in a bottle and sell it. I mean, we were improvising on something last night and we were playing the exact same notes."

In early November 1997—three weeks after the seventh anniversary of Art Blakey's death—Terence was back in the Big Apple for a three-week Jazz Messengers reunion gig that included a live recording for the Telarc label. The orchestrator of the reunion, saxophonist Benny Golson, had invited Terence to occupy the trumpet chair in the six-piece ensemble with fellow ex-Messengers Curtis Fuller, Geoff Keezer, Peter Washington, and accomplished drummer Lewis Nash honoring Blakey's stool.

> **BENNY GOLSON:** Art Blakey had a natural penchant for teaching. The man was didactic. And he intuitively taught many things that we benefited from. Even when he didn't have the drumsticks in his hands, he would feed things to us that were a direct reflection of his years ahead of us and all that experience. And we were like babes in a nest with our mouths wide open. That's why each member who went out with this Art Blakey Tribute Band was out there doing it not as a gig, per se, but because we loved Art. There was no one like him.
>
> **CURTIS FULLER:** Art would give you that superb confidence one needed in order to live up to his full potential. I wasn't the same musician when I came out of his band, and neither was Terence. When Terence came into the band he was timid like I was, but he came out a monster, you know. Art had such a tremendous influence on everybody he played with.
>
> **BENNY GOLSON:** Of course, Art had so many versions of the Jazz Messengers over the years, so what we tried to do was draw upon some of those wonderful moments by playing Messenger songs from all the different eras. My stuff came from the late 1950s, Wayne Shorter—who took my place—his stuff came from the early 1960s, then Cedar Walton and Curtis Fuller, then eventually Terence Blanchard in the mid-1980s. And on every show we played Terence's composition, "Oh, by the Way," and the audience loved it.
>
> I actually first met Terence while he was playing with Art Blakey. And over the years, I've gotten to know him better. In 1993, I asked him to join me in Europe for a three-week tour, and he played great. But then recently, I heard Terence at the Blue Note in New York, and he was a totally different trumpet player. His concept had changed; he now had more power, more range, which is to say, he was now more exciting. But I don't think Terence has reached where he's going. I still feel he is ascendant. He may not be at the top, but his foot is in the door, and they can't shut it on him because the man has talent. He's going straight ahead like a speeding bullet that has been spent from the muzzle. So get out of its way because its coming, ready or not! And I love him for that! That's the way I perceive Terence because he just keeps getting better and better. I hear it in his trumpet and I hear it in his pen. I've been around long enough to know what I'm hearing, and I love it!

Fed up with his recording company, Columbia Records, Terence walked out of his contract in 1998 and negotiated a new deal with Sony Classical. Four albums later, the label has shown a desire and ability to propel their overshadowed talent into the proverbial spotlight.

"There are some things in my performance career that I'm really thrilled about," Terence said at the time. "Going over to Sony Classical to make records is a very exciting prospect for me because they're not interested in limiting me to just jazz records. They want me to do bigger projects with orchestras and stuff like that. And working with Peter Gelb, the president of Sony Music, is so refreshing because he has such a love for music. It's like night and day compared to what I had to deal with at Columbia. So there will be a lot of things going on in the next few years that I'll be very happy about."

Ask Terence to reminisce over his final years at Columbia, and his face grows long with dissatisfaction. "I got tired of dealing with people at Columbia who don't like jazz the way I do. I got tired of their ineptness. I got tired of putting a lot of effort into my records and seeing nothing done about them. They wouldn't market or promote the records, and if they didn't sell according to what they projected, then it was my fault. I got tired of being in that kind of environment, and frankly, I got tired of their lies—that's basically what it all boils down to. I mean, *The Heart Speaks* was the last record I did with them, and at this big meeting they had promised me a big promotion with three videos and all this other stuff. Well, when they didn't end up coming across with any of it, I decided that I was no longer gonna let this record company define who I am. So I told Robin to call them up and talk to Tony McAnamy and tell him I want out of my deal. And Tony goes, 'Well, I don't think that will be a problem because the last record didn't do well.' But they did nothing to promote it! Now the irony in all of this is, if it didn't do anything, how did it get nominated for a Grammy?!

"But the thing that really made me upset about that was that after Miles Goodman died—at his memorial service—a friend of his gave me a letter Miles had written to him. And in the letter Miles said, 'We just made this record with Terence and Ivan called *The Heart Speaks*.' And his quote was, 'I think this is the one.' So Miles really believed in the project, and when I heard that quote from his letter, I was furious. I mean, you spend all your time and effort and creativity into putting a project together, and these assholes just sit back and say, 'Well, we don't think it's marketable.' And then the damn record gets nominated for a Grammy. So somebody was out there listening to it and somebody loved it. I mean, we went on a big tour, and wherever we played the music, people wanted that record. So I'm sitting here going, 'Well, these guys don't want to sell records. There's something else going on here.' It just wasn't logical.

"Now that I'm with Sony Classical, they have a totally different attitude toward selling records, which is refreshing. They don't have pop projections for selling records, which is a big plus because if they don't expect you to sell five hundred goddamn thousand records, then there's no pressure to do that."

Prior to striking a deal with Sony Classical, Terence directed the creative on an album for one of the label's operatic baritones, Jubilant Sykes. "When Peter Gelb called and invited me to work on this project, I swore he had the wrong number—until he called back! Jubilant is an amazing, passionate, and very sensitive musician with such a natural way of singing. So when I was given this opportunity, I was all for it."

The music, an anthology of traditional spirituals presented as jazz (once called the devil's music), gave Terence a chance to revisit his roots. "What we tried to do was take his world of classical music and my background in jazz and fuse them together to come up with a new interpretation of old Negro spirituals. Of course, I grew up in the South with a father who was always singing in the church, and I was always playing there, so these spirituals speak to the core of who I am."

Simply called *Jubilant*, the album was well received by jazz audiences upon its release in the spring of 1998. "I'm really happy people responded to the record favorably. It was a great experience working with Jubilant, and I had a great time taking this music out on the road with him. It's actually kind of funny because I wasn't sure how the tour would pan out. I mean, when you start talking about doing gospel/spiritual music in jazz venues, you'd think everybody would be running for the hills! When we did this one gig in Philadelphia, the woman who booked the club confessed to me afterward, 'I was so worried having you guys here, especially on Friday and Saturday nights talking about *Fix Me, Jesus*, but everybody was cool.'"

◆

Spring signifies a time of growth and renewal, when flowers bloom and beauty reawakens. In 1999, Sony Classical celebrated the season by releasing Terence's first album as a leader in three years, the longest recording hiatus of his career.

Entitled *Jazz in Film*, Terence's label debut is a collection of nine jazz compositions made famous in motion pictures. This inventive concept encompasses new orchestral arrangements by Terence for over thirty-five musicians and features a stellar lineup of such jazz soloists as Donald Harrison, Steve Turre, Kenny Kirkland, Reginald Veal, Carl Allen, and the legendary saxophonist Joe Henderson.

Joe Henderson: There were quite a few musicians there, probably one of the largest groupings of players on the jazz side that I have ever been in the studio with. And I found that to be rather interesting and unique. Terence had put together some interesting charts, which raised my level of appreciation and respect for the kind of talent that he has.

Previous to recording together in the studio, I was very well aware of who Terence was as a trumpet player and film composer, but I really didn't know him that well. We had played together a few times on the bandstand, and I recall Terence coming down to a gig I played in Torino, Italy, a few years ago where we had a nice casual chat. But I got to know him better during the recording session. Terence played with a great amount of professionalism. I was very impressed by that because it's always nice to see somebody who did their homework. Actually, we don't ever finish doing the homework; it's just an ongoing situation that's a part of who we are as jazz musicians.

Terence Blanchard: Well, Joe walks into the situation as the consummate professional: prepared and ready to play. Whenever I get the chance to work with one of the legends, it's a great learning experience and always a thrill. When I stand next to him, I still take a deep breath and go, "Damn, that's Joe Henderson!" When he took out his horn for the first time in rehearsal, it shook me up.

Having him on the record was like a crowning achievement for me. And to have him there, having a good time, being very productive, and being into the project meant a lot to me. I was so in awe of Joe just watching his every move during the session, trying to figure out how he was going to approach every tune.

I remember us taking a lunch break and I walked out of the studio, and I realized that he was still inside. So I walked back to see if he needed something to eat, and there he was at the piano going over the changes to all of the tunes. You think these guys reach a certain level where they can come in and just do what they do. But part of what they do is to have respect for the music and not treat it lightly. That was a big lesson for me.

It was interesting to listen to Joe on different takes. Just as I thought that I would have a clue as to how he would approach the changes of a certain tune, he would come up with another idea and his solo would take on a whole other feel. That's pretty amazing to witness. I mean, you've heard him do it on records, but to actually stand next to the guy and watch him in the middle of his process was a great learning experience.[3]

Playing with Donald Harrison again was a lot of fun, too. It was time for us to record something again; I've always loved his playing. He came in and sounded great. But what else can I say? That's Donald. On "The Pawnbroker," Donald's solo was the first take, and it was funny because it was just like old times. I was like, "Uh-oh, I gotta shift gears!" He made me rise to another level. And it was the same thing with Carl and Reginald. They added a great deal to this project as well. It was interesting because I was looking at these guys, and it started to dawn on me that we weren't [kids] anymore. There's been a lot of growth and maturity in all of these players, and that was a very inspiring thing for me to see.

Getting Kenny Kirkland [to record with me] was something I tried to do for years. So when he decided to do the session, I was real excited. Just the mere fact that he and Joe accepted, I thought we could stop there! But when we got to the rehearsal, Kenny was nowhere to be found! He had a reputation for disappearing sometimes, and so he gave us a little scare. Raymond Harris, my road manager at the time, went to the airport to look for him. But then Kenny came walking through the door and he ended up playing great on the record.

It's a different album for me in that I got these great jazz artists playing classic film themes. "The Pawnbroker" is from the movie with the same name by Quincy Jones. We also did Duke Ellington's *Anatomy of a Murder*, Jerry Goldsmith's *Chinatown*, Alex North's *A Streetcar Named Desire*, Bernard Herrmann's *Taxi Driver*, and we did a theme called "Why Are We So Afraid?" from a movie that André Previn did called *The Subterraneans*. We also have something from *Clockers* and *The Man with the Golden Arm*, which was one of Elmer Bernstein's first scores.

◆

Jazz in Film gave Terence a rare opportunity to bridge his dual careers. Additionally, the project saw him reunite with his former bandmates, collaborate with a beloved mentor, and take the music on an expansive tour with his regular group. However, his next Sony Classical release would be even closer to his heart.

Twenty years on the international performance circuit had Terence contemplating the rigors of such a life: "Missing family and losing the chance to see my kids grow all for playing a style of music that I love can take its toll on the soul."

This agonizing dilemma induced seven original compositions that expand on the familial themes of *Romantic Defiance.* The set of music, called *Wandering Moon*, explores a musician's loneliness on the road and the strain of being away from family.

The album is dedicated to Robin Burgess Blanchard, Terence's manager, wife, and mother of his two youngest children, daughters Sidney and Jordan. "While many of the tunes on the album are inspired by her," says Terence, "some are written just for her. 'Luna Viajera' (Traveling Moon) speaks to the feeling I get when I'm on the road and missing her. I look at the moon and realize it's the same moon that will pass or has already passed her way, and that brings me closer to her."

To communicate this music, Terence knew which musicians to hire—he wrote it with them in mind. "I wanted to use my band because we've been playing a lot together on the road, and it was important to me to document our development together. But I knew I wanted Dave Holland because of his style of music."

One of the most versatile bass players in jazz, Dave Holland came to international prominence when Miles Davis recruited him from England to join his fusion band in 1969. Since then, Holland has performed with Chick Corea's free jazz group Circle and led his own modern acoustic quintet. Currently, Holland is devoted to defying the economics of jazz by taking a thirteen-piece big band on the road.

DAVE HOLLAND: When I get offered recording sessions, I turn down the vast majority of them because the music is written for just any bass player. In the last few years, I've only done a few recordings other than my own. But I really wanted to do Terence's because I knew that he has a sensitivity in his writing, and I really felt a connection to this music. Terence had obviously given careful thought to who was going to be playing it because it wasn't written for just a generic bass player.

One of the things that I like to see in a composer is an ability to create a wide variety of settings for music. Composing for an improvisational setting is different than what Terence does in his film work. It requires a different approach because you're writing for people that are going to take that material and add their own creative ideas to it. So you have to leave room in the material for that to happen and also you have to write material with them in mind. And I saw all those things in the material he had for *Wandering Moon.*

TERENCE BLANCHARD: One of the definite joys of this business is getting the chance to work with your heroes. Sometimes you can get caught up in certain distractions in this business, but when you run across a guy like Dave Holland, he reminds you of what it's all about.

Dave came along at the tail end of the Miles Davis thing, and what's amazing about him to me is that he's not through yet. When some people get a taste of that kind of stuff, they'll rest on it forever. Dave's not one of those guys. He's still searching and trying different things. His passion about having new experiences playing music has always been a great inspiration to me.

When he accepted the project, Ed and I, we were just like overjoyed immensely because he's just one of those great musicians that you wish you get a chance to work with.

EDWARD SIMON: I've been wanting to work with Dave since I first heard him. He's one of my ideal bassists to play with. In fact, he was set to [guest on] a record with me, but it never happened because of scheduling conflicts. And then sometime after that, Dave called me to play a gig with him and his band, but I couldn't make it. So this was the first time we played together and it was great! He's phenomenal. I was so happy and felt very fortunate to have had that experience.

Dave Holland: I've known Edward for a while. I've seen him in a number of situations and I admire his work a lot. Of course, I was working closely with him on this session, going over the pieces and discussing how we were going to approach things from the rhythm section point of view. The rhythm section really works together as a team to create dialogue with the soloists and to create textures and movements in the music. And Ed's a master at that. He's a great accompanist, I think, and a great listener.

Eric Harland was a real joy to play with. I was very impressed by his composure in the studio and by his ability to remain focused on the music. Very often when young musicians are in a situation of playing with people they have respect for, it can be intimidating. I know that from my own experiences. You really have to stay focused on the music and to keep the spontaneity in your playing without tightening up. And Eric remained really loose all through the session. He's got a great feel, and he's able to really listen to what's going on around him, as well as play some interesting things at the same time. So he really entered into that dialogue that I was speaking of.

Edward Simon: Eric is a phenomenal player—very versatile and open, which I really like. I think he's a great asset to the band and I hooked up with him from the very beginning. We have very similar musical ideals, similar tastes, and we hear music in the same way.

Wandering Moon was also my first opportunity to play with Branford Marsalis. Well, he did sit in once when I was with Kevin Eubanks's band, but it was just a very brief thing. So this was really the first time that we had got a chance to play together. And that was great, too. He's a fantastic musician. We had a lot of fun.

Terence Blanchard: When I talked to [producer] Laraine Perri about getting an all-star to play the tenor parts, Branford was the first name that came to mind. He's one of those great musicians, man. He's always been kind of like the Michael Jordan to me. Like, whenever you step on the court, your game goes up a notch because you're playing with that type of person. It's been that way since we were kids.

The project gave us a chance to catch up and it was like old times. Even though I don't see him much anymore, Robin always laughs because whenever we do get together, you can't keep us from talking. So she would have to butt in just so we could get some music on tape. It was hard for us to get into the studio and record because we were reminiscing all day: "Man, you remember so-and-so?" But at a certain point, Robin was like, "OK, wait a minute now—the studio time is just ticking away!"

Branford Marsalis: I hadn't seen Terence in years. I got to a place where I had some personal issues that I was dealing with, and I kind of shut everybody out of my life for a while so I could get my shit together.

The thing that was really cool was that a few weeks before [Terence asked me to play on his record], I was on a float in New Orleans with my son for Harry Connick's Mardi Gras parade. I was wearing a mask because I didn't want people to know I was there. But the parade got stalled at a specific spot on St. Charles Avenue and it was so hot, so I took my mask off. So Harry starts talking to the people, and he says, "We got my friend Branford Marsalis over here!" And out of nowhere, Terence runs up with little Terence on his shoulders: "What's up, boy!" And as soon as I saw him, it was like, you know, all these feelings were coming out. And at that point I knew it was only a matter of time before we hooked up.

It was just funny, you know, how fate is. That float could have stopped anywhere. It was a seven-mile route, and there were a million people around. But we happened to be stalled right at the place where Terence was standing. And that was kind of like the cosmic signal for me. And when I saw him and he saw me, I knew that everything was cool.

I was pleased that Terence asked me to play on his record, but I'm on Columbia, and they don't want me to do any sideman projects. So we have a general policy that I'll do two songs on a record. But suddenly, Terence left Columbia and he's on Sony Classical, so now they really have a bug up their ass. There was all this political bullshit between [the two labels], and Columbia would have preferred that I didn't do it at all. But that was of little interest or consequence to me. So because it was Terence, I did three songs.

Terence knows I'm a good listener, and when you're playing with a trumpet player, it's more so the saxophone player's job to listen to the trumpet player, not the reverse. Trumpet is the lead instrument. So when I'm playing on his record, I'm not thinking about my solo. I'm going to do whatever I can do to make his music sound as good as it possibly can.

The music sounded so good thought *Down Beat* readers that they awarded *Wandering Moon* Best Jazz Album of 2000 and highlighted Terence as jazz artist and trumpeter of the year. In light of this achievement, Terence appeared on the magazine's cover with his idol Clark Terry, who was voted into its Hall of Fame that year.

Terence also received a Grammy nomination for Best Instrumental Soloist for his impassioned interpretation of the standard "I Thought about

You." He has been performing the ballad over the last few years as a tribute to his late friend Miles Goodman.

In fact, *Wandering Moon* contains many tunes that are dedicated to loved ones. In addition to "Luna Viajera," Terence's originals "My Only Thought of You" is for his wife, Robin; a bouncy number named "Sidney" is for his daughter; a tender ballad called "Sweet's Dream" honors trumpet great Harry Edison in the wake of his death; "Simplemente Simon" is for his longtime pianist; and a contrapuntal composition about Terence and his father is titled "Joe & O."

TERENCE BLANCHARD: After I did *Romantic Defiance*, I felt like I wanted to play other people's music for a while and investigate how they dealt with composing melody. I just wanted to get that ingrained in my ear and my subconscious before I thought about writing some more music. So after doing the Brazilian project and *Jazz in Film*, I was ready to return to playing my own music.

When I sat down to write, I knew I wanted to investigate this whole dilemma about being a traveling musician and a family person. I turned thirty-eight in the year 2000. And I remember when I was kid, I kept saying, "Damn, I'm going to be thirty-eight at the turn of the century; I'm going to be old!" And that's right about the point in life where most men have a midlife crisis. So it makes you think; you sit down and take stock of yourself and contemplate the things that really matter to you. I really have fun doing what I do: writing music and touring around the world with it. But at the end of the day, the place I want to be is at home with my family. People think that we live a glamorous lifestyle, which we do. But at the same time, it's a very hard life.

BRANFORD MARSALIS: Being on the road definitely puts a strain on your relationship with family members. That's part of the gig. It can be a miserable experience. I miss my wife and my son; I miss my house and my bed, everything. The bus rides are a drag, the planes are always late, the weather sucks, and you're sleep deprived. But I try to be patient. I sneak in naps when I can, try to be on time, and play the shows. When it starts getting on my nerves, I think about how much better it is than having to work for a living at a job that you hate and have to speak to a boss that you don't respect.

EDWARD SIMON: I have a wife and young son, and I certainly miss my family a great deal when I'm out on the road. We travel so much that after a while you feel like you don't have a home. And then when you do come home, it's just for a few days, and then you're back out again. So those are the kind of things that every musician that tours goes through. And it's only natural for Terence to express those feelings in his writing.

Branford Marsalis: Terence had been working with his composition instructor, my godfather, Roger Dickerson. His compositions are based on some of the things they were working on together. *Wandering Moon* had all the earmarks for artistic success. It's an album full of great music from a fertile, creative mind.

Edward Simon: With *Wandering Moon,* Terence made an effort to move in a different direction. He's trying to stretch with his writing but still within the realms of his particular influences and experiences. He dedicated one piece to me called "Simplemente Simon," which I like very much. It's actually a piece that I may have written because he used certain devices that I use when I write my tunes. So Terence definitely made an effort to bring it into my world. And, in general, some of his writing on the record is closer to my world. So that's been a very welcoming process for me, which has made our collaboration much more enriched.

I've been with Terence for seven years now, and I think we've developed a certain kind of sound together. Perhaps it's not as intimate as the one Terence had with Troy because they played together very long and come from a similar background. They had a great rhythmic connection, too, and they knew how to "burn out," as musicians call it. With us, it's more of a certain sensibility in the music. Being a pianist, I play somewhat of a delicate instrument, so I like to work more with the nuances of the music, the different touches, colors, and sounds. When we get into those [sensitive] realms of playing, I know what Terence wants and we hook up—harmonically, too. We're beginning to know what each other is like more and more. It's kind of strange—you always feel like you are beginning even though you may have been at it for a long time.

Terence Blanchard: I've really grown to appreciate Ed as a musician and as a friend. He's been with me for a long time, and he has really helped define the sound of the band through his background as a Latin musician and his interest in world music. He's definitely contributed to giving the band a broader perspective.

◆

The broader perspective Terence admires in others continues to influence his own work. In planning his next Sony Classical recording, he and producer, Laraine Perri, decided on the music of prolific American songwriter Jimmy McHugh. Terence was attracted to the strong melodic content of McHugh's writing and relished the idea of playing alongside some of his favorite singers. "I always enjoy playing with singers. To me, they're musicians who have mastered a unique instrument. The human voice has more timbre and color on one note than any musical instrument."

Terence enticed Grammy Award winners Cassandra Wilson, Dianne Reeves, and Diana Krall along with acclaimed newcomer Jane Monheit to support him and his quintet on eleven interpretations of McHugh's songs. "As a feat of booking alone, this is a marvel," praised *Vanity Fair*. "Blanchard's album has an almost cinematic sense of narrative drive. Listening to him weave lines around his singers is like listening to volleys of great dialogue. He plays the most coolly expressive trumpet in jazz, transmuting the instrument's repertoire of smears, growls, peeps, and blasts into an astonishingly fluid language both luxurious and controlled."[4]

"Let's Get Lost," performed with Krall on vocals and piano, is the first track and title of the album. Lesser-known tunes are Reeves's "I Can't Believe That You're in Love with Me" and "Can't Get out of This Mood," and Monheit's cover of "Too Young to Go Steady." More popular fare is covered by Monheit on "I Can't Give You Anything but Love" and by Wilson on "Don't Blame Me" and "On the Sunny Side of the Street." Classics like "I'm in the Mood for Love" and "Exactly Like You" get new and inventive instrumental arrangements by Edward Simon.

"Jimmy McHugh didn't develop a big name like some other composers," says Terence, "but he has such a long list of timeless hits that people know. It was a challenge interpreting his tunes, and it was interesting to discover that no matter how you arrange them, they retain their essence."

◆

Observing the midafternoon traffic out on Columbus Avenue, Terence perks up on his bar stool at the Iridium Restaurant and smiles. "I'm excited about the future—I really am. There's a lot of things in their infancy right now that I'm looking forward to, particularly a couple of film projects that could set me up pretty well in that vein. I've been in the film industry for a while, but it's been a struggle to really get established."

Supermodel Gia Carangi was The Face in the late 1970s. Her exotic looks appeared on the cover of every major fashion magazine at least once. By 1986, she was dead, one of the first celebrities to have been struck down by AIDS.

HBO, a U.S. cable network reputed for its bold programming, acquired the film rights to her story and commissioned Michael Cristofer to direct. Cristofer was the established screenwriter of such major Hollywood movies as *Falling in Love*, *Bonfire of the Vanities*, and *Mr. Jones* but had never assumed the director's chair. He immediately enlisted veteran producer Marvin Worth, who made a career out of producing screen biographies, like *Lenny*, *The Rose*, *Patty Hearst,* and *Malcolm X*.

MICHAEL CRISTOFER: Marvin came aboard and really took care of me, getting me a great line producer and helping me a lot in preproduction. When it came to scoring the picture, I had said to Marvin, "What I'd really love to have in here is a lot of work with a single instrument. We should get somebody who's a composer but a performer, too." I was thinking about a couple of people here in Woodstock and suddenly he just sat up in his chair and said, "My God, Terence! Terence should do this."

My first impression of Terence was that for somebody who played the way he did, and for somebody who had done so many edgy films with Spike Lee, I was really surprised that he was so quiet. He generated a real surprising simplicity to me in his manner, his quietness and his straightforwardness. There was nothing to suggest, you know, Spike Lee, who's a walking Coney Island, or even your idea of a strange and mysterious jazz musician. I was really taken with that because he was so direct and so simple and so open.

When we talked about the film, he seemed to feel deeply about it and he really identified the essentials of what was going on in different scenes, which was really interesting to me. So I was really surprised and impressed by Terence when I first met him.

Unfortunately, we had so little money for this picture and everything happened so fast, but Terence managed, on our measly budget, to really put a full score together. However, we had a much better situation on this last picture, *Original Sin*. We had a few more bucks, which allowed Terence a little more time to write and allowed us a little more time to communicate.

◆

Gia was first screened on HBO in early 1998 and at year's end would be showered with awards, including Outstanding Directorial Achievement for Television from the Director's Guild of America and a Golden Globe Award for its star, Angelina Jolie. On the success of *Gia*, Cristofer was tapped to do another small film called *Body Shots* and then a major studio picture for MGM entitled *Original Sin*, reuniting him with Jolie and Blanchard.

Set in the exotic world of Cuba in the 1880s, *Original Sin* is a sexy thriller about a wealthy coffee merchant (Antonio Banderas) and his American mail-order bride (Jolie). When he arrives at the docks to meet her, he is pleasantly surprised to find that she is not the plain woman he was expecting. But the surprises continue until the story takes a fateful turn.

MICHAEL CRISTOFER: We had a little pressure on us this time because, for one, they originally wanted to release the picture [several months before they did]. But then, the head of the studio came down and said, "We can't keep rushing the way we're rushing. Let's just wait." And thank god for that because Terence would have been writing on toilet paper!

Another thing they were intent about was the music for the picture—not that they had any clear or good ideas, but they had a lot of ideas. I had been experimenting with a temp score, but it was extremely difficult because there's not a lot of music around that you can dip into for a nineteenth-century erotic suspense-thriller taking place in Cuba. But I did manage to find some great source music that conveyed to Terence what I thought the music should be like.

I was using everything from the period because it's so interesting to me. In 1880, there was the classical music being composed in Cuba, and there was music in that period written by Louis Gottschalk that was very popular. There was a lot of French-African influenced music that was coming to Cuba from Haiti and the Spanish-Cuban feel of music that was beginning to evolve out of the combination of African and classical music. Also, the American influence was great because so many of the sugar plantations in Cuba were owned by Americans, so there was music coming from New Orleans. And that whole mix of the African influence, and what Gottschalk was doing was beginning to produce jazz. So it was very interesting to use all those elements and then have somebody who is a jazz artist as the composer.

All of this information, of course, was just too much for the studio, and they just thought, "Well, what the *fuck* is he going to do?!" They were terrified. And they were already nervous because it's a period picture. So they just kept saying, "It's got to be modern." And I kept saying, "It's got to sound like the period." Their biggest concern was that it was going to sound like a Merchant–Ivory film, so they kept shuffling over to me Cuban music from the fifties—1950s—saying, "Shouldn't it sound like this?" And I kept saying, "No!"

I kept Terence out of all of that for a long time but then I started to tell him a little bit. I said, "Look, I'm in a little bit of trouble here, so we have to be careful." Then we started second-guessing ourselves. Back and forth, he would send me a cue and then I would call him to talk about it. He said, "I thought I would change this around and then do that." And finally I said, "Forget everything I said about this. Let's just follow our own instincts because that's the only way we're going to be happy with what we've got." And he called me back a couple of days later and told me that he was really happy that I said that to him.

They don't give film composers any time to do anything, and so, they're under enormous pressure just to be able to produce the score in the amount of time they're given. So they have to go with their instincts and with whatever conversations you've had to sort of shape those instincts. There's no time, unless you're a machine, which a few of these guys are, but Terence is not. So finally you have to say, "Do what you feel and follow your instincts." I gave him the road map, which is the temporary score, and left everything up to him. And he came out with wonderful entrances and exits in the scenes that were not typical. His music would

> begin at odd moments in the scene and leave in odd moments, finishing way before the scene was over. And then toward the end of the scene, another cue would come in and bridge us into the next scene. It was great. And I think MGM really loved it because Terence did what I thought should happen—somehow combine all of the musical elements.
>
> The score is very orchestral and romantic, and very rhythmic, too. And, aside from conducting the orchestra, Terence performed on the score. He loathes to do that, but I refused to not have him there somewhere.
>
> The two things that I want to say about the whole experience are, number one, it was a chance to spend time with him and Robin and get to know them better as people, and that was terrific because I just feel Terence is an extraordinary human being and I was happy to experience that closer. But the other thing, which I think was very frustrating for me, was I wrote the script for this picture, too, and while we were mixing the film, I was sitting there thinking, "If I could just get rid of this *fucking* dialogue, I could listen to this music." And I felt so strongly about that. I said, "Jesus, I could have left him more space. I could have relied on him more because what he came up with is so great." And I should've taken the chance and left some more space because there were some things that were happening in Terence's music that were so terrific and to have to bury them or turn down that volume was painful.

◆

In addition to reuniting with Cristofer on *Original Sin*, Terence was rehired by Kasi Lemmons to score her film *The Caveman's Valentine*. Based on the acclaimed novel by George Dawes Green, Lemmons's anticipated follow-up to *Eve's Bayou* is about a formerly devoted family man and Juilliard-trained musician who now lives in a New York City cave. Played by Samuel L. Jackson, the character wages a one-man battle against an imaginary power broker who he feels is responsible for all of society's ills. When he discovers a corpse outside his cave, he launches an obsessive quest for answers that leads him back to the bowels of the "civilized" world.

The film is produced by Danny DeVito's Jersey Films, the company behind *Pulp Fiction* and *Erin Brockovich*. *The Caveman's Valentine* premiered at the 2001 Sundance Film Festival and received a theatrical release later in the year.

"Since [the main character] is a classically trained pianist from Harlem, it really opened up a lot of musical possibilities. I tried to bring another aspect from his background and culture because, growing up in Harlem, he was obviously exposed to certain types of ethnic music. So in addition to writing a couple of piano concertos, I used a lot of African drum rhythms and stuff like that. It was a really interesting project to work on," says Terence.

Lemmons knew it would be a challenge to convince Terence to perform on his score, so she began cajoling him as soon as they arrived at the studio in Seattle. The concertos were to be performed by Awadagin Pratt, but scant scheduling prohibited Terence from familiarizing Pratt with all the music. So Terence would compromise with Lemmons and perform several cues on the piano himself.

"This is the first time I've done that on film. I mean, I've done sync stuff on piano but never played with an orchestra. And I don't practice the piano, so the only time I play it is when I'm composing. And there were some things that I had to play that were kind of difficult, so I started practicing a couple of days before in the studio. And that was some funny shit 'cause my hands started to swell and got real hot 'cause I wasn't used to playing those pitches. It was deep, man. I had to stop. I said, 'Wait, I'm gonna fuck up my hands!'

"There are always feature film projects on the horizon," says Terence, smiling sideways, knocking on the wooden bar top, "but there are some great TV projects that I've been real lucky to write for." He's alluding to his abundant work with director Lee Rose on award-winning films like *The Color of Courage*, *Navigating the Heart*, and *The Truth about Jane*.

Their latest effort is an ambitious four-part miniseries for Showtime called *A Girl Thing* that chronicles various women's issues and stars a slew of notable actresses. In one series, a jazz fan, played by Kate Capshaw, tells her date, Elle McPherson, "I'm going to take you to hear Terence Blanchard play." And so, the trumpeter makes his second cameo appearance in the movies playing on stage in a jazz club.

"I ain't never had this kind of activity. In [2000], I worked on seven film projects and after Kasi's film I kept saying, "I'm going to take a vacation. I *need* to take a vacation." We were in Seattle; I was tired; I was broke down, trying to get through that because I knew I had *Original Sin* and *A Girl Thing* to work on. So I kept saying when that was all over, I was going to take a break. But then Robin goes, 'Gregory Hines just called you; he wants you to score his new film about "Bojangles" Robinson.' And I said, 'Oh, wow, Gregory Hines? Wow, that's cool!' I mean, for me, it's like, I better do it while I can. I don't want to ever become presumptuous and think that, 'Oh, I'm the man!' and that calls will always be coming in. This business doesn't work that way.

"I never thought I would be writing this much for film. I'm just thankful for the opportunities I've been given. But you know," he pauses and reaches for some more wood to knock on, "I've been really lucky with it so far."

After a prolific 2000, Terence composed and conducted scores for several more films, including Spike Lee's documentary *Jim Brown: All American*, a Robert Redford production called *People I Know*, and Ron Shelton's police drama *Dark Blue*. Set in April 1992, *Dark Blue* stars Kurt Russell as an LAPD detective investigating a racially charged homicide in the week leading up to the verdict of the Rodney King trial. Al Pacino leads an all-star cast in *People I Know*, a film loosely based on the famous New York publicist Bobby Zarem.

More work with Spike will follow with a film called *The 25th Hour*, which stars Edward Norton in a story about a man's last day before serving a seven-year prison term for drug dealing.

Dave Grusin: I think from a career standpoint, Terence is doing very well. I know he's gotten extremely busy with film work, and I just hope he's not getting frustrated by being buried with deadlines because that takes its toll after a while, and it doesn't become as much fun as it once was. I'm very fond of Terence's jazz music, more now than ever. He continues to amaze me. He keeps growing as a trumpet player and as an improviser, and it seems like he's finding more and more specifically his own voice, which I love to see. And once you commit to a film project, it doesn't matter what they tell you about the schedule; it's a big commitment. And once you say yes, you're no longer in control of your own destiny; you're forced to give up your own choices and go with the company.

Ray Brown: I hadn't had the privilege of playing with Terence until recently [on my album *Some of My Best Friends Are Trumpet Players*]. I had heard him play a lot with the Messengers and in different settings since then, so I was looking forward to having him on the record. Terence is a killer trumpet player, a great musician, composer, and arranger. He does everything, and he does it well.

I was there when jazz musicians started doing film scores. Back in the fifties and sixties, it was stylish to have a prominent jazz musician scoring a film. That door may have closed because it seems to be a little tougher to do it now. But when that door opened, a lot of guys like Johnny Mandel and Henry Mancini ran through it. These former musicians were doing scores for major Hollywood films. And I find that with most of these guys, the really serious composers, it takes up all of their time. I didn't see them out at night in clubs playing gigs. I don't mean that it's not possible to do; I'm just saying what I've seen. They just no longer had time for their instrument. I mean, you don't see Quincy Jones playing trumpet anymore. Mancini was a great piano player, and he got away from that when he started composing scores. Johnny Mandel was a French horn and trombone player, and you don't see him playing horn anymore.

The trumpet is a very demanding instrument, so that may be something that Terence has to face at one time or another. I mean, I think he's got the potential to go to the top of the mountain as a jazz musician.

TERENCE BLANCHARD: I don't know how to respond to all of this film work coming together now because I am at a period where I want to slow down and refocus on my playing. You get so engrossed in writing the film that you don't get a chance to spend time with your instrument the way you'd like. I feel very fortunate to have the film career that I do, but I'm at a point in my life where I know what I want—which is to focus on becoming the greatest jazz musician I can be. So I would love to be able to just sit at home and practice for a while.

◆

Despite a desire to reduce his workload, Terence could not resist an offer to share his experience and knowledge with some of the finest aspiring jazz musicians in the country. In the fall of 2000, he accepted a prestigious commission as artistic director of the Thelonious Monk Institute.

The conservatory, located on the University of Southern California campus, offers a two-year master's program to a limited number of students (up to eight per year). In offering a unique program where established musicians can pass on their expertise to young talent, the institute evokes the spirit of its namesake. For decades, Monk was known to conduct lessons from his apartment on West 63rd Street in Manhattan.

In his role as artistic director, Terence works with the students in the areas of artistic development, arranging, composition, and career counseling. He also participates in master classes and community outreach activities associated with the college program.

"Out of my desire to give something back to the jazz community—just like my teachers did—I wanted to get involved. In fact, I've always said that if I wasn't a musician, that I would like to be a teacher. So I was glad to get involved and to be a part of this unique program that fosters such an open and accessible environment. And the students here are amazing, really self-motivated with strong musical visions and a bright future ahead of them."

Although Terence's own future looks very bright, he takes little for granted. He is a man marked by humility, one who believes conceit spoils the finest genius. So whatever musical projects, media coverage, or peer adulation comes his way in the future, you can be sure this contemporary cat will take it all in stride, accrediting and involving most of the people in this book.

ALEX STEYERMARK: I think that Terence is known as someone who writes deeply felt, beautiful music. He's not somebody that comes to mind to write something for an action movie—although I'm sure he has the chops to do it. But I think that his music resonates on an emotional level that's quite special. When people think of music that moves you in that way, then they think of Terence. People know who he is in Hollywood and elsewhere. I remember hearing comments on the score that he did for *4 Little Girls*—and there's not a lot of score in it—but what's there is beautiful, and I think it helps support the film emotionally. And I think that it's truthful music. You know, I don't think anyone ever feels like Terence is trying to pull a fast one.

Dave Holland: I met Terence quite some years ago—I'd say in the mid-1980s. We had a chance to play together at a session in New York. My first impression of him was the sound that he produced on the trumpet—which is always the first thing that I notice in a musician—the quality of the sound that they make. And Terence had this wonderful warmth to his sound, which, now that I know him, reflects his character, too. He's a very warm individual. After that, I watched his career develop and I have a great admiration for his writing abilities, not only with his group but with the scores that he's written for film. And I think he's a talent that also keeps developing. He very much keeps his eye on how to improve his craft, improve his creativity, and expand it—and he's very open-minded, which I think is also a great quality in a musician.

Mulgrew Miller: On stage, Terence is certainly a very warm and charismatic person, but also very confident and assertive. Though off stage—and I think I can speak from experience because I've had a rather intimate relationship with him as a friend—I've found Terence to be a very level-headed individual. He's always been focused on what he wanted to attain and achieve. But, you know, we've also had a lot of discussions about some of the deeper things in life. Terence is a very spiritual person, and he's always extremely interested in those kind of things.

Clark Terry: We've played on few occasions together, and as far as music is concerned, Terence is not selfish at all—he's very loving and compatible with other musicians. On a couple of occasions we did a concert with a bunch of trumpets where we had me, Sweets [Harry Edison], and Doc Cheatham, the old-timers, and we had two young players: Terence and Roy Hargrove. And I think Terence is a marvelous performer. He's a very studious person, and very few people know how musically talented Terence really is. He's a great piano player and a marvelous, marvelous composer. There are not too many young musicians who have the know-how to be able to do film scores, and he does them great. I guess we have sort of a mutual admiration for each other because every time I see him I get a [music] lesson as well. I love him. I think he's a marvelous, giving, and outgoing person. I can't say enough beautiful things about him. Those of us who have been established and have been on the scene for a long time, we're always very proud to see a young talented gentleman like him come on the scene. So we've all welcomed Terence with open arms.

JOE HENDERSON: Different players arrive at their sound at different periods in their careers, some a bit faster than others. After hearing Terence up close in the studio recently, I would say that I could recognize his sound probably within a bar. To me, that's a pretty strong observation. Terence has his own identifiable fingerprint, his own voice, which is a hell of an accomplishment when you consider all of those great trumpet masters [of the past]. But he's managed to come through with something that is quite uniquely his own, which is the ultimate goal for a player.

Sometime after I was invited to play on his record, Terence came and played with us in Chicago. I thoroughly enjoyed it and I think he did as well. I definitely have high regard for Terence and the image that he's projecting out there. I just have really good feelings about Terence, his talent, his work ethic, and the position he has established for himself out here as a musician.

SONNY ROLLINS: I've never said this to Terence's face because I didn't think it was necessary. But now that I have this opportunity to express how I feel about him, I'm really happy to do so: Terence Blanchard is a very gifted young musician. And not only is he a gifted musician but also a good example and role model for the young black musicians coming up today because he's a gentleman. He leads his life in a very exemplary fashion. I mean, it's wonderful to know [that I've had an influence on Terence] because it's a joint effort out here; we have to help each other.

Paul Jeffrey, who was one of Terence's teachers at Rutgers University, is a very close friend of mine. We both like to discuss all the young guys coming up, and Terence's name always comes up. I'm one of his biggest fans. Whenever I see him playing some place or when I hear one of his movie scores, it just makes me feel very proud—actually, I think that would be more true to the point. He makes me feel very proud to see such a young man coming up in our business that's handling himself in such an exemplary manner and I certainly wish him all the best.

TERENCE BLANCHARD: I've basically devoted everything to being a jazz musician, so I feel really blessed to have been around such great teachers and great musicians throughout my life. They've had such a strong influence on me, and they have all been really nice people. Their help has always been out of love. It was never like they were trying to mess with me. I've yet to run into any big assholes who've rubbed me the wrong way, so I feel really lucky to have had such wonderful experiences.

You know, there will always be those moments when the road starts taking its toll, you're tired and want to be home with your family, but

> every once in a while, there are those moments when you're playing with other great musicians and you have such a great time playing. It's hard to describe the feeling, but it's like a wholeness. And that's the carrot that's always dangled in front of you in this business; that's the drug. Because once you get a shot of that stuff, you're running after that carrot for months and months and months. That's the idea because you remember how great that was. But if you're conscious of it, you'll never re-create it. It's the type of thing you can't control; it always happens unexpectedly. So you just have to go out there each time and try to have as much fun as the spectators are hopefully having, then just maybe you'll get the opportunity to take another bite of that carrot.

◆

When music lovers around the world gather to experience the dazzling artistry of Terence Blanchard, hoping he has all the harmonious ingredients to create those magical moments, I am reminded of the time he so gregariously chomped into that dangling carrot at the Top O' the Senator. Though we will never again appear together in the same room at the same time, the group of us share an indelible imprint in our collective memories.

Here, despite his eclectic interests and passion for film scoring, is where Terence finds the musical moments he most treasures. And while this central focus looms large in his life, Terence Blanchard remains a man unequivocally committed to his lovely wife, Robin, and his four precious children.

Notes

1. Ted Panken, "Sincere Sounds," *Down Beat* (December 2000): 44.
2. Jim Macnie, "CD Reviews," *Down Beat* (October 1995): 48.
3. Bill Milkowski, "Cinematic View," *Jazz Times* 29, no. 4 (May 1999): 66.
4. Bruce Handy, "Horn Again," *Vanity Fair* (June 2001): 78.

In loving memory of

Joseph Oliver Blanchard

February 25, 1914–December 30, 1998

At a time of reflecting on my relationship with my dad, I am wondering what I could say that would give you an idea of how I felt about him as a child and young man growing up.

I loved my dad for building my character and showing me the way to manhood.

My father always took an interest in what I was doing and would become my friend, which was great. It only became a problem when my friend would turn into a taskmaster at any given time, correcting me anywhere, no matter who was there.

I went through those years thinking that my dad was so uncool, that he just didn't have a clue. As an adult, I now realize that he had all the right answers—not the popular ones, the right ones.

And that's what I love and respect most about my dad, how he knew when to be a friend and when to be a father. And I would really hate it if I could not be as great a father to my kids as my father was to me.

Love You Always,
Terence

CHRONOLOGY

1962 Born in New Orleans, Louisiana, on March 13.
1967 Begins formal music lessons studying piano.
1970 Takes up the trumpet.
1973 Performs with Branford and Wynton Marsalis in a summer camp.
1978 Enrolls in the famed New Orleans Center for Creative Arts (NOCCA).
1979 Joins the New Orleans Civic Orchestra.
1980 Earns scholarship to Rutgers University to study music; tours the United States with the Lionel Hampton Orchestra.
1982 Leaves Rutgers University prematurely to join Art Blakey's Jazz Messengers; moves to Brooklyn, New York.
1984 Jazz Messengers win Grammy Award for Best Performance by a Group for *New York Scene*; assembles the Blanchard/Harrison Quintet and wins Gran Prix du Disque for *New York Second Line*.
1985 Marries Jackie DeMagnus.
1986 Leaves Jazz Messengers to tour with Blanchard/Harrison Quintet.
1988 Performs on his first film soundtrack for Spike Lee's *School Daze*; wins Gran Prix du Disque for *Black Pearl*; son Terence Oliver II born.
1989 The Blanchard/Harrison Quintet disbands; takes a year-long sabbatical to reconstruct his embouchure; hired as trumpet instructor to actor Denzel Washington for *Mo' Better Blues*.
1990 Returns to the performance circuit with his own band, a new manager and recording contract with Columbia Records; records debut album as a leader, *Terence Blanchard*.
1991 Composes and conducts first film score for Spike Lee's *Jungle Fever*; records second jazz album, *Simply Stated*; daughter Olivia Ray Blanchard born.

1992 Composes and conducts epic film score for Spike Lee's *Malcolm X*; rearranges score for jazz quintet recording, *The Malcolm X Jazz Suite*.

1993 Performs with Sonny Rollins at Carnegie Hall; records tribute album to Billie Holiday with string orchestra, *The Billie Holiday Songbook*.

1994 Composes several film scores, including *Sugar Hill*, *Assault at West Point*, *The Inkwell*, *Trial by Jury*, and Spike Lee's *Crooklyn*.

1995 Receives Emmy nomination for Best Original Score in a Documentary for *The Promised Land*; *Romantic Defiance* released; moves home to New Orleans.

1996 Gets Grammy nomination for Best Latin Jazz Performance for *The Heart Speaks*; collaborates with film mentor, Miles Goodman, on *'Til There Was You*; marries Robin Burgess.

1997 Composes film scores for *Eve's Bayou* and *4 Little Girls*; daughter Sidney Bechet Blanchard born.

1998 Signs new recording contract with Sony Classical; produces and performs on spiritual album, *Jubilant*.

1999 Amalgamates talents on *Jazz in Film* with Joe Henderson, Donald Harrison, and a posthumous Kenny Kirkland; daughter Jordan Cozart Blanchard born.

2000 Named artistic director of the Thelonious Monk Institute at the University of Southern California; wins *Down Beat* Jazz Artist, Trumpeter, and Jazz Album of the Year honors for his recording *Wandering Moon*; earns Grammy nomination for Best Instrumental Soloist.

2001 Celebrates the music of Jimmy McHugh on *Let's Get Lost* with singers Diana Krall, Jane Monheit, Dianne Reeves, and Cassandra Wilson; receives Grammy nomination for Best Instrumental Soloist; succeeds Ellis Marsalis as director of jazz studies at the University of New Orleans.

2002 Performs trumpet for actor Val Kilmer in *The Salton Sea*; composes film scores for *People I Know* starring Al Pacino, *Dark Blue* starring Kurt Russell, and Spike Lee's *The 25th Hour* starring Edward Norton; tours with the Newport Jazz All-Stars featuring Joe Lovano and Cedar Walton; performs the music of Billie Holiday with his band, a string quartet, and prominent Broadway vocalists at Carnegie Hall and other big-city venues.

DISCOGRAPHY

Bandleader

Terence Blanchard (1991) (Columbia). Personnel: Terence Blanchard, trumpet; Sam Newsome, Branford Marsalis, tenor sax; Bruce Barth, piano; Rodney Whitaker, bass; Troy Davis, Jeff "Tain" Watts, drums

Simply Stated (1992) (Columbia). Personnel: Terence Blanchard, trumpet; Sam Newsome, tenor sax; Antonio Hart, alto sax; Bruce Barth, piano; Rodney Whitaker, bass; Troy Davis, drums

Malcolm X Jazz Suite (1993) (Columbia). Personnel: Terence Blanchard, trumpet; Sam Newsome, tenor sax; Bruce Barth, piano; Tarus Mateen, bass; Troy Davis, drums

Billie Holiday Songbook (1994) (Columbia). Personnel: Terence Blanchard, trumpet; Bruce Barth, piano; Chris Thomas, bass; Troy Davis, drums; Jeanie Bryson, vocals

Romantic Defiance (1995) (Columbia). Personnel: Terence Blanchard, trumpet; Kenny Garrett, tenor sax; Edward Simon, piano; Chris Thomas, bass; Troy Davis, drums

The Heart Speaks (1996) (Columbia). Personnel: Terence Blanchard, trumpet; Ivan Lins, vocals, piano; Oscar Castro-Neves, guitar; Pauhlino Da Costa, percussion; Edward Simon, piano; David Pulphus, bass; Troy Davis, drums

Jazz in Film (1999) (Sony Classical). Personnel: Terence Blanchard, trumpet; Steve Turre, trombone; Joe Henderson, tenor sax; Donald Harrison, alto sax; Kenny Kirkland, piano; Reginald Veal, bass; Carl Allen, drums

Wandering Moon (2000) (Sony Classical). Personnel: Terence Blanchard, trumpet; Brice Winston, Branford Marsalis, tenor sax; Aaron Fletcher, alto sax; Edward Simon, piano; Dave Holland, bass; Eric Harland, drums

Let's Get Lost (2001) (Sony Classical). Personnel: Terence Blanchard, trumpet; Brice Winston, tenor sax; Edward Simon, Diana Krall, piano; Derek Nievergelt, bass; Eric Harland, drums; Diana Krall, Jane Monheit, Dianne Reeves, Cassandra Wilson, vocals

Blanchard/Harrison

New York Second Line (1984) (Concord). Personnel: Terence Blanchard, trumpet; Donald Harrison, alto sax; Mulgrew Miller, piano; Lonnie Plaxico, bass; Marvin "Smitty" Smith, drums

Discernment (1986) (Concord). Personnel: Terence Blanchard, trumpet; Donald Harrison, alto sax; Mulgrew Miller, piano; Phil Bowler, bass; Ralph Peterson Jr., drums

Nascence (1986) (Columbia). Personnel: Terence Blanchard, trumpet; Donald Harrison, alto sax; Mulgrew Miller, piano; Phil Bowler, bass; Ralph Peterson Jr., drums; Jeff Haynes, percussion

Crystal Stair (1987) (Columbia). Personnel: Terence Blanchard, trumpet; Donald Harrison, alto sax; Cyrus Chestnut, piano; Reginald Veal, bass; Carl Allen, drums

Black Pearl (1988) (Columbia). Personnel: Terence Blanchard, trumpet; Donald Harrison, alto sax; Cyrus Chestnut, piano; Reginald Veal, bass; Carl Allen, drums; Monte Croft, vibes; Steve Thornton, percussion; Mark Whitfield, guitar

The Jazz Messengers

Oh, by the Way (1982)
Blue Night (1983)
New York Scene (1984)
Dr. Jeckyle (1985)
New Year's Eve at Sweet Basil (1985)
Live at Kimball's (1986)

Hard Champion (1987)
The Art of Jazz (1989)
The Legacy of Art Blakey (1998)

Sideman

Various artists, *Eric Dolphy and Booker Little Remembered Live at Sweet Basil* (1986)
Various artists, *Fire Waltz* (1986)
Benny Green, *Prelude* (1988)
Ralph Moore, *Images* (1988)
Ralph Peterson, *V* (1989)
Alvin Queen, *Jammin' Uptown* (1989)
Cedar Walton, *As Long as There's Music* (1990)
J. J. Johnson, *Let's Hang Out* (1992)
Various artists, *Swing into Christmas* (1994)
Various artists, *Color & Light: Jazz Sketches on Sondheim* (1995)
Billy Childs, *The Child Within* (1996)
Orquestra Was (Don Was), *Forever's a Long Time* (1997)
Jubilant Sykes, *Jubilant* (1998)
Joe Jackson, *Symphony No. 1* (1999)
Cedar Walton, *Roots* (1999)
Ray Brown, *Some of My Best Friends Are Trumpet Players* (2000)
Grover Washington Jr., *Aria* (2000)

FILMOGRAPHY

Composer

Jungle Fever (1991), director: Spike Lee
Malcolm X (1992), director: Spike Lee
Sugar Hill (1994), director: Leon Ichaso
Assault at West Point (1994), director: Harry Moses (television)
The Inkwell (1994), director: Matty Rich
Crooklyn (1994), director: Spike Lee
Trial by Jury (1994), director: Heywood Gould
The Promised Land (TV) (1995), director: Anthony Geffen
Clockers (1995), director: Spike Lee
Soul of the Game (TV) (1996), director: Kevin Rodney Sullivan
Get on the Bus (1996), director: Spike Lee
'Til There Was You (1997), director: Scott Winant
4 Little Girls (1997), director: Spike Lee
Eve's Bayou (1997), director: Kasi Lemmons
Gia (TV) (1998), director: Michael Cristofer
Free of Eden (TV) (1999), director: Leon Ichaso
A Saintly Switch (TV) (1999), director: Peter Bogdanovich
The Color of Courage (TV) (1999), director: Lee Rose
Having Our Say (TV) (1999), director: Lynne Littman
The Tempest (TV) (1999), directors: Jack Bender and Bonnie Raskins
Summer of Sam (1999), director: Spike Lee
Navigating the Heart (TV) (2000), director: David Burton Morris
The Truth about Jane (TV) (2000), director: Lee Rose

Love & Basketball (2000), director: Gina Prince-Blythewood
Next Friday (2000), director: Steve Carr
Bamboozled (2000), director: Spike Lee
A Girl Thing (TV) (2001), director: Lee Rose
Bojangles (TV) (2001), director: Joseph Sargent
The Caveman's Valentine (2001), director: Kasi Lemmons
Original Sin (2001), director: Michael Cristofer
Glitter (2001), director: Vondie Curtis Hall
Jim Brown: All American (2002), director: Spike Lee
People I Know (2002), director: Daniel Algrant
Barbershop (2002), director: Tim Story
Dark Blue (2002), director: Ron Shelton
The 25th Hour (2002), director: Spike Lee

Featured Performer

School Daze (1988), composer: Bill Lee
Do the Right Thing (1989), composer: Bill Lee
Mo' Better Blues (1990), composer: Bill Lee
Housesitter (1992), composer: Miles Goodman
Backbeat (1994), composer: Don Was
Primal Fear (1996), composer: James Newton Howard
Random Hearts (1999), composer: Dave Grusin
Things You Can Tell Just by Looking at Her (2000), composer: Ed Shearmur

INDEX

INDEX

ABOUT THE AUTHOR

Anthony Magro is a writer and independent filmmaker in Toronto, Canada. His passion for jazz was galvanized as a teenager by a recording by John Coltrane, and he soon began writing about the music. His short films, which he wrote, produced, and directed, have been featured in North American festivals. Mr. Magro is keen to adapt this, his first book, into a documentary, make feature films, and continue writing about jazz musicians.